Language Links

Grammar and vocabulary for reference and self-study

ADRIAN DOFF AND CHRISTOPHER JONES

PRE-INTERMEDIATE

CAMBRIDGE
UNIVERSITY PRESS

CAMBRIDGE UNIVERSITY PRESS
Cambridge, New York, Melbourne, Madrid, Cape Town, Singapore, São Paulo

Cambridge University Press
The Edinburgh Building, Cambridge CB2 8RU, UK

www.cambridge.org
Information on this title: www.cambridge.org/9780521608695

First published 2007

Produced by Kamae Design, Oxford

Printed in Italy by Legoprint S.p.A

A catalogue record for this book is available from the British Library

ISBN 978-0-521-60869-5 paperback and audio CD pack
ISBN 978-0-521-60870-1 paperback

Introduction

This is the second level of *Language Links*. There are two levels:
Level 1: Beginner > Elementary
Level 2: Pre-intermediate

Why *Language Links*?

Language Links combines grammar, vocabulary and phrases to give the range of language you need to communicate effectively in English. To talk about money, for example, you need not only vocabulary *(credit card, bill, receipt)*, but also verb forms *(I paid, I bought, It cost)* and phrases such as *Can you lend me ...? Can we have the bill?*

This book provides **links** which take you from one unit to another, so that you can explore the language in whatever direction you want to go, and in whatever order you choose.

What *Language Links* contains

Language Links includes all the basics of English you need at this level. It includes:
– grammar areas (verb tenses, question forms, passive forms, phrasal verbs ...)
– vocabulary areas (clothes, food, work, accidents, holidays ...)
– basic 'concepts' (quantity, frequency, age, distance ...)
– common verbs (*bring/take, find/lose, see/watch, forget/remember ...*)
– prepositions (*near, round, by, since ...*)
– useful phrases (*Why don't we ...? Would you mind ...? You should ...*)

You can use *Language Links* for self-study without a teacher. All the language is presented with clear examples and illustrations, and all key language items and examples are recorded on the CD. Answers to the exercises are in the Answer Key.

How to use the book

There are various ways to use the book:
1 **Focus on a particular area you want to practise.** So, for example, you might want to do some practice of past simple questions, or find out how to use *something* and *anything*, or learn how to ask directions, or learn some transport vocabulary. Use the Contents or the Index to find the unit you want, and go straight there.
2 **Go from one unit to the next in sequence.** For example, you might want to study and practise the past and present perfect tenses, so you could work your way through a series of units, starting with *Unit 83* and going on to *Unit 92*.
3 **Use the links** to go from one unit to another. For example, you're on *Unit 33: Rooms, flats and houses*, and you're practising sentences such as *The flat is near the shops* or *It's not far from the town centre.* You might want to know more about *near* and *not far from*, so follow the link – it takes you to *Unit 12: Distance*.

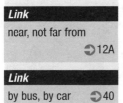

Link
near, not far from
➲ 12A

Link
by bus, by car   ➲ 40

Unit 12 shows you sentences like *It's 10 minutes from the university by bus.* You might want to learn more about phrases like *by bus*, so follow the link – it takes you to *Unit 40: Transport*. In this way, you can go from unit to unit in whatever order you choose, and find out more about language points as you come across them.

Links called RU1, RU2 are to the Reference Units at the end of the book. These units focus on general grammatical features, such as infinitives, -*ing* forms and phrasal verbs.

Contents

Numbers

A Vocabulary   Measurements

Link
→ 11   How high …?

Link
How …?, What …?
→ 95

How big / What size is the room?	How fast are we going?	How much does it weigh?	What's the temperature?

6m x 3m.	18m².	120 kph.	10 kg.	23°.
(= 6 metres by 3 metres)	(= 18 square metres)	(= 120 kilometres per hour)	(= 10 kilograms or kilos)	(= 23 degrees)

1 Complete the questions and write the answers.

a – <u>How fast</u> is he driving?
  – <u>30 kilometres per hour</u> . (30 kph)

b – _____ in Oslo?
  – _____ . (5°)

c – _____ is the pool?
  – _____ . (30m x 20m)

d – _____ is your office?
  – _____ . (90m²)

e – How much _____ you _____?
  – _____ . (82 kg)

B Vocabulary   Small numbers

Links
only   → 6C

half a kilometre

She only lives ½ km from her office, but she always takes the car to work. In fact, only 10% of people in cities walk to work.

one and a quarter litres

1¼ LITRES for the price of 1 litre –
¼ LITRE FREE!

The world is still getting warmer: temperatures will go up by 0.9 degrees in the next 20 years.

one point seven kilos

In the USA, people eat about 90 kg of meat and fish a year – that's 1.7 kg a week.

ten per cent   a quarter of a litre   nought point nine degrees

$\frac{1}{4}$	$\frac{1}{2}$	$1\frac{1}{2}$	1.4	0.9	10%
a quarter (of a ...)	half (a ...)	one and a half	one point four	nought point nine / zero point nine	ten per cent (of ...)

2 Complete what the people say.

a 'It's <u>one and a half kilometres</u> to the next petrol station.'

b 'Only _____ of people voted for the new bridge.'

c 'Prices went up by _____ last month.'

d 'We need _____ of flour and _____ of water.'

e 'You can buy _____ of potatoes for €3.50.'

prices up by 0.7%

½ kilo flour
¼ glass water

POTATOES
2½ kg
ONLY €3.50

1.5 km

THE NEW BRIDGE
YES: 23% NO: 67%

C Phrases — *over, under, exactly ...*

Links

more than, less than ➔ 27
a bit ➔ 14A

Link

tall, high ➔ 11

It's exactly 5.2 cm.	It's	just over / a bit more than	5 cm.			
It's exactly 4.9 cm.	It's	just under / a bit less than	5 cm.	*or*	It's almost / nearly	5 cm.

3 Write these measurements in two ways.

a It weighs *exactly 24.8 kg* .
  It weighs *nearly 25kg* .

b I was going at _____ .
  I was going at _____ .

c She's _____ tall.
  She's _____ tall.

d It's _____ high.
  It's _____ high.

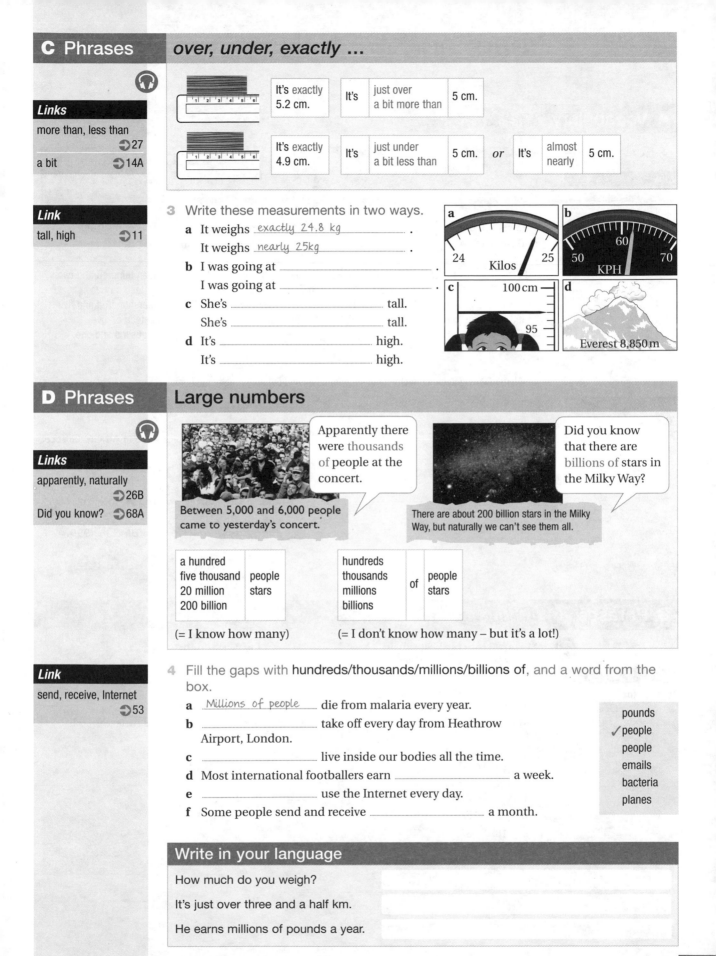

a 24 Kilos 25
b 50 60 70 KPH
c 100 cm 95
d Everest 8,850 m

D Phrases — Large numbers

Links

apparently, naturally ➔ 26B
Did you know? ➔ 68A

Link

send, receive, Internet ➔ 53

Apparently there were thousands of people at the concert.

Between 5,000 and 6,000 people came to yesterday's concert.

Did you know that there are billions of stars in the Milky Way?

There are about 200 billion stars in the Milky Way, but naturally we can't see them all.

a hundred five thousand 20 million 200 billion	people stars		hundreds thousands millions billions	of	people stars

(= I know how many)   (= I don't know how many – but it's a lot!)

4 Fill the gaps with **hundreds/thousands/millions/billions of**, and a word from the box.

a *Millions of people* die from malaria every year.
b _____ take off every day from Heathrow Airport, London.
c _____ live inside our bodies all the time.
d Most international footballers earn _____ a week.
e _____ use the Internet every day.
f Some people send and receive _____ a month.

pounds
✓ people
people
emails
bacteria
planes

Write in your language

How much do you weigh?	
It's just over three and a half km.	
He earns millions of pounds a year.	

11

2 Years and centuries

Link
⟹85 **Past simple (1)**

Link
was born, died ⟹45

A Vocabulary — Years

JUAN JOSE FLORES
First President of Ecuador
1800–1864

He was born in eighteen hundred and he died in eighteen sixty-four.

BILL CLINTON
President of the USA
1993–2001

He was President from nineteen ninety-three to two thousand and one.

1650	sixteen fifty	1400	fourteen hundred	1802	eighteen hundred and two *or* eighteen oh two
1775	seventeen seventy-five	1700	seventeen hundred	1905	nineteen hundred and five *or* nineteen oh five
1844	eighteen forty-four	1900	nineteen hundred		
1993	nineteen ninety-three	2000	two thousand	2001	two thousand and one

Link
was, were ⟹83

1 Write the years in words.

a   seventeen fifty-four _____   He was born in 1754 in Paris.

b   _____   The 2004 Summer Olympics were in Athens, Greece.

c   _____   Emperor Hirohito was born in 1901.

d   _____   Shakespeare started writing Hamlet in 1600.

e   _____   King Hussein of Jordan died in 1999.

f   _____   The First World War started in 1914.

B Phrases — *in the eighties*

Link
from ... to ⟹7A

Mozart wrote his best music between 1782 and 1787.

⬇

Mozart wrote his best music in the seventeen eighties.

I was a student from 1982 to 1987.

⬇

I was a student in the nineteen eighties *or* in the eighties.

2 Complete the table.

a	1650–1659	the sixteen fifties		
b	1720–1729	_____		
c	1870–1879	_____		
d	1930–1939	_____	*or*	the thirties
e	1960–1969	_____	*or*	_____
f	1990–1999	_____	*or*	_____

3 Rewrite the phrases in *italics*.

  a He was born *between 1752 and 1757.*   *in the seventeen fifties*

  b I was at university *from 1993 to 1996.*

  c My family lived in Buenos Aires *from 1921 to 1928.*

  d The Troggs were a rock band *around 1965–66.*

  e This house was built *between 1830 and 1840.*

C Phrases

Link

was (invented) ➜ 94

in the 19th century

Glasses were invented
in the early 13th century.

Pencils were invented
in the 16th century.

The microscope was invented
in the late 17th century.

in the	(early) (late)	13th 16th 17th	century

the 13th (thirteenth) century = 1200–1299
the 16th (sixteenth) century = 1500–1599

4 Look at the time line. When were the things invented?

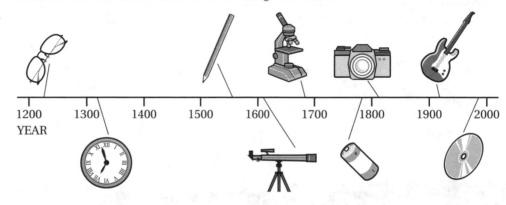

  a CDs <u>were invented in the late 20th century</u> .

  b The camera _____ .

  c Batteries _____ .

  d The telescope _____ .

  e The electric guitar _____ .

  f The clock _____ .

Link

camera, batteries
➜ 34C

Write in your language

His mother died in nineteen eighty-nine.

She was born in the nineteen twenties.

This house was built in the late 18th century.

3 Age

A Phrases — *She's in her thirties*

Link

twenties, thirties ➔2

her, his, their ➔20A

manager, pilot ➔42A

WHO'S WHO AT BusinessAir

We're a young team at BusinessAir, the airline for people in business. The director, Kathryn Scott, is in her forties. Our five pilots are in their thirties. And the sales manager is still in his twenties.

Director	**Pilot**	**Pilot**	**Sales manager**
Kathryn Scott	Keith Chen	Maria Fernandez	Mel Long
41	36	33	27

| I'm He's She's They're | in | my his her their | twenties. thirties. forties. | (= 20–29 years old) (= 30–39 years old) (= 40–49 years old) |

1 How old were these people when they died?

a He was in his nineties.

b ....

c ....

d ....

e ....

f ....

Winston Churchill 1874–1969

Joseph Stalin 1879–1953

John F. Kennedy 1917–1963

Lady Diana Spencer 1961–1997

Indira Gandhi 1917–1984

Mao Zedong 1893–1976

B Phrases — *older, younger, the same age*

Links

older, younger ➔27

same ➔31

brother, sister, cousin ➔44

OK, this is me, with the hat on, and this is my older brother. He's three years older than me … And this is my younger sister. She's a year younger than me … And this is my cousin. We're the same age.

| (my) | older younger | brother sister | He's She's | (three years) (a year) | older younger | than (me). | We're the same age. |

2 Read the sentences and write the people's ages.

Roberto

This is Roberto with his brothers and sisters.
Paula is three years younger than Roberto.
Paula and Riccardo are the same age.
Marco is seven years older than Riccardo, and a year younger than Bella. Bella is 21.

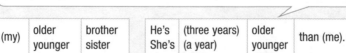

Bella	21
Marco	....
Riccardo	....
Paula	....
Roberto	....

3 Complete the sentences. Use words from the box.

than	
older	
brother	
younger	
sister	
brothers	
years	

a Marco is seven _years_ _older_ _than_ Paula.

b Riccardo has two _____ _____ and one _____ _____ .

c Paula is eight _____ _____ _____ Bella.

d Roberto is _____ _____ Bella, but _____ _____ Paula.

e Marco is Roberto's _____ _____ .

4 Write sentences about you and your family.

_____

_____

_____

_____

> I have a cousin, Mary. She's three years younger than me.

> My father is ten years older than my mother.

C Vocabulary *baby, child, teenager ...*

teenager young adult middle-aged person old person

child

baby

0 10 20 30 40 50 60 70 80

Child Adult ➡

Nouns	baby/babies, child/children, teenager(s), young adult(s)
Adjectives	young, middle-aged, old (person, man, woman, people ...)

5 Change the phrases in (brackets). Use words from the box above.

a This isn't a hotel. It's a home for _old people_ *(people of 70–90)*.

b The Harry Potter books were written for _____ *(people of 8–12)*, but _____ *(people of 15–16)* and _____ *(people over 21)* enjoy reading them.

c I rang the bell. _____ *(A woman in her 50s)* opened the door and said 'Hello'.

d This town needs a good place for _____ *(people between 13 and 17)* to go in the evening.

e Tickets cost £1.50 for _____ *(people under 13)*, and nothing for _____ *(people under 2)*.

Write in your language

My mother's in her sixties.	
He's five years older than me.	
My younger brother's just a baby.	

4 Time phrases (1)

A Vocabulary · *in time, on time, early, late*

MEETING
11.00 a.m. Room 501

I was early for the meeting. I arrived at 10.30.

Most people arrived in time for the meeting. They were there before 11.00.

The meeting started on time, at 11.00.

George was 20 minutes late for the meeting.

on time = at the correct time   *in time (for)* = early enough, having enough time

Links

start, finish	➲65
verb + -ed	➲85A

1 Complete the sentences, using **early**, **late**, **in time** or **on time**.

a The concert started _late_____ . (It started at 7.15.)
b The lecture finished _____ . (It finished at 7.45.)
c We arrived at the wedding _____ . (We arrived at 12.30.)
d We got to the station _____ . (We got there at 12.20.)
e The train left London _____ . (It left at 12.30.)
f The train arrived in Manchester _____ . (It arrived at 4.30.)

CONCERT
7:00 PM

Lecture
6.00 – 8.30 pm

Trains
London 1230
Manchester 1545

Wedding
Sat. 12th July
3.00 pm

B Phrases · *at, in, on, by*

Links

so	➲98C
so that	➲98D
by post, by email	
	➲24B
by email, visit our website	➲53

The plane leaves at 8.00 in the evening, so we should be at the airport by about 6.30, so that we have time to check in.

"We hope to finish building the stadium by early July," Mr Green said yesterday. "So we'll certainly be ready for the World Cup in October."

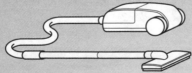
Buy now!
Offer closes on 20th June!

How to pay:
By post Send a cheque for £65. Your cheque should reach us by 15th June.
By email Visit our website at www.

at + times	at	2 o'clock the end of the year		
on + days	on	Monday 15th June	by	2 o'clock the end of the year Monday 15th June October 2010 the evening
in + months, years, parts of the day	in	October 2010 the evening		

(by = not after*)*

2 Fill the gaps with words from the boxes.

a

> at ✓by in on

I've got to finish my report __by__ Sunday night, so that it's ready for the meeting .... Monday. I won't have time .... the morning, because the meeting starts .... 9.00.

b

> by in on

'We're starting work on the new road .... April, and it will be ready .... the end of this year,' a minister said at a meeting .... Friday.

c

> at by in on

The plane leaves .... 6.30 .... the afternoon and arrives in Tokyo early .... Tuesday morning. So we'll probably be at the hotel .... lunchtime.

Links

until, till	➲7A
don't	➲81A
didn't	➲86A

C Grammar — *not ... until*

> I finished work at 5.00, but it was snowing, so I didn't get home until 8.30.

> The post was very slow. I posted the letter on Monday, but it didn't get there till Friday.

> School holidays are very late this year. They don't start until July.

till = until

(= at 8.30, not before) (= on Friday, not before) (= in July, not before)

3 Complete the sentences. Choose sentences from the box, and change them using **not ... until** or **not ... till**.

They finished it in 2006.	We'll get there this evening.	It will open next week.
✓I woke up at 10.30.	The meeting started at 12.00.	We'll see you on Monday.

a I wanted to get up early today, but _I didn't wake up until 10.30_ .
b We're still about 300 kilometres away, so ....
c I arrived at 10.30, but ....
d They started work on the new stadium in 2001, but ....
e We're away for the weekend, so ....
f They haven't finished work on the new restaurant yet, so ....

Write in your language

The train left on time, but it arrived late.	
I'm out tonight, but I'll be home by 11.00.	
The meeting didn't start until 10.30.	

5 Time phrases (2)

A Phrases — *this week, last month, next year*

Links

I saw	85B
I'm (see)ing	82
I'll (see)	78
I'm going to (see)	79

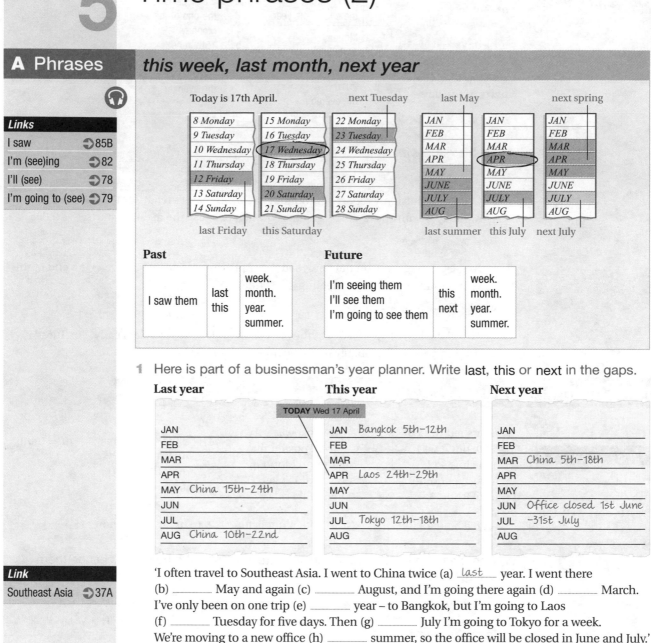

Today is 17th April.

8 Monday	15 Monday	22 Monday
9 Tuesday	16 Tuesday	23 Tuesday
10 Wednesday	17 Wednesday	24 Wednesday
11 Thursday	18 Thursday	25 Thursday
12 Friday	19 Friday	26 Friday
13 Saturday	20 Saturday	27 Saturday
14 Sunday	21 Sunday	28 Sunday

next Tuesday · last May · next spring

last Friday · this Saturday · last summer · this July · next July

Past

I saw them	last / this	week. / month. / year. / summer.

Future

I'm seeing them / I'll see them / I'm going to see them	this / next	week. / month. / year. / summer.

1 Here is part of a businessman's year planner. Write **last**, **this** or **next** in the gaps.

Last year

JAN	
FEB	
MAR	
APR	
MAY	China 15th–24th
JUN	
JUL	
AUG	China 10th–22nd

This year

TODAY Wed 17 April

JAN	Bangkok 5th–12th
FEB	
MAR	
APR	Laos 24th–29th
MAY	
JUN	
JUL	Tokyo 12th–18th
AUG	

Next year

JAN	
FEB	
MAR	China 5th–18th
APR	
MAY	
JUN	Office closed 1st June
JUL	–31st July
AUG	

Link

Southeast Asia 37A

'I often travel to Southeast Asia. I went to China twice (a) _last_ year. I went there
(b) _____ May and again (c) _____ August, and I'm going there again (d) _____ March.
I've only been on one trip (e) _____ year – to Bangkok, but I'm going to Laos
(f) _____ Tuesday for five days. Then (g) _____ July I'm going to Tokyo for a week.
We're moving to a new office (h) _____ summer, so the office will be closed in June and July.'

B Phrases — *today, tomorrow, three days ago*

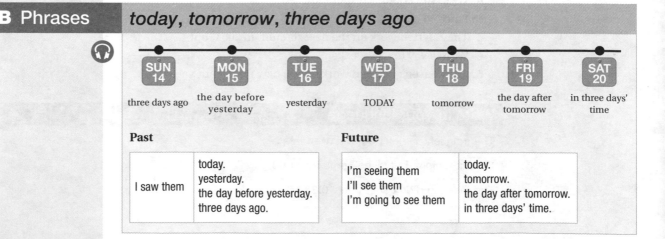

SUN 14	MON 15	TUE 16	WED 17	THU 18	FRI 19	SAT 20
three days ago	the day before yesterday	yesterday	TODAY	tomorrow	the day after tomorrow	in three days' time

Past

I saw them	today. / yesterday. / the day before yesterday. / three days ago.

Future

I'm seeing them / I'll see them / I'm going to see them	today. / tomorrow. / the day after tomorrow. / in three days' time.

Link
theatre, play ➲54

2 Look at this person's diary. Today is Wednesday the 17th. Complete the sentences.

a She came back from holiday _5 days ago_ .

b It's her birthday ...., but she's having a party ....

c She went to the sports centre ...., and she's going again ....

d She went to London ....

e She loves the theatre. She went to a play .... and she's going again ....

Th 11	Holiday
F 12	↓
Sa 13	Theatre
Su 14	
M 15	Sports centre
Tu 16	Meeting in London
(W 17)	Sports centre
Th 18	Birthday
F 19	Theatre
Sa 20	Birthday party

C Phrases

three months ago, in three months

Link
move, leave school ➲45

We moved here five years ago.

I bought it a few days ago.

He's retiring in six months.

I'm expecting the baby in three weeks.

Past

three six a few	days weeks months years	ago

Future

in	three six a few	days weeks months years

We can also say:
in three weeks' time
in three months' time
in a few years' time

3 Think of the date now. Write these sentences using … **ago** or **in** …

a I saw her last Thursday. ....

b She's going to England next January. ....

c I went swimming the day before yesterday. ....

d He left school in 2002. ....

e They're getting married in June. ....

f I met Michèle last summer. ....

Write in your language

They got married last summer.	
They're arriving the day after tomorrow.	
She came back from holiday two weeks ago.	

6 *already, just, only ...*

A Grammar — *already, still, yet*

Links

has (done) ➲ 90
hasn't (done) ➲ 91
leave school, go to college ➲ 45

Like most other 16-year-olds, Sandra Willis goes to school and lives at home with her parents. But unlike her friends, Sandra earns a lot of money. In her free time, she designs birthday cards and sells them over the Internet. Last year she earned £9,000, and this year she has earned more than £16,000 – and it's still only June!

What does she want to do when she leaves school? 'I don't really know yet,' Sandra says. 'I'll probably go to art college.'

Look at these sentences about Sandra Willis:

She is still at school.
She still goes to school.

She isn't 17 yet. (= She's still 16.)
She hasn't left school yet.

She is already quite rich.
She already earns a lot of money.
She has already earned more than £25,000.

We use *yet* in negatives and questions. It comes at the end of the sentence:

> She hasn't left school yet.
> I don't know yet.
> Has she gone to college yet?

still and *already* come
– before the main verb:

> She still goes ...
> She already earns ...
> She has already earned ...

– after the verb *be*:

> ... is still at school.
> ... is already quite rich.

1 Add **already**, **still** or **yet** to these sentences.

a It was 10 o'clock in the morning, but everyone was *still* asleep.

b She's only 20, but she has _____ finished university.

c He's nearly 30, but he _____ plays computer games.

d He's starting university soon, but he hasn't found a room _____ .

e Hurry up, or we'll be late! It's _____ 7 o'clock.

f I'm _____ at the office, so I'll be home late this evening.

g I'd like to read that book. Have you finished it _____ ?

B Grammar — *just*

Links

➲ 90 **Present perfect (1)**
➲ 82 **Present continuous**

I've just **arrived** at the airport.

I'm just **checking** in my luggage.

I'm just about to get on the plane.

just + present perfect tense   *just* + present continuous tense   *be just about to ...*

NOW   NOW   NOW

2 What is the woman saying?

a <u>I'm just getting some money.</u>

b ....

c ....

d ....

e ....

f ....

a
get some money

b
get on the bus

c
have a coffee

d
buy some flowers

e
have an accident

f
watch the news

C Grammar   *only*

Link

got a job, applied for
→42C

Delete Reply Reply All Forward Print

I've got a new job with a company called Extel. They make computers. I applied for it a few weeks ago,

It's quite a small company. There are only 30 people, and only 10 of them work full-time. Everyone is really friendly, and it feels like a family more than a company. *(only = not more)*

I only started last week, but I already know everyone here. *(only = not before)*

The manager is really nice. He's only 28, and he's very friendly to everyone. He knows an incredible amount about computers, so he's very interesting to talk to. *(only = not older)*

At the moment, I only work on Monday, Tuesday and Wednesday, but they say that I might work more next month. *(only = not the other days)*

Link

subject   →RU6

only comes

– before the main verb:	– after the verb *be*:	– before the subject of the sentence:
I only work … I only started …	He's only 28 … There are only …	Only 10 people work full time.

3 Add only to these sentences.

a We~~only~~arrived yesterday, so we're quite tired.

b She's 30, but she's got a well-paid job as a company manager.

c I don't want to go to bed yet – it's 9 o'clock.

d She's got three small children, so she works in the mornings.

e 50 people came to the concert.

f He lives in the next street, but I don't see him very often.

Write in your language

I think they're still asleep.	
We're just about to have dinner.	
They only arrived last weekend.	

A Phrases

from … to, until, for

Links

(work)ed, went	➲85
(we)'ll	➲78
we're (go)ing, we're (stay)ing	➲82B
1996, 2002	➲2

> I worked in Mexico for six years, from 1996 to 2002. Then I went to the USA.

> We're going to Turkey this summer. We're staying for two weeks – we'll be there until 18th July.

Past

1996 ◄——— (6 years) ———► 2002

I worked in Mexico.

I worked in Mexico	for 6 years. from 1996 to 2002. until 2002.

Future

4th July ◄——— (2 weeks) ———► 18th July

We'll be in Turkey.
We're staying in Turkey.

We'll be in Turkey We're staying in Turkey	for 2 weeks. from 4th to 18th July. until 18th July.

1 Here is part of the curriculum vitae (CV) of an English teacher. Continue the sentences with phrases from the box.

from 1998 to 2003
✓until 1989
for 2 years
for 3 years
for 4 years

Curriculum Vitae	
1981–89	Watson's School, Liverpool
1989–93	University of Manchester (English)
1993–96	Taught English in Valencia, Spain
1996–98	South London Business College (Business and Computing)
1998–2003	Taught business at International Business School, Cairo, Egypt

a She was at school in Liverpool _until 1989_ .

b She studied business _____ .

c She lived in Spain _____ .

d She worked in Egypt _____ .

e She was at Manchester University _____ .

2 Read the text, and fill the gaps with **from, to, until** or **for**.

Lisa, Nina and Max all work for a company in London.
They want to have a meeting in April.

Lisa is on holiday (a) _until_ 23rd April.
She's also going to Paris (b) _____ three days,
(c) _____ 28th (d) _____ 30th April.

Nina will be in the office (e) _____ 22nd April, and then she's going to Madrid
(f) _____ three days, (g) _____ 25th April.

Max is going to Moscow on 20th April. He'll be there (h) _____ three days. He's
also going on holiday (i) _____ a week, (j) _____ 27th April
(k) _____ 4th May.

Now complete the table. When can they meet?

_____

	APRIL										
	20	21	22	23	24	25	26	27	28	29	30
LISA		―Holiday―									
NINA											
MAX											

How long …?

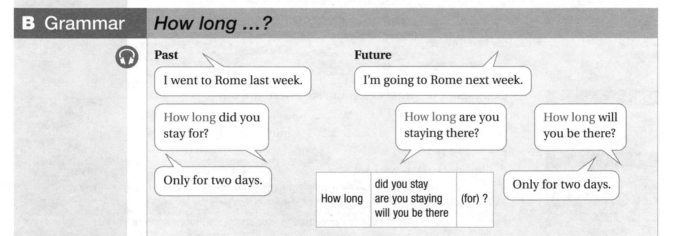

Past

I went to Rome last week.

How long **did you** stay for?

Only for two days.

Future

I'm going to Rome next week.

How long **are you** staying there?

How long **will** you be there?

How long	did you stay / are you staying / will you be there	(for) ?

Only for two days.

3 Write questions with **How long …?** Use the verbs in brackets.

a We're playing football on Monday. _How long are you playing?_ (play)
b I went to Brazil last summer. _____ (stay)
c I lived in Oman when I was a child. _____ (live there)
d My sister's visiting us next week. _____ (stay)
e I played tennis yesterday. _____ (play)
f I'm going to Rome tomorrow. _____ (be there)

Write in your language	
They worked in Egypt for five years.	
We're staying here until next Saturday.	
How long did you stay at the party for?	

8 How long ...? (2): *up to now*

A Grammar — They've lived there for six months

Links

lived, didn't (get)	⮕85, 86
ago	⮕5
still	⮕6A
for (six months)	⮕7

Ian Coe left school at 15 and started work in a car factory. But he didn't get a car. 'I lived in the town centre, and I walked to work,' he says. 'I didn't need a car.'

Ian is now 55, and he still works in the car factory. Six months ago, he and his wife Mary moved to a village in the country – and they had a problem. 'There are only two buses a day,' says Ian. 'If you live here, you need a car!'

So two weeks ago, Ian and Mary got their first car. And next week, they're having their first driving lessons.

Look at these sentences about Ian and Mary:

Ian has worked in a car factory for forty years.

```
HE STARTED
WORK              40 years              NOW
X──────────────────────────────────────●
                              (He still works there.)
```

They have lived in the country for six months.

```
THEY
MOVED             6 months              NOW
X──────────────────────────────────────●
                              (They still live here.)
```

They have had a car for two weeks.

```
THEY GOT
A CAR             2 weeks               NOW
X──────────────────────────────────────●
                              (They still have a car.)
```

Present perfect tense + *for* ...

He has/He's	worked in a car factory		forty years.
They have/They've	lived in the country	for	six months.
	had a car		two weeks.

| NOT |
| He works ... for 40 years. |

Link

⮕90 **Present perfect (1)**

Link

nearly, over, about ⮕1C

1 Complete the sentences with verbs from the table.

I've	been
She's	had
He's	known
It's	lived
We've	worked
They've	

a Whose car is that? _It's been_ outside our house for two days.

b He's my oldest friend. _____ him for nearly 20 years.

c I need a new coat. _____ this one for about 10 years.

d She's not back at work yet – _____ ill for several weeks.

e _____ a microwave for six months now – and we've only used it once!

f _____ in Turkey for over five years, and he still can't speak Turkish.

g He knows everyone in the company – _____ here for over 30 years.

B Phrases — since, for

We've been here since Saturday.

They arrived on Saturday. Today is Monday.

| They've been here | since Saturday. |
| | for two days. |

```
                              NOW
SATURDAY      2 days       (Monday)
X──────────────────────────────●
```

We've been married since June.

They got married in June. Now it's December.

| They've been married | since June. |
| | for six months. |

```
                              NOW
JUNE          6 months     (December)
X──────────────────────────────●
```

2 Complete the sentences. Use **for** or **since**.

  a We've had our car <u>since</u> 1999.
  b He's lived here _____ 35 years.
  c I've been awake _____ 8 o'clock.
  d She's worked there _____ April.
  e The shop has been closed _____ 20 minutes.
  f I've known him _____ last summer.
  g They've been on holiday _____ 12th May.
  h This meat has been in the fridge _____ 10 days.

3 Write true sentences about yourself. Use **since** or **for**.

  I've known _____ .
  I've lived _____ .
  I've had _____ .
  I've been _____ .

> *I've known Emma since 1995.*
> *I've lived in this flat for 10 years.*

C Grammar   *How long …?*

> How long has the company been here?

> Since 2002.

> How long have you worked for Bitco?

> For just over three years.

The computer company Bitco has been in the town of Corley since 2002, and now has over 1,000 workers. The manager, Mike Sands, has worked for Bitco for just over three years. He talked yesterday about Bitco's plans to open a new factory in the town.

Sentence

| The company has been here since 2002. |
| I've worked for Bitco for three years. |

Question

| How long | has the company been here? |
| | have you worked for Bitco? |

4 Complete the journalist's questions. Use **How long …?** and the present perfect.

  a – <u>How long has the exhibition been</u> open?
     – For two days.
  b – _____ an artist?
     – Since 1995.
  c – _____ in Paris?
     – Since 1990.
  d – _____ friends?
     – Since 1945.
  e – _____ together?
     – For 20 years.
  f – _____ married?
     – For two weeks.

> An exhibition of paintings by French artist Marie Genot opened two days ago. Genot came to live in Paris in 1990, and has worked as an artist since 1995.

> Dancers Jon and Lynne Freeman have been friends since 1945, and they've worked together for 20 years – and 2 weeks ago they finally got married.

Write in your language

I've known them for 10 years.	
They have been married since 1995.	
How long have you had those jeans?	

9 *always, usually ...*

Frequency adverbs

Links

arrive, don't arrive
➔81

on time, late ➔4A

> Do you get to work on time?

> Yes, I **always** get to work on time. I arrive at 7.45 and start work at 8.00 – I'm **never** late.

> I **usually** get to work on time. I **sometimes** arrive a few minutes late, if there's a lot of traffic.

> I'm **hardly ever** late for work – maybe once or twice a year.

> I'm **not usually** late for work. We start work at 9.00, and I **nearly always** get there by 8.45.

```
          HARDLY EVER              SOMETIMES               NEARLY ALWAYS
0% ◄─────────────────────────────────────────────────────────────► 100%
       NEVER              NOT USUALLY            USUALLY            ALWAYS
```

Frequency adverbs usually come
– before a main verb:

I	always usually hardly ever	get to work on time. arrive late.

– after *am, is* or *are*:

I'm	always usually hardly ever	on time. late.

Negative sentences:

I don't usually arrive late.

I'm not usually late.

1 Rewrite these sentences with frequency adverbs, so they're true about you.

Link

by ➔4B

> I always get up early.
> I'm not usually tired in the morning.

  a I get up early. ....
  b I'm tired in the morning. ....
  c I leave the house by 7.30. ....
  d I'm late for work. ....
  e I have a big lunch. ....
  f I go to bed early. ....
  g I'm asleep by 10.30. ....

often, not often

We don't know very much about our neighbours.

We don't see them **very often**, because they're **often** away for several days – and when we see them, they never speak to us.

And they **aren't often** at home during the day – at least, we **don't often** see them. But we **often** hear music coming from the house late at night ...

often comes

– before a main verb:

We often hear music.

– after *am/is/are*:

They're often away.

Negative sentences:

We don't often see them. *or*
We don't see them very often.

They aren't often at home. *or*
They aren't at home very often.

2 What else does the man say? Put the sentences in the right order.

a the visitors often weekend have at they   They often have visitors at the weekend.
b often open curtains the aren't
c very they letters get often don't
d green a the see outside I taxi often house
e empty the the often is winter house in
f into go garden they don't the often

C Phrases

from time to time

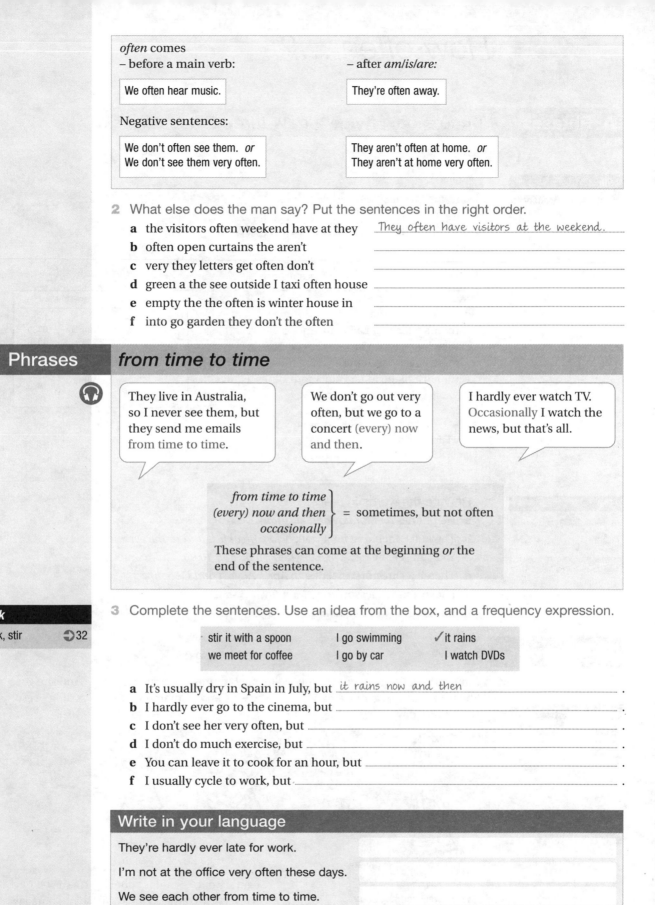

They live in Australia, so I never see them, but they send me emails from time to time.

We don't go out very often, but we go to a concert (every) now and then.

I hardly ever watch TV. Occasionally I watch the news, but that's all.

from time to time
(every) now and then } = sometimes, but not often
occasionally

These phrases can come at the beginning *or* the end of the sentence.

Link

cook, stir   ➲ 32

3 Complete the sentences. Use an idea from the box, and a frequency expression.

stir it with a spoon	I go swimming	✓ it rains
we meet for coffee	I go by car	I watch DVDs

a It's usually dry in Spain in July, but *it rains now and then* .
b I hardly ever go to the cinema, but .
c I don't see her very often, but .
d I don't do much exercise, but .
e You can leave it to cook for an hour, but .
f I usually cycle to work, but .

Write in your language

They're hardly ever late for work.	
I'm not at the office very often these days.	
We see each other from time to time.	

10 How often …?

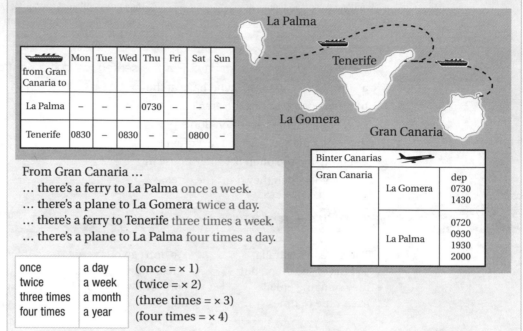

A Phrases

Link
↪40   Transport

once a day, twice a day, three times a week

⛴ from Gran Canaria to	Mon	Tue	Wed	Thu	Fri	Sat	Sun
La Palma	–	–	–	0730	–	–	–
Tenerife	0830	–	0830	–	–	0800	–

La Palma

Tenerife

La Gomera

Gran Canaria

Binter Canarias ✈		
Gran Canaria	La Gomera	dep 0730 1430
	La Palma	0720 0930 1930 2000

From Gran Canaria …
… there's a ferry to La Palma once a week.
… there's a plane to La Gomera twice a day.
… there's a ferry to Tenerife three times a week.
… there's a plane to La Palma four times a day.

once	a day	(once = × 1)
twice	a week	(twice = × 2)
three times	a month	(three times = × 3)
four times	a year	(four times = × 4)

Link
on Monday, at 9.00,
in April   ↪4

1 Rewrite the words in *italics*.

a He phones *on Monday and Saturday*.   twice a week

b They take their dog for a walk *before breakfast and in the evening*. ....

c You can see the news *at 9.00, 12.00, 5.00 and 10.00*. ....

d There's a Directors' meeting *in April, August and December*. ....

e I have a music lesson *every Monday*. ....

f Buses come *at 11.00 a.m. and 4.30 p.m.* ....

B Phrases

every

Link
every   ↪17

Mona is very fit. She walks to work every day.   She goes to the gym every two days.   She plays tennis every weekend.   She runs a marathon every three months.   And she goes skiing every year.

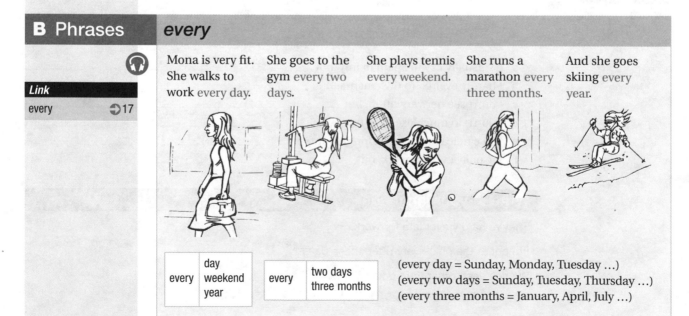

every	day weekend year		every	two days three months

(every day = Sunday, Monday, Tuesday …)
(every two days = Sunday, Tuesday, Thursday …)
(every three months = January, April, July …)

2 Complete the sentences with **every** and an expression from the box.

> morning   2 hours   ✓summer   4 years   month   76 years

a They go camping _every summer_ .
b There's a train to Paris _____ .
c Halley's Comet comes _____ .
d I pay my phone bill _____ .
e He takes his dog for a walk _____ .
f They have a new president _____ .

Halley's Comet, 1986

Link

2000, 2002   ➲2

3 What do these sequences mean? Write phrases with **every**.

a 10.00, 10.10, 10.20, 10.30 ...   = _every ten minutes_
b Monday, Thursday, Sunday ...   = _____
c 2000, 2002, 2004, 2006 ...   = _____
d Sunday 7th, Sunday 14th, Sunday 21st ...   = _____
e 8.00 a.m., 12.00, 4.00 p.m., 8.00 p.m. ...   = _____
f 1800, 1850, 1900, 1950, 2000 ...   = _____

C Grammar *How often ...?*

Links

How often ...?   ➲95C
do/does ...   ➲81

> How often is there a train to the airport?

> Once an hour.

> How often do buses go to the airport?

> Every 15 minutes.

How often	is there ...	How often	do ...
	are there ...		does ...

4 Read the holiday information. Write questions with **How often ...?**

a – _How often are there buses to the city centre?_
– Every 30 minutes.
b – _____
– Once a week.
c – _____
– Three times a week.
d – _____
– Twice a week.
e – _____
– Three times a day.
f – _____
– Once a day.

> The postman comes at 9.00 every morning.

> They clean the apartments on Monday, Wednesday and Friday.

> ✓ There are two buses to the city centre every hour.

> Planes fly to Madrid at 0800, 1200 and 1700 every day.

> There's a boat to the island on Tuesday and Friday.

> There are concerts every Sunday.

Write in your language

I have an English lesson three times a week.	
She has a holiday every six months.	
How often is there a train to London?	

How high …?

A Vocabulary tall, short

Link
➲25   Adjectives

Link
slice of …, piece of …
➲13C

a tall person   a short person

a long tail   a short tail

a high ceiling   a low ceiling

a wide street   a narrow street

thick slices of bread   thin slices of bread

a deep pool   a shallow pool

1 What's the opposite?

   a a high fence   _a low fence_

   b wide feet

   c thick glass

   d a narrow river

   e a long piece of rope

   f a short tree

   g shallow water

   h a low wall

Buildings, trees and mountains can be _tall_ or _high_.

2 Write the best word.

   a He wears _thick_ glasses.

   b She's got _____ hair.

   c We're coming to a _____ bridge.

   d Now we're coming to a _____ bridge.

   e Don't walk on the ice – it's very _____ .

   f It's a very _____ tunnel.

B Phrases   _He's two metres tall_

Links
nearly   ➲1C
2.5, 1.5   ➲1B

My brother has a very small car.
It's 2.5 metres long.
It's 1.5 metres wide.
And it's 1.3 metres high.
The problem is, my brother's nearly 2 metres tall.

	long
… (2 metres)	wide
	high
	tall

3 Look at the pictures. Write sentences.

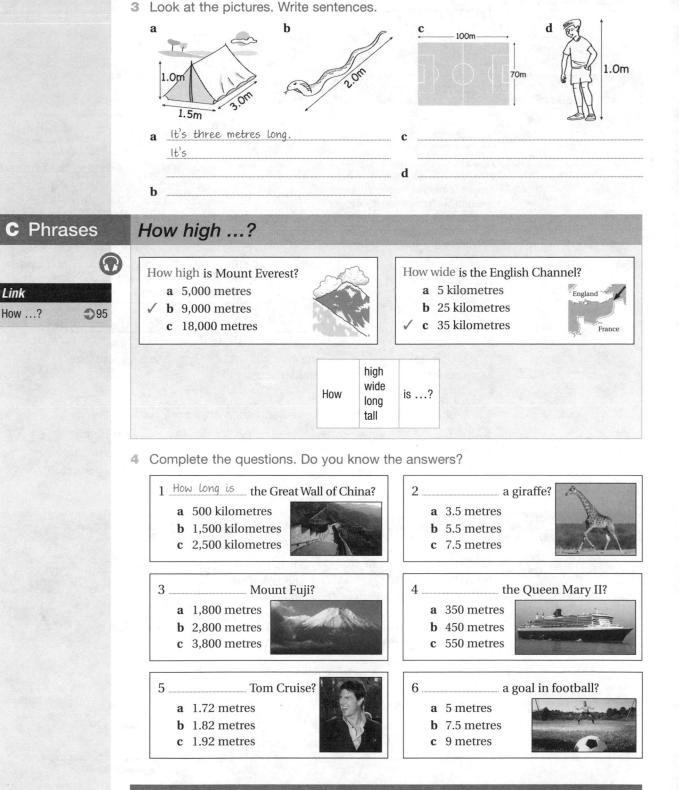

a It's three metres long.

It's ....

....

b ....

c ....

....

d ....

C Phrases

Link

How ...? ➲95

How high ...?

How high **is Mount Everest?**
  a 5,000 metres
  ✓ **b** 9,000 metres
  c 18,000 metres

How wide **is the English Channel?**
  a 5 kilometres
  b 25 kilometres
  ✓ **c** 35 kilometres

England

France

How	high wide long tall	is ...?

---

4 Complete the questions. Do you know the answers?

1 How long is the Great Wall of China?
  a 500 kilometres
  b 1,500 kilometres
  c 2,500 kilometres

2 .... a giraffe?
  a 3.5 metres
  b 5.5 metres
  c 7.5 metres

3 .... Mount Fuji?
  a 1,800 metres
  b 2,800 metres
  c 3,800 metres

4 .... the Queen Mary II?
  a 350 metres
  b 450 metres
  c 550 metres

5 .... Tom Cruise?
  a 1.72 metres
  b 1.82 metres
  c 1.92 metres

6 .... a goal in football?
  a 5 metres
  b 7.5 metres
  c 9 metres

Write in your language

It's a very narrow bridge.

Mount Kilimanjaro is 5,900 metres high.

How tall are you?

12 Distance

A Phrases — *near, not far, a long way*

Hi John.
I've found a new flat. It's quite nice – it's close to the river, and it's not far from the city centre, so it's quite near the shops.
But it's a long way from the university – I have to take a bus every morning.

10 km → 8

1 centre   4 railway station   7 cinema
2 sports club   5 university   8 airport
3 bus station   6 library

MY FLAT

near (to)
close to

quite near (to)
not far from

a long way from

1 Look at the map. Complete these sentences about the flat.

a It's _not far from_ the centre.
b It's _____ the airport.
c It's _____ the bus station.
d It's _____ the railway station.
e It's _____ the library.
f It's _____ the cinema.
g It's _____ the sports club.

B Phrases — *2 kilometres from, 15 minutes from*

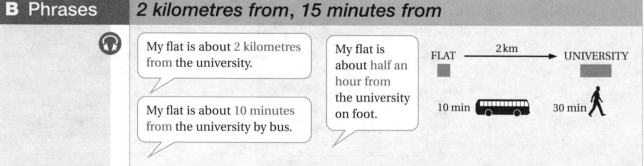

My flat is about 2 kilometres from the university.

My flat is about 10 minutes from the university by bus.

My flat is about half an hour from the university on foot.

FLAT — 2 km → UNIVERSITY

10 min   30 min

Link

by bus, by car   ➲ 40

2 Write sentences about these places.

a _Munich is 80 kilometres from the Alps._
   It's about 1 hour from the Alps by car.

b _____

c _____

d _____

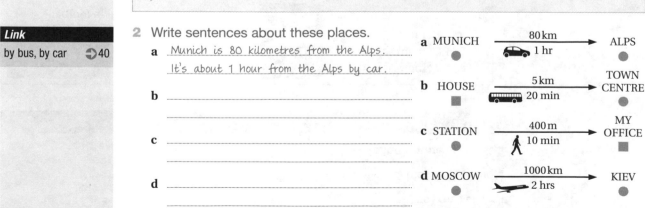

a MUNICH — 80 km — 1 hr — ALPS

b HOUSE — 5 km — 20 min — TOWN CENTRE

c STATION — 400 m — 10 min — MY OFFICE

d MOSCOW — 1000 km — 2 hrs — KIEV

How far …?

Link

How …?   ➲95C

BUENOS AIRES
51km
→

How far is it to Buenos Aires?

How far away is Buenos Aires?

About 50 kilometres.

3 Write questions for these answers.

a – How far is it to Montreal?

– It's a long way – nearly 2000 kilometres.

b –

– It's about half a kilometre up the road, on the right.

c –

– It's not far – about two minutes on foot.

d –

– It's about 10 minutes away by bus.

e –

– It's about an hour by bus, or 25 minutes by taxi.

Airport
30 km ✈

P
500 m
↱

Montreal
1980 km

Town
centre 3 km
↑

station 🚶

It's 300 km southwest of Sydney

Link

southwest of, north of
          ➲37B

Canberra is 300 km southwest of Sydney.
Brisbane is 800 km north of Sydney.
Kalgoorlie is a small town 600 km east of Perth.

Darwin
Mount Bruce ∧
Alice Springs
∧ Uluru
Townsville
Brisbane
Kalgoorlie
Perth • Albany
Adelaide
Mount Bogong
∧
Sydney
Canberra
0   1500 km
Melbourne

4 Find these places.

a a mountain 500 km southwest of Alice Springs   Uluru

b a town 500 km northeast of Albany

c a town on the coast, about 400 km southeast of Perth

d a mountain 1000 km north of Perth

e a city on the coast, 800 km northeast of Melbourne

f a mountain about 200 km southwest of Canberra

Links

Scotland   ➲38B
cousin   ➲44A

5 Write about friends and relatives. Where do they live?

My cousin lives in Scotland. She lives in a village near Glasgow.

Write in your language

My flat is a long way from the city centre.

We're 10 minutes from the airport by car.

It's about 60 km northeast of London.

A Grammar — Countable or uncountable?

Links

plenty of, lots of, how much ➲14

How many …? ➲15C

Walking in the Andes

Some things to remember

- You're walking at over 3,000 metres, so the sun is strong. Take sunscreen, a hat and plenty of water.
- It's a long way from one village to the next. So be sure you always have plenty of time.
- Always take some food with you. Biscuits are good, because they don't take much space in your backpack.
- Look after your money: always keep it in a money belt.

metre	hat	village
biscuit	backpack	money belt

sunscreen	water	time
food	space	money

These are countable nouns. They have a singular and a plural form. We can say:

a backpack	one metre
backpacks	metres
some backpacks	how many metres?

NOT ~~some backpack, how many metre~~

These are uncountable nouns. They have only a singular form. We can say:

water	sunscreen
plenty of water	some sunscreen
how much water?	lots of sunscreen

NOT ~~a water, waters~~

1 Countable or uncountable? Write C or U.

   a   _U_   I don't eat *meat*.

   b   Is this jacket made of *leather*?

   c   They sell *vegetables*.

   d   We've got plenty of *wood*.

   e   Let's buy some *fruit*.

   f   Do you like *jazz*?

   g   How much *petrol* have we got?

   h   Would you like a *sandwich*?

B Vocabulary — *chocolate*, *a chocolate*

Link

paper, glass, wood ➲52B

Some words can be countable or uncountable:

chocolate	a chocolate	paper	a paper (= a newspaper)	coffee	a coffee (= a cup of coffee)

hair	a hair	glass	a glass	wood	a wood

2 Choose the best answer.

a Let's buy *a paper* / *some paper*. I want to see what's on at the cinema.

b I'll have a cheese sandwich and *a small coffee* / *some small coffee*, please.

c Give me *a paper* / *some paper* and I'll draw a map.

d Be careful! There's *a glass* / *glass* on the road.

e He has long blond *hair* / *hairs*.

f Is that table made of *a wood* / *wood*?

C Phrases

a piece of paper

Link
packet, carton, bottle
➡52A

a piece of paper	a slice of pizza	a packet of rice	a bottle of wine	a carton of orange juice	a bar of chocolate

pieces of cake	slices of salami	a kilo of sugar	a litre of oil	a jug of water	a loaf of bread (plural: loaves)

3 Choose the **two** best words.

a a *carton* / *piece* / *loaf* / *bottle* of milk   carton, bottle

b a *bottle* / *slice* / *litre* / *piece* of cheese

c a *piece* / *carton* / *bar* / *slice* of chocolate

d a *bar* / *litre* / *jug* / *packet* of lemonade

e a *slice* / *loaf* / *bottle* / *bar* of bread

4 What are these?

a slices of toast or pieces of toast

b

c

d

e

f

Write in your language

How much food have we got?	
There isn't much space in the car.	
I'd like a piece of paper, please.	

14 How much …?

Links
→15 **How many?**
→13 **Countable and uncountable nouns**

A Phrases — *a little, a bit, a lot, plenty*

Have we got any bread?

Yes. A bit.

Yes. A little.

Is there any milk?

Yes. Lots.

Yes. A lot.

Yes. Plenty.

We've got There's	a little a bit of	bread.

NOT ~~a little of bread~~

We've got There's	a lot of lots of plenty of	milk.

Link
have got →66

1 Look at the picture. Answer the questions.

a Have we got any milk? Yes. _A bit_ .

b Is there any rice? Yes. ____ .

c Is there any cheese? Yes. ____ .

d Have we got any sugar? Yes. ____ .

e Is there any yoghurt? Yes. ____ .

f Have we got any butter? Yes. ____ .

(picture labels: Yoghurt, Butter, Butter, Yoghurt, Yoghurt, Butter, RICE, SUGAR)

2 Now write complete sentences.

a _We've got a bit of milk._

b ____

c ____

d ____

e ____

f ____

B Phrases — *a lot of, not much, very little*

Link
Denmark, Japan →38

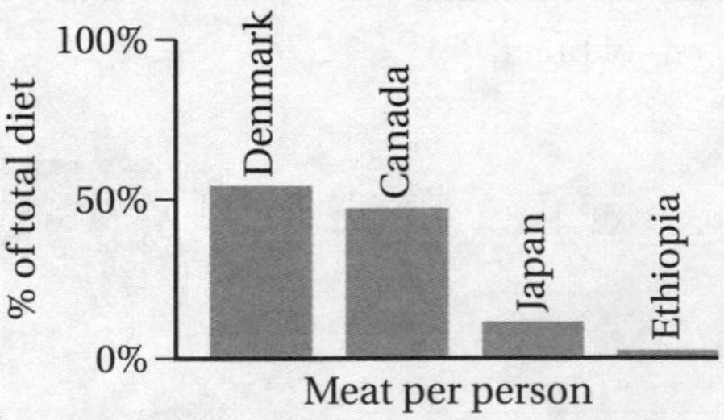

% of total diet — 100%, 50%, 0% — Denmark, Canada, Japan, Ethiopia — Meat per person

In Denmark, people eat a lot of / lots of meat.

In Canada, people eat quite a lot of meat.

In Japan, people don't eat much / a lot of meat.

In Ethiopia, people eat very little meat.

a lot of *lots of*	*quite a lot of*	*not much* *not a lot of*	*very little*

a little is positive: Would you like *a little* milk in your coffee?

very little is negative: He doesn't go out much – he's got *very little* money.

3 Look at the diagrams and write sentences.

  a In Canada, *people eat very little rice* .

  b In Iceland, _____ .

  c In Japan, _____ .

  d In Denmark, _____ .

  e In Ethiopia, _____ .

  f In China, _____ .

  g In Vietnam, _____ .

Sugar

Iceland | Vietnam | Ethiopia | Japan

Rice

Denmark | Canada | China

C Phrases

Links

uncountable nouns
➲13

How much ...? ➲95

How much ...?

How much bread is there?

Lots. I bought some this morning.

How much time have we got for lunch?

Only half an hour.

***How much* + uncountable noun**

| How much | money ...? |
| | time ...? |

4 Complete the questions. Write **How much** + a word from the box.

  a – _How much food_ shall we take?

   – Quite a lot – I expect we'll be quite hungry.

  b – _____ is there in the car?

   – Not much – we can take one more person.

  c – _____ did you use?

   – Not much – I only had a quick shower.

  d – _____ have you got?

   – Not much, but I've got a credit card.

  e – _____ is there in the car?

   – Plenty – I filled it up yesterday.

  f – _____ did you do yesterday?

   – Lots – I was in the office until 10.30.

water
work
space
money
petrol
✓food

Write in your language

There's plenty of oil, but not much rice.	
We've got very little money.	
How much time have we got?	

15 How many …?

A Phrases — *a few, several, lots of*

Links
→ 13 Countable and uncountable nouns
→ 14 How much?

Links
someone → 16A
was/were (watch)ing → 87A

In the street …

Someone was playing the violin. **A few** people were watching.

Two people were playing the guitar. **Several** people were watching.

Someone was juggling. **Lots of** / **A lot of** people were watching.

a few   *several*   *lots of / a lot of*

Link
nearly, over → 1C

1 Change the words in *italics*. Use **a few**, **several** or **lots of / a lot of**.

  a He loves reading – he's got *nearly 200 books* in his room.   <u>lots of books</u>

  b On my birthday, I went out for a meal with *3 friends*.   ....

  c You can buy these boxes in *5 or 6 different colours*.   ....

  d There were *over 100 people* on the beach – we couldn't find a place to sit down.   ....

  e I took *40–50 photos* of their wedding.   ....

  f There were *2 or 3 people* in the café.   ....

B Phrases — *a lot, not many, very few*

Link
in the north/south/centre of → 37

Look at the map of Argentina.

Lots of / **A lot of** people live around Buenos Aires.

Quite a lot of people live in the north of the country.

Not many / **Not a lot of** people live in the centre of the country.

Very few people live in the south.

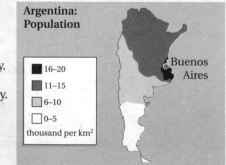

Argentina: Population

- ■ 16–20
- ■ 11–15
- □ 6–10
- □ 0–5

thousand per km²

a lot of lots of	quite a lot of	not much not a lot of	very few

⟵——————————————————————————⟶

a few is positive: We had a nice evening. *A few* friends came for dinner.

very few is negative: The party wasn't very good. *Very few* people came.

2 Look at the maps of Australia and Ireland. Complete the sentences.

a _Lots of people live_ around Sydney.

b _____ in the centre of Australia.

c _____ along the east coast of Australia.

d _____ around Dublin.

e _____ in the west of Ireland.

f _____ in the north of Ireland.

C Phrases — *How many ...?*

Links

were there	➥ 84
How many ...?	➥ 95C

Do you know?

How many passengers were there on the Titanic?	**2,227.**
How many lifeboats did it have?	**20.**
How many people died in the disaster?	**1,560.**

How many + **plural noun**

How many	passengers ...? people ...?

---

3 Read the texts and complete the questions. What are the answers?

There are 206 bones in your body. About 120 of these are in your hands and feet.

There were 69,000 people at the 2002 World Cup Final between Brazil and Germany. Ronaldo scored two goals, and Brazil won the match 2–0.

There are about 6,000 languages in the world. In Nigeria, people speak 500 different languages.

a _How many bones_ are there in your hands and feet?   _About 120._

b _____ did Ronaldo score?   _____

c _____ are there in the world?   _____

d _____ were there at the Final?   _____

e _____ do people in Nigeria speak?   _____

f _____ are there in your body?   _____

Write in your language

They have several children.	
He has very few friends.	
How many people came to the funeral?	

16 *someone, something ...*

someone, something, somewhere

She's talking to someone. somebody.
(= we don't know who)

There's something under the bed.
(= we don't know what)

He's from somewhere in India.
(= we don't know where)

Link

has/have (gone) ➜ 90

1 Complete these sentences. Use someone/somebody, something or somewhere.

a He's got _something_ in his pocket. (a gun? a phone?)

b There's _____ at the door. (a neighbour? the postman?)

c He's gone home to get _____ . (his pen? his money?)

d I know I've left my glasses _____ . (on the table? in my coat?)

e He's living _____ in Brazil. (in Rio? in São Paolo?)

f _____ has written you a letter. (your parents? a friend?)

anyone? anything? anywhere?

Is anyone anybody sitting here?

Have we got anything to eat?

Is there anywhere cheap to stay?

Sentence	Question
someone	anyone
somebody	anybody
something	anything
somewhere	anywhere

2 Complete the questions, and match them with the answers.

a Is there _anything_ good on TV? ___4___

b Did you go _____ interesting last summer? _____

c Has _____ seen my dictionary? _____

d Did you do _____ interesting last night? _____

e Did _____ phone while I was out? _____

f Does _____ know the time? _____

1 No, we just went to a café.

2 Yes. It's 2.30.

3 Yes – we went to Canada.

4 I don't know. Look in the newspaper.

5 I think it's on my desk.

6 Yes. Your brother.

C Phrases — *no-one, nothing, nowhere, none*

Link

none ⮕18A

How much petrol have we got?

None.

What's on TV?

Nothing.

3	
2	A. Blair
1	G. Dimarco

Who lives in Flat 3?

No-one. *or* Nobody.

CAR PARK 1 FULL
CAR PARK 2 FULL
CAR PARK 3 FULL
CAR PARK 4 FULL

Where can I park?

Nowhere.

Positive	Negative
some	none
someone	no-one
somebody	nobody
something	nothing
somewhere	nowhere

Link

Who …? ⮕96

3 Answer these questions. Use none, no-one/nobody, nothing or nowhere.

a Who's in the bathroom? *No-one.*

b What are you doing? ....

c How much money have we got? ....

d Where did you go last night? ....

e Who did you see last night? ....

f What do you want to eat? ....

D Phrases — *not … anyone, not … anything*

Link

no ⮕18A

Michelle was bored. She had no friends in this town – in fact, she knew nobody. She did nothing all day and she went nowhere in the evening.

Michelle was bored. She didn't have any friends in this town – in fact, she didn't know anybody. She didn't do anything all day and she didn't go anywhere in the evening.

no	=	not … any
no-one	=	not … anyone
nobody	=	not … anybody
nothing	=	not … anything
nowhere	=	not … anywhere

Link

There was, there were ⮕84

4 Here are some more sentences about Michelle. Complete the sentences.

a There was nothing to read. = There *wasn't anything to read* .

b She .... = She didn't have any money.

c She saw nobody all day. = She ....

d There .... = There wasn't anywhere to go.

e She .... = She didn't have anybody to talk to.

f There were no videos to watch. = There ....

Write in your language

They live somewhere in France.	
Is anybody sitting here?	
I don't want anything to eat.	

41

17 *every, all, the whole*

A Grammar *every, all the*

Holiday villas

HOLIDAY VILLAS
- 3 LUXURY ROOMS
- AIR-CONDITIONING
- SEA VIEW

Link
all ⟳18

Every villa has three rooms.
Every room has air-conditioning.
Every villa has a view of the sea.

All the villas have three rooms.
All the rooms have air-conditioning.
All the villas have a view of the sea.

every + singular

| Every | room
villa | has … |

all the + plural

| All the | rooms
villas | have … |

Link
plane crash, fire ⟳50

1 Complete these sentences. Write **every** or **all the** plus a word from the box.

   a Have you closed <u>all the windows</u> ?

   b She's been to _____ in Europe.

   c _____ are closed today. It's a holiday.

   d Could you put _____ in the dishwasher?

   e _____ in the street has its own garage.

   f Pictures of the plane crash were in _____ .

   g A fire destroyed _____ in the university library.

   h _____ in their flat is a different colour.

house
plates
books
room
shops
country
newspapers
✓windows

B Phrases *all day, the whole day*

Links
every ⟳10
from … to, until ⟳7A

0°
−30°
−60°
JAN   JUNE   DEC

I felt ill,
so I stayed in bed all day.
              the whole day.
(= from morning to evening)

In Antarctica,
it stays cold all year.
          the whole year.
(= from January to December)

all day = from morning to evening
every day = on Monday, Tuesday, Wednesday, Thursday …

2 Re-write the sentences, changing the parts in *italics*.
Use phrases from the table.

	morning
	afternoon
all	evening
the whole	night
	week
	summer

a Were you at home *from 6.00 p.m. to midnight*?

   Were you at home the whole evening?

b We talked *until 6.00 in the morning*.

   _____

c They stayed in London *from Monday to Sunday*. _____

d I'd love to stay in bed *until lunchtime*. _____

e We spent *from June to September* in Italy. _____

f He watched TV *from 12.00 to 6.00 p.m.* _____

C Phrases — *everyone, everything, everywhere*

Link

➲16 **someone, something …**

VILLAGE FLOODED

The village of Twyford in Devon was flooded at the weekend. Water rose suddenly to 10 metres in the village centre, and everyone had to leave their homes. 'It was terrible,' said a resident. 'Suddenly there was water everywhere. It all happened very quickly, but fortunately, everyone was rescued, by boat or by helicopter.' On Monday, the villagers could return to their homes, but many found that there was serious damage. One resident told us, 'Everything in the house was destroyed – furniture, carpets, papers – everything.'

> Everyone had to leave their homes.

> There was water everywhere.

> Everyone was rescued, by boat or by helicopter.

> Everything in the house was destroyed: furniture, carpets, papers – everything.

Links

was (rescued), was (destroyed) ➲50B, 94

there was ➲84

fire, thieves, steal, police ➲50

3 Complete the sentences. Use **everyone, everybody, everything** or **everywhere**.

FIRE IN OFFICE

JEWELLERY STOLEN

a There was smoke *everywhere* _____ .

b _____ left the building in time.

c 'We had to leave _____ on our desks.'

d _____ was destroyed in the fire.

e There was glass _____ .

f The police want to talk to _____ who was in the shop.

g 'They took _____ in the shop.'

Write in your language

Every room in the hotel has its own balcony.	
We stayed there all evening.	
Everything was destroyed in the fire.	

18 *all, both, most, some …*

A Grammar — *all, most, some, none*

Links

all	➲17
none	➲16

All (the) countries in Europe are members of the United Nations.
Every country in Europe is a member of the United Nations.

Most (of the) countries in Europe are members of the EU.

Some (of the) countries in Europe use the euro.
No countries in Europe use the US dollar.
None of the countries in Europe use the US dollar.

all	*most*	*some*	*none*

All Most Some No	countries people	*or*	All (of) Most of Some of None of	the	countries people	NOT ~~most of countries~~ ~~some of people~~ ~~the most people~~

Link

is (spoken), are (sold), is (taught) ➲93

1 Complete these sentences. Use words from the table (add **of** if necessary).

 a He has read *all* the books in the library. (100%)
 b Spanish is spoken in _____ countries in South America. (80%)
 c _____ the players in the team are Italian. (30%)
 d _____ the rooms in the Hotel Astor have baths. (0%)
 e I'm afraid _____ the tickets are sold for tomorrow's concert. (100%)
 f French is taught at _____ schools in Britain. (90%)

B Grammar — *all of them, most of them, none of them*

All these people were at school together in the 1960s.

Most of the people are women.
⟶ Most of them are women.

None of the people are wearing hats.
⟶ None of them are wearing hats.

2 Here are more sentences about the people in the photo. Correct them.

All	
Most	of them ...
Some	
None	

a All of them are men.   Some of them are men.

b Some of them are sitting. ....

c Most of them have glasses. ....

d All of them have short hair. ....

e Some of them are over 40. ....

f All of them are smiling. ....

both, one, neither

 Here is some luggage at an airport.

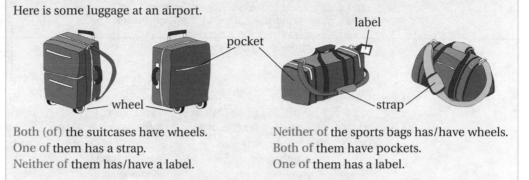

Both (of) the suitcases have wheels.   Neither of the sports bags has/have wheels.
One of them has a strap.   Both of them have pockets.
Neither of them has/have a label.   One of them has a label.

Two people or things: ✓✓   ✓✗   ✗✗
                        both one neither

3 Which pieces of luggage belong to Mike and Irina?

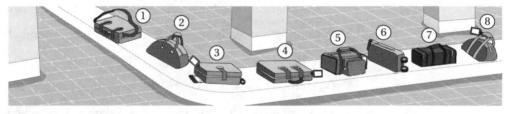

Mike has two pieces of luggage. Both of them are suitcases.
Neither of them have wheels. One of them has a label.   Answer: ...., ...
Irina also has two pieces of luggage. One of them is a suitcase with
wheels. Both of them have labels. Neither of them has pockets.   Answer: ...., ...

4 Choose the best answer.

a Peter and John are good friends. *Both* / *All* / *None* of them like fishing.

b This is a photo of Sue, Anne and me. *Both* / *All* / *None* of us work in the same office.

c Chad, Niger and Mali are in Africa. *Both* / *Neither* / *None* of them are on the coast.

d I met my husband in 1995. *Both* / *All* / *Neither* of us were on a plane to New York.

e I invited Sue and Nick to the party, but *both* / *neither* / *none* of them came.

f Anna and her husband always travel by bus. *Both* / *Neither* / *One* of them can drive.

Write in your language

Most of the people here are students.	
Neither of them are married.	
Both those suitcases are mine.	

19 other, another ...

A Grammar — *other, another, the other*

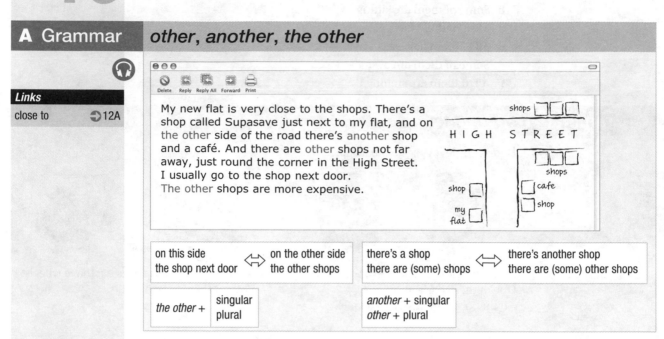

Links

close to ➲12A

My new flat is very close to the shops. There's a shop called Supasave just next to my flat, and on the other side of the road there's another shop and a café. And there are other shops not far away, just round the corner in the High Street. I usually go to the shop next door.
The other shops are more expensive.

HIGH STREET
shops
cafe
shop
shop
my flat

on this side		on the other side		there's a shop		there's another shop
the shop next door	⟺	the other shops		there are (some) shops	⟺	there are (some) other shops

the other +	singular		*another* + singular
	plural		*other* + plural

1 Add **other**, or change **a** to **another**.

  other

a There's no phone here, but there's one in the ⟍room.

    another

b There's a toilet on the ground floor, and there's ~~a~~ ⟍ toilet upstairs.

c I've read this book. Have you got any books by Ian Rankin?

d I'm not staying with Peter. I'm staying with some friends.

e This is my husband when he was twenty – and here's a picture of him.

f One brother lives in London, but he's got a brother in Canada.

g Mary's at university, but all my friends are still at school.

B Grammar — *another, some more*

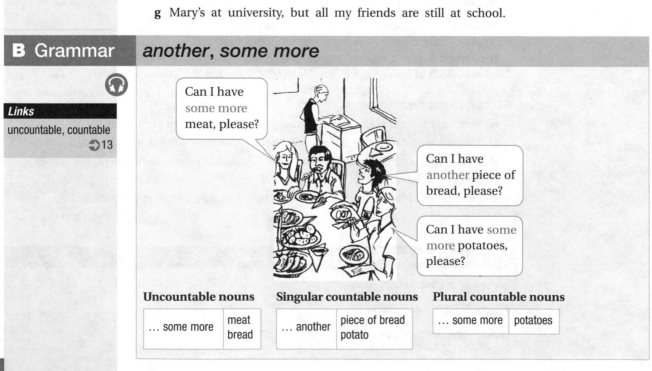

Links

uncountable, countable ➲13

Can I have some more meat, please?

Can I have another piece of bread, please?

Can I have some more potatoes, please?

Uncountable nouns		**Singular countable nouns**		**Plural countable nouns**	
... some more	meat bread	... another	piece of bread potato	... some more	potatoes

2 You're at the table. Ask for more food and drink. Write **some more** or **another**.

a Can I have _some more_ lamb, please?

b Can I have .... vegetables, please?

c Can I have .... glass of orange juice, please?

d Can I have .... piece of chicken, please?

e Can I have .... salad?

f Can I have .... banana?

g Can I have .... water?

C Grammar   *something else, someone else, somewhere else*

Link

➲16   **someone, something …**

Do you want coffee, or shall we have something else?

Where's the waitress?

She's serving someone else.

It's cold here. Let's sit somewhere else.

something else	*someone* ⎱ *else*	*somewhere else*
= another thing, a different thing	*somebody* ⎰ = another person, a different person	= another place, a different place

Link

different   ➲31

Link

Let's …, Why don't you …?   ➲75

3 Complete the sentences. Use **someone/somebody else**, **something else** or **somewhere else**.

a We've watched enough TV. Let's do _something else_ .

b This isn't my car. It belongs to ....

c They used to live here, but now they've moved ....

d I'm not interested in football. Let's talk about ....

e If you don't want those books, why don't you give them to .... ?

f You can sleep in my bed, and I'll sleep ....

Write in your language

There's another phone in the bedroom.	
Would you like some more fish?	
I don't like it here. Let's go somewhere else.	

20 mine, yours …

A Grammar

Link

I think, I expect ➲70

It isn't mine

> Is that your mobile?

> No, it isn't mine. I think it's yours.

> OK. I've got our passports, but I can't find John's.

> Don't forget your suitcase.

> Oh, that isn't ours. I expect it's hers.

Possessive adjectives

It's They're	my your his her our their	mobile. case. passport.
	John's	

⇨

Possessive pronouns

It's They're	mine. yours. his. hers. ours. theirs.
	John's.

yours, hers, ours, theirs
NOT
~~your's, her's, our's, their's~~

Link

bigger, better ➲27A

1 Rewrite the words in *italics*, using possessive pronouns.

a – Could I have my drink, please?
  – *Which is your drink*, the tea or the coffee?   *Which is yours?*
  – Oh, *the coffee is my drink* …
  … *The tea is Maria's drink.*

b They have two cars. *The Honda is his car* …
  … and *the VW is her car.*

c – I think their flat is *better than our flat.*
  – Really? *Our flat is bigger.*
  – Yes, but *their flat is nearer the centre.*

B Phrases

It belonged to Isaac Newton

This telescope once belonged to Isaac Newton.
(= it was Isaac Newton's)

This island belongs to the Onassis family.
(= it's the Onassis family's)

These jewels belong to the Queen of Britain.
(= they're the Queen's)

…	belong belongs belonged	to …

2 Write sentences with a form of **belong to**.

a Abraham Lincoln

b Princess Diana

c Bill Gates

d Prince Charles

e Elvis Presley

f William Shakespeare

a It belonged to Abraham Lincoln.

b _____

c _____

d _____

e _____

f _____

C Grammar

Links

Whose …?, Who …?
➲ 95, 96

do, does ➲ 81

Whose coat is this?

These people had guests for the weekend. When they left, the guests didn't take everything with them …

Whose scarf is this?

Who does this coat belong to?

Whose gloves are these?

Who do these boots belong to?

Whose	…	is this? are these?

Who	does this do these	…	belong to?

Links

might be, may be, probably ➲ 71

was (wear)ing ➲ 87

tie, boots ➲ 51

3 The guests left some other things. Write questions with **Whose …?** or **Who …?**

a – Whose tie is this? _____ *or*
Who does this tie belong to?
– It may be Colin's. He was wearing a tie.

b – _____ ?
– They're probably Jan's. He smokes.

c – _____ ?
– They're Alice's. She was wearing them last night.

d – _____ ?
– It may be Angus's. He speaks Italian.

e – _____ ?
– It might be Matt's. He drives a VW.

f – _____ ?
– It's Oliver's.

book

tie

earrings

ring

cigars   key

Write in your language

These keys aren't mine. Are they yours?

This dress belonged to my mother.

Whose mobile is this?

21 *myself, my own ...*

A Grammar — *introduce yourself ...*

Link

cut ➲49A

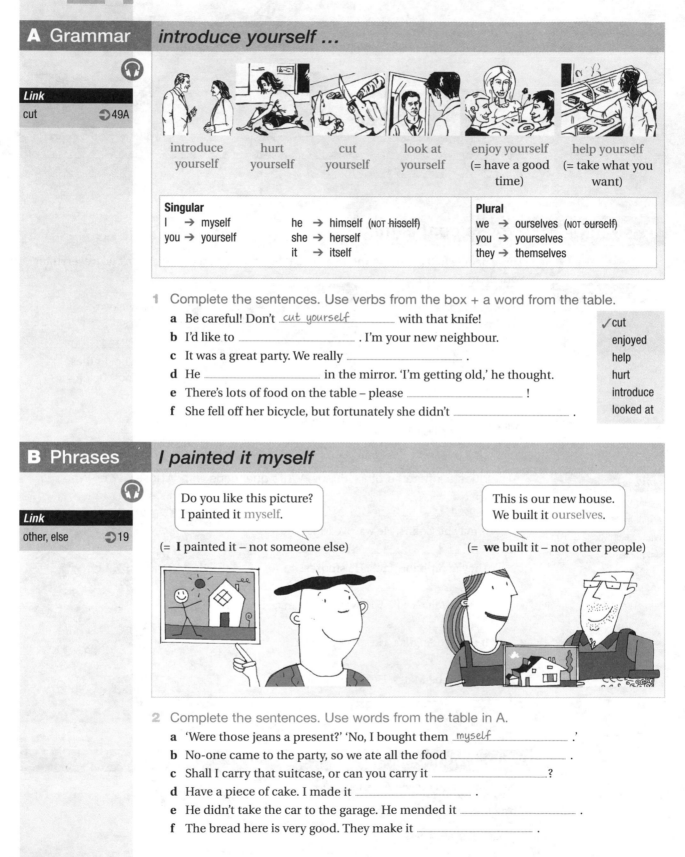

introduce yourself   hurt yourself   cut yourself   look at yourself   enjoy yourself (= have a good time)   help yourself (= take what you want)

Singular			Plural	
I → myself	he → himself (NOT ~~hisself~~)		we → ourselves (NOT ~~ourself~~)	
you → yourself	she → herself		you → yourselves	
	it → itself		they → themselves	

1   Complete the sentences. Use verbs from the box + a word from the table.

   a   Be careful! Don't <u>cut yourself</u> with that knife!

   b   I'd like to _____ . I'm your new neighbour.

   c   It was a great party. We really _____ .

   d   He _____ in the mirror. 'I'm getting old,' he thought.

   e   There's lots of food on the table – please _____ !

   f   She fell off her bicycle, but fortunately she didn't _____ .

> ✓cut
> enjoyed
> help
> hurt
> introduce
> looked at

B Phrases — *I painted it myself*

Link

other, else ➲19

> Do you like this picture?
> I painted it myself.

(= **I** painted it – not someone else)

> This is our new house.
> We built it ourselves.

(= **we** built it – not other people)

2   Complete the sentences. Use words from the table in A.

   a   'Were those jeans a present?' 'No, I bought them <u>myself</u> .'

   b   No-one came to the party, so we ate all the food _____ .

   c   Shall I carry that suitcase, or can you carry it _____ ?

   d   Have a piece of cake. I made it _____ .

   e   He didn't take the car to the garage. He mended it _____ .

   f   The bread here is very good. They make it _____ .

my own, our own

Links

work, leave, business ⟳ 42

make ⟳ 63A

For 10 years, Claire Mancini worked in a large supermarket, but then she decided to leave and start her own business. She opened the first Pasta Company shop in 2003, and she now has 20 shops in 15 different towns. 'We make our own pasta, and we make 15 different pasta sauces,' Claire told me. 'And we also sell other Italian food: cheese, ham, coffee, olives, olive oil.'

It's her own business = she doesn't work for other people.

We make our own pasta = we don't buy it from other people, we make it ourselves.

3 Complete the sentences. Use words from the table.

my your his her its our their	own	vegetables language shower car sandwiches flat

a She doesn't buy lunch at the office. She always brings *her own sandwiches* .

b They didn't come with us. They came in
....

c We've got a large garden, so we can grow
....

d It's a lovely room. It's really big, and it's got ....

e I'm renting a room at the moment, but I'd like to buy ....

f If you can't say it in English, say it in ....

on my own, on her own

1

The café was nearly empty, and she was sitting in a corner on her own.

(= she was alone, no-one was with her)

2

No-one taught me to read. I learnt on my own at the age of four.

(= she learnt without help, she taught herself)

4 Look at the phrases in *italics*. Do they mean **alone** or **without help**?

a He enjoys travelling *on his own*.   *alone*

b I can't move the piano *on my own* – it's too heavy.   *without help*

c He's 95, but he can still go up and down stairs *on his own*.   ....

d Everyone went out, and I stayed in the house *on my own*.   ....

e In 1995, she spent six months in England *on her own*.   ....

f Shall I tell you what to write, or can you do it *on your own*?   ....

Write in your language

I'd like to introduce myself. I'm John.

Did you paint this yourself?

They grow all their own vegetables.

A Phrases

in the middle, on the right

Claudia   Stefan   Arzu   Julia   Florian

Jana   Max   me   Friederike   Rafaela   Philip

| on the | left
right | | at the | front
back | | in the middle |

This is me, in the middle, with long dark hair.
And there's Rafaela at the front, on the right – the one with glasses.
And that's Stefan at the back, on the left – he's got his eyes closed!

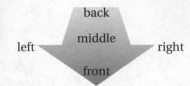

back

left   middle   right

front

We can also say:
in the front row, in the back row, in the middle row, at the side

Links

top, trainers ➡ 51
he's got, she's got
➡ 66A

1 Find these people in the photo.

   a She's in the middle row, on the left. She's got a light top.   *Claudia*

   b He's in the middle row, on the right. He's short.

   c She's at the back.

   d She's at the front, on the left.

   e He's at the front, on the right.

   f She's at the front, in the middle. She's wearing a scarf.

B Phrases

behind, at the back

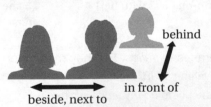

behind

in front of

beside, next to

Stefan is at the back (of the photo).

Friederike is at the front (of the photo).

Philip is   on the right
at the side   (of the photo).

He's behind Claudia.

She's in front of me.

He's   beside
next to   Rafaela.

2 Say two things about each of these people:

   a Me   *I'm in the middle of the photo, and I'm behind Friederike.*

   b Arzu   *She's*

   c Claudia

   d Florian

   e Jana

at the top, at the bottom

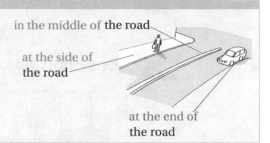

at the top of **the page**

at the side of **the page**

at the bottom of **the page**

in the middle of **the road**

at the side of **the road**

at the end of **the road**

3 Where could you find these things? Use words from both boxes.

a <u>at the top of a mountain</u>

b ....

c ....

d ....

e ....

f ....

g ....

top	page
side	corridor
middle	building
bottom	mountain
end	road
	field

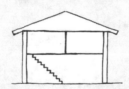

a Mount Murdoch 1675m

b 56th floor – *Panorama* restaurant

c – 63 –

 **d**

 **e**

 **f**

 g

upstairs, downstairs

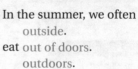

There's a kitchen downstairs, and there are two bedrooms upstairs.

In the winter, we eat inside. indoors.

In the summer, we often outside. eat out of doors. outdoors.

4 Choose the best answer.

a It rained all weekend, so the children had to play (*indoors*)/ *downstairs* .

b Let's sit *inside* / *outside* in the garden.

c It's too cold to stay *downstairs* / *out of doors*. Why don't you come in?

d The toilet is *upstairs* / *downstairs* , by the front door.

e I was tired, so I went *upstairs* / *outside* and went to bed.

f My shoes are very dirty. I think I'll leave them *indoors* / *outside* .

Write in your language

She's at the back, on the left.	
Don't stand in the middle of the road!	
He lives at the end of the street.	

23 Direction

A Phrases | Direction prepositions: *past*, *towards*, *round* ...

A bee flew into the room.	It flew towards me.	It flew past my nose.	Then it flew under the table ...
... and round the room.	Then it flew through the window ...	... out of the house ...	... and over the wall.

into   *over*   *past*   *towards*
out of   *under*   *round*   *through*

Link

went, came ➜ 85B

1 What are these directions? Complete the phrases.

a We went _over_ the bridge.
b I walked _____ the bridge.
c He came _____ the corner.
d We went _____ the gate.
e The ball went _____ the goal.
f The ball went _____ the chair.
g She came _____ the shop.
h He walked _____ me.
i We drove _____ the house.

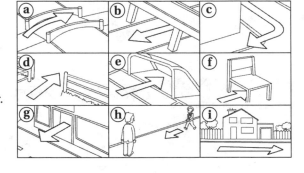

B Phrases | Prepositions: *across*, *along*, *up*, *down* ...

Link

floor, bookshelf, curtain
➜ 33

1 The mouse came out of its hole, ...
2 ... ran across the floor, ...
3 ... climbed up the leg of the table, ...
4 ... and climbed on the table.
5 Then it jumped onto the bookshelf, ...
6 ... ran along the bookshelf, ...
7 ... jumped off the bookshelf, ...
8 ... climbed down the curtain, ...
9 ... and went back into its hole again.

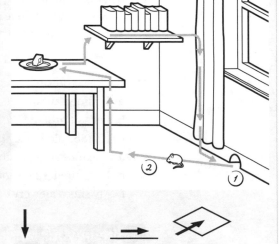

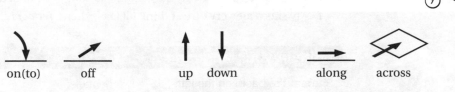

on(to)   off   up   down   along   across

2 Look at the picture of the mouse again. Write numbers 3–9 in the picture.

3 Choose the **two** best words in each sentence.

  a They ran across *the field* / *the street* / *the gate*.   <u>the field, the street</u>

  b Go *across* / *through* / *under* the bridge and turn left.

  c The road runs along *a river* / *a railway* / *a hotel*.

  d You'll go past *a river* / *a hotel* / *a church*.

  e The mouse ran *up* / *across* / *down* the table leg.

  f He walked *through* / *past* / *towards* me.

C Phrases   Giving directions

Link

➲ 36   **In the street**

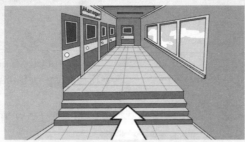

'Go up the stairs, then go along the corridor until you come to a door that says 'Manager'. Go past that door, and my office is the second door on the left.'

'Go through the main entrance, and go round to the back of the building. You'll come to a wall with a gate in it. Go through the gate, and across a courtyard. You'll see my office in front of you.'

Go	up … along … round …

You'll	come to … see …

… until you	come to … see …

You'll see it	on the left. on the right. in front of you. straight ahead.

4 Look at the pictures above. Where do the directions go to?

5 Look at the picture and write directions to the statue.

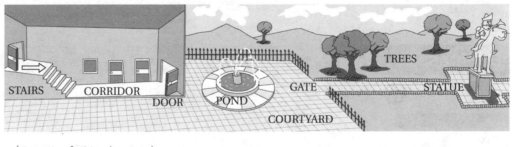

STAIRS   CORRIDOR   DOOR   POND   GATE   TREES   STATUE   COURTYARD

'Go out of this door and

                                                 I'll meet you by the statue.'

Write in your language

He came out of the house and ran towards me.

Go down the stairs and along the corridor …

… until you come to a door on your right.

24 *by, with, without*

A Phrases — *a novel by Isabel Allende*

Links

was written, was painted ➔94

painting, play, film ➔54

a novel by Isabel Allende

a painting by Edouard Manet

= Isabel Allende wrote it.
or It was written by Isabel Allende.

= Edouard Manet painted it.
or It was painted by Edouard Manet.

1 Do you know what these are? Write sentences, using a word from the box and **by**.

a Otello .... It's an opera by Verdi. ....

b Guernica ....

c Tao Te Ching ....

d Macbeth ....

e War and Peace ....

f Seven Samurai ....

book
play
film
opera
painting

B Phrases — *by train, by fax, by cheque*

Links

by train ➔40A

pay, credit card ➔47

We can use *by* to talk about:

travel	communicating	paying money
How did you get to London?	How shall I send this letter?	How shall I pay you?
We went by train.	Send it by fax.	You can pay by cheque.

2 Add phrases to the lists. Choose words from the box.

credit card bus email post plane taxi

We went ...
......by train......
....
....
....

Send it ...
......by fax......
....
....

You can pay ...
......by cheque......
....
....

We also say:
I went there *on foot*.
(= we walked)
I paid *in cash*.
(= with money)

Link

If … would ⮕80B

3 Complete these sentences about yourself.

  a I usually travel to work or school _____ .

  b If I wanted to send a photo to a friend, I would send it _____ .

  c If I bought a TV, I would pay for it _____ .

C Phrases *with*

Link

use ⮕64A

Light the blue paper.
Use a match.

⬇

Light the blue paper
with a match.

Clean the shoes.
Use a soft cloth.

⬇

Clean the shoes with
a soft cloth.

Links

glue, sellotape ⮕64B

cut, stir ⮕32

4 Complete these instructions. Use **with** and an expression from the box.

  a Write your name __with a black pen__ .

  b Cut the meat into pieces _____ .

  c **Stir the soup** _____ .

  d Wash your hands _____ .

  e Clean the oven _____ .

  f Stick the sheets of paper together _____ .

soap and water

✓ a black pen

a sharp knife

glue or sellotape

a large spoon

an old toothbrush

D Phrases *with, without*

a room with a
balcony

a room without a
balcony

a shirt with a collar

a shirt without a
collar

5 Choose **with** or **without**.

  a Don't go out *with* / *without* your coat. It might be cold later.

  b These glasses are no good. I can see better *with* / *without* them.

  c I'd like coffee *with* / *without* two sugars, please.

  d Can you lend me some money? I came out *with* / *without* my wallet.

  e Do you want your chicken *with* / *without* potatoes or *with* / *without* rice?

  f I don't know what colour his eyes are. I've never seen him *with* / *without* sunglasses.

Write in your language

Have you got any plays by Chekhov?

Cut up the vegetables with a sharp knife.

You can pay by credit card or in cash.

25 Adjectives

A Vocabulary — Opposite adjectives

a full bottle · an empty bottle · a light room · a dark room · a light bag · a heavy bag

a fast car · a slow car · a strong man · a weak man · a dangerous place · a safe place

an easy formula · a difficult formula · a quiet engine · a loud / a noisy engine · a quiet / an empty street · a busy / a crowded street

1 Which **two** adjectives could go in each sentence?

  a She's a very ___?___ driver.   (~~loud, difficult,~~ safe, fast)

  b They live in a ___?___ part of town.   (noisy, slow, dangerous, weak)

  c Be careful. The suitcase is quite ___?___.   (full, difficult, heavy, dry)

  d I usually wear ___?___ colours.   (dry, light, easy, dark)

  e Chess is a ___?___ game.   (dangerous, difficult, slow, wet)

  f It's very ___?___ here in the winter.   (dark, wet, strong, fast)

B Grammar — *quite, very, really*

The hotel was quite nice. Our room was very big, and the bed was really comfortable.

It was quite a nice hotel. We had a very big room with a really comfortable bed.

very really quite	nice comfortable

a	very really	nice room comfortable bed
quite a		

2 Complete the sentences.

  a The restaurant wasn't very good.   It wasn't _a very good restaurant_ .

  b Our balcony was quite big.   We had _____ .

  c The bathroom was very small.   The room had _____ .

  d The beach near the hotel was really nice.   There was _____ .

  e The town wasn't very interesting.   It wasn't _____ .

  f Our holiday was quite relaxing.   We had _____ .

C Grammar · *so, such*

> I had a wonderful evening. The party was so good, and the people were so interesting!

> I had a wonderful evening. It was such a good party, and I met such interesting people.

so + adjective

| so | good |
| | interesting |

such (a) + adjective + noun

| such | a good party |
| | interesting people |

3 Here are some other things the people said. Add **so** or **such**.

a They have _such_ a lovely flat!

b It has _____ big rooms.

c Everyone was _____ friendly!

d She was wearing _____ a beautiful dress!

e The chairs were _____ comfortable!

f I'm _____ tired!

D Phrases · *I found it interesting*

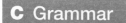

Links

➲ 46   happy, angry, friendly …

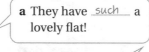

> It was an exciting match. They scored twice in the last two minutes.

> We roast chicken in it. We find it really useful.

> I'm not very good at Chinese. I find it quite difficult.

CHINESE LEVEL 1

> I don't have any problems with it. I think it's an easy language.

> I enjoyed that book. I found it very interesting.

> I thought it was quite a sad book. I cried at the end.

> I found Blue Moon very boring. I fell asleep!

SHREK 2 · BLUE MOON

> I laughed a lot in Shrek 2. I thought it was really funny.

Present

| I find it | interesting. |
| I think it's | an interesting book. |

Past

| I found it | interesting. |
| I thought it was | an interesting book. |

4 Add sentences. Use **I find / I found …** or **I think / I thought …** and an adjective.

a I'm glad I went to the lecture.   _I found it very interesting._

b I couldn't finish the crossword. _____

c I really like our new dishwasher. _____

d I didn't enjoy English at school. _____

e I always watch 'Time to Laugh' on TV. _____

f I learned Italian in three weeks. _____

Write in your language

The suitcase isn't heavy – it's nearly empty!

It's quite a dangerous place.

I thought that film was really funny.

26 Adverbs

Adjectives and adverbs

Link
⮕25 **Adjectives**

I'm sorry we gave him the job – he isn't very good. He's a very slow worker, and he isn't very careful. And he's often late for work.

I'm sorry we gave him the job – he doesn't work very well. He does everything very slowly and not very carefully. And he often arrives late for work.

The words in blue are adjectives. We use adjectives before a noun or after the verb be:

He's a very slow worker.
He isn't very good.
He's often late.

The words in blue are adverbs. We use adverbs with a verb:

He does everything very slowly.
He doesn't work very well.
He often arrives late.

Many adverbs are formed from adjective + –ly:

Some adverbs have the same form as adjectives:

good is irregular:

Adjective	Adverb
slow	slowly
careful	carefully
late	late
good	well

1 Are the words in *italics* adjectives or adverbs? Write **adj** or **adv**.

a They live in a *beautiful* flat. _adj_   **f** I got up *quickly* and had breakfast. ....

b He speaks English very *clearly*. ....   **g** Is Johannesburg a *dangerous* city? ....

c I have to get up *early* tomorrow. ....   **h** Have a rest. You work too *hard*. ....

d You don't need to drive so *fast*. ....   **i** I'm tired. I slept *badly* last night. ....

e I thought the film was really *bad*. ....   **j** I'll get a *late* bus home. ....

2 Choose the **two** best adverbs from the box to go in each sentence.

quietly	clearly	safely	hard	beautifully
late	✓fast	easily	fast	✓dangerously

a I don't want to go with him. He drives too _fast_ .
dangerously .

b She spoke very .... I couldn't understand a word.
....

c I enjoy reading her letters. She writes so ....
....

d I hope you got home .... last night.
....

e Of course he's tired. He works really .... every evening.
....

Sentence adverbs

Here are parts of a newspaper story. All the adverbs in blue can come at the beginning of a sentence.

Links

so   98C
downstairs, outside
                 22D

FARMER SEES 'BRIGHT LIGHT'
A farmer told journalists he saw a 'bright light' in the sky above his farm near Opole, in southern Poland.

1 It was about 2.00 in the morning. I couldn't sleep, so I got up and went downstairs to the kitchen. Suddenly, all the lights went out, and there was a sound outside like a large plane.

2 Naturally, I was frightened, but I went to the window and looked out. I saw a bright light in the sky just above the house, and there was a really strong wind.

3 Fortunately, I had a camera, so I took several photos.

4 I watched the light for over an hour. Eventually, it moved away and the sound got quieter. A few minutes later, the lights in the house came on again.

5 Unfortunately, I was alone in the house, so no-one else saw it.

6 I listened to the weather reports. Apparently, there were no winds that night anywhere in southern Poland.

3 Look at the adverbs. Which means:

a This wasn't surprising. ___2___
b It was a good thing. ....
c It was a bad thing. ....
d after a long time ....
e very quickly ....
f I heard (or read) this. ....

4 Complete the sentences. Use one of the adverbs from B, and a phrase from the box.

a Have you heard the news about Nick and Fiona?
    Apparently they're getting married next month.
b The tickets cost €50 each. ....
    .... with me.
c I was just crossing the road, when ....
    .... round the corner.
d She's got a job in Paris, but she doesn't speak French.
    .... for her.
e I had an interview for a job at Mitsubishi, but ....
f I didn't like London at first, but .... living there.

a car came
I had plenty of money
I started to enjoy
it's very difficult
I didn't get it
✓they're getting married

Write in your language

He came to work late yesterday.

Unfortunately, I don't speak English very well.

Suddenly, the door opened.

Comparatives

A Grammar *cheaper, more expensive*

Links

⮞28   **Superlatives**

⮞25   **Adjectives**

Links

short, long, thin ⮞11

> Which laptop is better?

The Xpert is more powerful than the Atom. It's lighter, and it has a bigger screen. But it's more expensive.
The Atom is faster than the Xpert, and it's cheaper. But it's heavier, and it has a smaller screen.
So they're both good, but the Xpert is better.

XPERT
BIG SCREEN! 30x24
LIGHT! 2.5 kg
FAST! 5.8 GHz
POWERFUL!
1280 MB RAM

ATOM
BIG SCREEN! 28x22
LIGHT! 2.7 kg
FAST! 6.2 GHz
POWERFUL!
1024 MB RAM

The Xpert is	lighter more expensive	than the Atom.

Short adjectives: adjective + -er		**Long adjectives: more + adjective**

light	➤	lighter	**Double consonant + -er**			powerful	➤	more powerful
fast	➤	faster	big	➤	bigger	expensive	➤	more expensive
cheap	➤	cheaper	*thin*	➤	*thinner*	....	➤	....
small	➤	smaller				....	➤	....
....	➤	....	**Words ending in -y: ~~y~~ + -ier**					
....	➤	....	heavy	➤	heavier			
			....	➤	....			

Irregular:	good	➤	better
	bad	➤	worse

1 What are the comparative forms of these adjectives? Write them in the table.

✓thin   warm   difficult   short   easy   comfortable

2 Write sentences with **two** comparisons. Use adjectives from the box.

cheap   comfortable   easy   expensive   fast   powerful   ✓short   ✓warm

Link

and, but   ⮞98A

a The black coat <u>is shorter than the white coat</u>,
but <u>it's warmer</u>.

b Book 1 ....,
and ....

c First class is ....,
but ....

d The Solo Plus ....,
and ....

Have you got anything shorter?

Links

too   ➜29

something, anything
    ➜16

Have you got …?
    ➜66C

This coat's too long …

… I need something shorter.

… Have you got anything shorter?

3 Add sentences with **I need…** or **Have you got…?**

a I like these jeans, but they're too narrow. _Have you got anything wider?_

b This paper's too thick. _____

c This dictionary is very big. _____

d I like this dress, but it's a bit too dark. _____

e It's a lovely camera, but it's too expensive. _____

f This jug is too small. _____

more, less, fewer

Links

➜14 **How much …?**

➜15 **How many …?**

Links

uncountable nouns
    ➜13

more, less   ➜1C

Britain in 1960

Population: 55 million
Cars: 3,000,000
Trains: 3,000 every day
Working day: 9 hours

Britain now

Population: 58 million
Cars: 18,000,000
Trains: 2,600 every day
Working day: 8 hours

There are more people in Britain now (than in 1960). There is more traffic on the roads. There are more cars, but fewer trains.
People do less work, and have more free time.

Uncountable nouns		Countable nouns	
more	traffic	more	people
less	free time	fewer	cars

4 Can you guess the facts? Write **more**, **less** or **fewer**.

a There are _fewer_ small shops now than in 1960.

b _____ people smoke cigarettes than in 1960.

c There are _____ churches than in 1960.

d People eat _____ fish than in 1960.

e People have _____ children than in 1960.

f People eat _____ meat than in 1960.

Write in your language

This coat is warmer than my old one.

Have you got anything cheaper?

People do less work now than in 1960.

28 Superlatives

A Grammar — the cheapest, the most expensive

Link
➲27 Comparatives

The silver ring is the cheapest.
(= It's cheaper than the diamond ring, and it's cheaper than the gold ring.)

The diamond ring is the most expensive.
(= It's more expensive than the silver ring, and it's more expensive than the gold ring.)

SILVER $120   GOLD $350   DIAMOND $2,500

	Adjective	Comparative form	Superlative form	Irregular
Short adjectives	cheap	cheaper	the cheapest	good, better, the best
Long adjectives	expensive	more expensive	the most expensive	bad, worse, the worst

Links

intelligent, lazy,
hard-working ➲46C

tall, short, thin ➲11

1 Write the superlative forms.

old, older, __the oldest__   lazy, lazier, _____

young, younger, _____   fit, fitter, _____

tall, taller, _____   intelligent, more intelligent, _____

short, shorter, _____   hard-working, more hard-working, _____

thin, thinner, _____

2 Think about people in your family. Who is ...

… the oldest?   … the tallest?   … the most hard-working?   … the best singer?

… the youngest?   … the fittest?   … the most intelligent?   … the best cook?

Link

grandmother, uncle
➲44A

Look at the example, and write some sentences.

__In my family__ _____

_____

_____

_____

_____

_____

> In my family …
> My grandmother is the oldest.
> The tallest person is my uncle.
> My sister is the best cook.
> The fittest person is my brother.

B Vocabulary — the hottest place in the world

Link

the world, Africa, Asia
➲37A

Q What's the wettest place in the world?

A Mawsynram, India. (11,900 mm rain every year)

Q What's the largest lake in Africa?

A Lake Victoria. (69,500 km^2)

Link

5.5m, 57.8°C ⮕1B

3 Complete the quiz questions. Use words from the boxes.

a What's _the tallest animal_ in the world?
The giraffe (5.5 m)

b What's _____ in Asia?
The Yangtse (6380 km)

c What's _____ in the world?
El Azizia, Libya (57.8°C)

d What's _____ in South America?
Brazil (8.5 million km²)

e Who's _____ in the world?
Alice Walton ($20 billion+)

f What's _____ in the world?
The blue whale (175 tonnes)

large	animal
tall	country
long	woman
rich	place
heavy	river
hot	

4 Look at the examples, and write sentences about your own country.

_____

_____

_____

_____

Edinburgh is the most beautiful city in Britain.
Celtic is the best football team in Scotland.
London is the largest city in Britain.

C Grammar — *the most, the least, the fewest*

Links

⮕14 **How much …?**
⮕15 **How many …?**

Links

Russia, China ⮕38
Countable nouns,
uncountable nouns ⮕13
use ⮕64
make ⮕63

Russia, Canada, the USA and China are the four
largest countries in the world.
China has the most people. Canada has the fewest people.
Russia produces the most oil. Canada produces the
least oil.

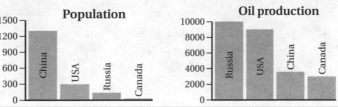

Population | Oil production

Countable nouns

the most the fewest	people

Uncountable nouns

the most the least	oil

5 What do you think? Fill the gaps with **the most**, **the least** or **the fewest**.

a The USA makes _____ cars.
b Canada uses _____ electricity.
c China has _____ trees.
d China grows _____ rice.

e Russia has _____ trees.
f The USA uses _____ electricity.
g Russia makes _____ cars.
h Canada grows _____ rice.

Write in your language

I'm the tallest person in my family.

It's the most beautiful city in Europe.

Which country uses the most electricity?

29 too

It's too high

Link
low, high, narrow, wide
↳11A

The lorry can't go under this bridge.
The bridge is too low.
The lorry is too high.

The lorry can't go over this bridge.
The bridge is too narrow.
The lorry is too wide.

1 What's the problem? Use **too** + words from the box.

big	small	long	short	high	low

a The sleeves *are too long* .
   The trousers _____ .
b The card _____ .
   The envelope _____ .
c The window _____ .
   The ladder _____ .
d The chair _____ .
   His legs _____ .

He worries too much

He worries about money, about
his work, about his children,
about his car, about his flat ...

⟹ He worries too much.

2 Write sentences with **too much**. Use verbs from the box.

a She has 60 cigarettes a day.   *She smokes too much.*
b He goes to sleep at 8.30 in the evening and
   wakes up at 9.30 in the morning.   _____
c She goes to the office at 6.00 a.m., and comes
   back home at 9.00 in the evening.   _____
d He has 3 eggs for breakfast, a large lunch,
   coffee and tea in the afternoon, and then a
   large dinner.   _____
e Yesterday she bought a new coat, today she
   bought a TV and a camera, and tomorrow she's
   getting a new car ...   _____
f Cars are too expensive in Britain.   _____

cost	sleep	spend
eat	✓smoke	work

too much, too many

OVERWEIGHT BRITAIN

40% of British adults are overweight – because they eat too much, and they eat the wrong things. Many people in Britain eat

- too much sugar
- too much chocolate
- too many burgers
- too many chips.

too much + uncountable noun			*too many* + plural countable noun	
too much	chocolate sugar		too many	burgers chips

3 Four people say what they eat. Complete the sentences with **too much/many**.

a 'I think I eat _too much_ cheese, and I certainly eat _____ butter.'

b 'I eat _____ sugar, _____ sweets and _____ chocolate.'

c 'I probably have _____ sweet drinks, like lemonade and cola.'

d 'I don't eat very healthy meals: I eat _____ pizzas and _____ ice-cream.

4 Add **too**, **too much** or **too many** to these sentences.

a I'm afraid you're ⌄too⌄ late – the train's gone .

b I think he's very boring – he talks .

c We never go to the town centre on Saturday – there are always people there .

d I can't see you next week – I've got work .

e They spend money on clothes .

f I can't drink this coffee – it's strong .

g I think they paid for their flat .

Write in your language

We ate too much last night.

You spend too much money.

There are too many cars in the town centre.

30 *enough*

A Grammar   *We haven't got enough milk*

We've got enough eggs and we've got enough flour, but we haven't got enough milk.

Pancakes
3 eggs
150g flour
$\frac{1}{2}$ litre milk

enough + **noun**	enough	eggs
	not enough	milk

NOT ~~enough of eggs~~

Links

make (a cake) ➜ 63A
has/hasn't got ➜ 66

1   Someone wants to make a banana cake. He's got these things: Write sentences.

a   *He hasn't got enough*   eggs.
b   .... flour.
c   .... bananas.
d   .... butter.
e   .... sugar.
f   .... lemons.

Banana Cake
300 g sugar
4 eggs
500g flour
2 lemons
200g butter
5 bananas

Link

food, time, space
➜ 13A

2   Complete the sentences. Use **enough** + a word from the box.

a   You can't put the photocopier here – there isn't *enough space* .
b   Come back for lunch. I think there's .... for everyone.
c   We can't visit the museum today. We haven't got ....
d   There will be 8 people at the meeting. Are there .... in the room?
e   We can't buy a new car. We haven't got ....
f   There's too much sport on TV, and there aren't ....

money
chairs
films
food
✓ space
time

B Grammar   *It isn't long enough*

This ladder isn't long enough.   This ladder is long enough.

adjective + *enough*

is	(long) enough
isn't	

NOT ~~enough long~~

Link

long, tall, wide ➲11

3 What's the problem? Complete the sentences. Use the adjectives in the box.

strong   big   ✓long   tall   old   wide

a
d

a Those curtains are no good.
   They _aren't long enough_ .

b Sorry, you can't see Terminator 3.
   You _____ .

c I can't change the light bulb.
   I _____ .

d Don't try to lift that box.
   You _____ .

e I can't take five people in my car.
   It _____ .

f The piano won't go through the door.
   The door _____ .

b
e
c
f

C Grammar   *She's old enough to drive*

Link

leave school ➲45

Maria is 17 years old.

In Britain …

At 16 you can:
- leave school
- get married
- buy a lottery ticket

At 17 you can:
- drive a car
- ride a motorbike
- give blood

At 18 you can:
- vote
- buy fireworks

At 21 you can:
- drive a bus

She can buy a lottery ticket.
She's old enough.

She can't vote.
She isn't old enough.

She's old enough to buy a
lottery ticket.

She isn't old enough to vote.

Link

and, but, or ➲98A

4 Anna is 15, Nina is 16 and Rose is 19. Match them with the sentences.

a _____ She's old enough to get married, but she isn't old enough to drive a car.

b _____ She isn't old enough to get married or leave school.

c _____ She's old enough to vote and drive a motorbike.

Now write sentences.

d Anna / give blood   _Anna isn't old enough to give blood._

e Nina / leave school   _____

f Anna / buy fireworks _____

g Rose / vote   _____

Write in your language

We've got enough money to take a taxi.

Sorry – there isn't enough time.

It isn't warm enough to go swimming.

31 *the same, different ...*

A Vocabulary — *the same, similar, different*

Look at these houses.

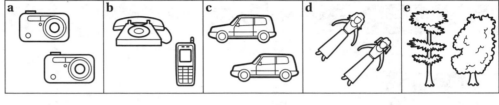

They're (exactly) the same.   They're similar.   They're (completely)
(= almost the same)   different.

Link
exactly   ➔ 1C

1 Look at the pictures. Are they **the same**, **similar** or **different**?

a *They're the same.*   d ....

b ....   e ....

c ....

B Phrases — *the same name, different names*

Peter and Paul are twins. They are the same age, they
have the same surname and they live in the same
house. But they aren't exactly the same: they have
different first names, different hairstyles, and they
wear different clothes.

2 Sue and May are friends. Which things are **the same** and which are **different**?

Name: Sue Green	Name: May Dunn
Address: 7 Bridge Road, York	Address: 23 West Street, York
Age: 25	Age: 25
Job: Computer programmer	Job: Shop assistant
School: York High School	School: York High School

a They have *different names* . (name)

b They live in .... (town)

c They live in .... (street)

d They are .... (age)

e They have .... (job)

f They went to .... (school)

the same as, different from

Link
mine, ours, yours ➲20

They live in New Street.
We live in New Street, too.

They live in **the same** street **as** us.

They live in New Street, but we live in George Street.

They live in a **different** street **from** us.

3 Write the words in (brackets) in the correct order.

a I often see them. They live _in the same street as us_ . (us / as / street / same / the / in)

b We can't go on holiday together, because she has holidays _____
_____ . (me / from / a / time / different / at)

c Their children are _____ , so they often
play together. (age / same / the / ours / as)

d We have two televisions at home, because my husband watches _____
_____ . (me / programmes / from / different)

e Your camera was _____ , but I think yours is better.
(as / price / same / mine / the)

like, similar to

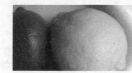

A lime is $\begin{matrix} \text{like} \\ \text{similar to} \end{matrix}$ a lemon, but it's green and it's smaller.

lime   lemon

Links
smaller, bigger ➲27A
looks like ➲62B

4 Match the pictures with the sentences. Complete the last two yourself.

a _3_ It's similar to a horse, but it's got stripes.
b ____ They're like scissors, but they are stronger, and you use them in the garden.
c ____ It's like a large spoon, but it's deeper.
d ____ It's like an orange, but it's smaller.
e ____ _____ , but it's bigger.
f ____ _____ , but it's got one wheel.

Write in your language

They live in the same street as us.

My brother and I went to different schools.

It's like an apple, but it's smaller.

32 Food and cooking

A Vocabulary — Food

Links

a slice of, pieces of
➲ 13C

with ➲ 24

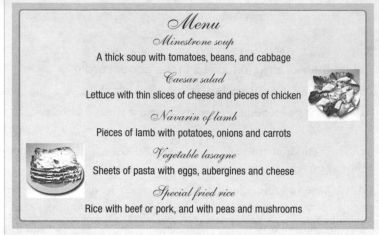

Menu

Minestrone soup
A thick soup with tomatoes, beans, and cabbage

Caesar salad
Lettuce with thin slices of cheese and pieces of chicken

Navarin of lamb
Pieces of lamb with potatoes, onions and carrots

Vegetable lasagne
Sheets of pasta with eggs, aubergines and cheese

Special fried rice
Rice with beef or pork, and with peas and mushrooms

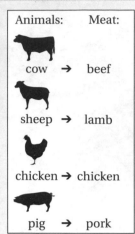

Animals:		Meat:
cow	→	beef
sheep	→	lamb
chicken	→	chicken
pig	→	pork

1 Find words for food in the menu. Write them in three lists:

Meat — lamb ....

Vegetables — potatoes ....

....

Other — cheese ....

Link

(We) had ➲ 85B

2 Think of a meal you had in the last week. Write a sentence about it.

....

....

> For lunch yesterday we had beef with rice and mushrooms.

B Vocabulary — Cooking

You can **cook** food, or you can eat it **raw**.

cooked food   **raw** food (= not cooked)

Some ways to cook food:

boil (= cook in water)   fry (= cook with fat or oil)   bake (= cook in the oven)   roast (= cook in the oven with fat or oil)   grill

a **boiled** egg   a **fried** egg   **baked** potatoes   **roast(ed)** meat   **grilled** fish

Verbs	cook	boil	fry	grill	roast	bake	–
Adjectives	cooked	boiled	fried	grilled	roast(ed)	baked	raw

3 Which of these have you eaten? Write ✓✓ (= I often eat this), ✓ (= I have eaten this, but I don't often eat it) or ✗ (= I've never eaten this).

.... baked potatoes .... fried aubergines .... raw fish .... roast beef

.... boiled potatoes .... grilled chicken .... boiled rice .... raw lamb

C Vocabulary Recipes

CHICKEN STEW

4 to 6 chicken pieces	2 cups of water	oil
1 onion	salt, pepper	a large pan
2 potatoes		

Cut the potatoes and onions into slices.

Pour some oil into the pan.

Put the chicken, potatoes and onions in the pan and fry them for 10 minutes.

Add the water, salt and pepper.

Put a lid on the pan, and cook it slowly for an hour.

Stir it occasionally with a spoon.

Cut the onions into	slices pieces.		Pour	the oil water	into the pan.		Put	the onions in the pan. the lid on the pan.

4 Complete the sentences. Use each word from the box **once**.

How to cook rice

You need: 1 cup of rice, 2 cups of cold water, salt

(a) Put _____ the rice in a pan. Then (b) _____ the water over the rice, and (c) _____ a little salt. (d) _____ it very fast for a minute or two. Then (e) _____ it once with a spoon, (f) _____ a lid on the pan, and leave it to (g) _____ very slowly for 15 minutes.

add
cook
✓ put
stir
boil
pour
put

5 Cover the first part of Section C. Write the recipe for chicken stew, using these notes.

- onions / potatoes / slices
- oil / pan
- fry chicken / potatoes / onions / 10 minutes
- water / salt / pepper
- lid / pan
- cook slowly / 1 hour
- stir / spoon

Cut the onions and _____
_____
_____
_____
_____
_____
_____

Write in your language

We had a salad with thin slices of beef.

I like grilled fish, but I've never eaten raw fish.

Pour some oil into the pan, then add the onions.

33 Rooms, flats and houses

A Vocabulary Rooms and furniture

Link

cooker, fridge, stereo
➲34

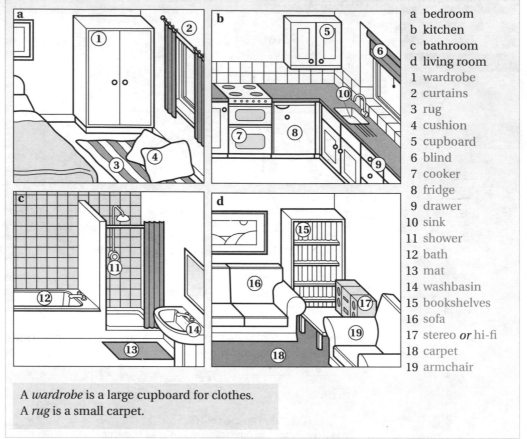

a bedroom
b kitchen
c bathroom
d living room
1 wardrobe
2 curtains
3 rug
4 cushion
5 cupboard
6 blind
7 cooker
8 fridge
9 drawer
10 sink
11 shower
12 bath
13 mat
14 washbasin
15 bookshelves
16 sofa
17 stereo *or* hi-fi
18 carpet
19 armchair

A *wardrobe* is a large cupboard for clothes.
A *rug* is a small carpet.

1 Complete the diagrams. Use words from the list.

carpet ____ ____
(on the floor)

curtains ____
(in the window)

shower ____
(used for washing) ____

fridge ____
(they use electricity)

cupboard ____
(you keep things in or on them)

Link

It's got ➲66

2 Which room is the woman describing?

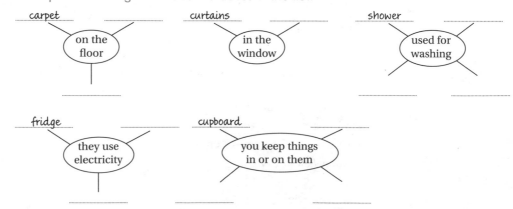

It's a nice room. It's got a bed in the corner, and a big wardrobe for your clothes. And there's a rug and some nice pictures on the wall.

____

Now choose two other rooms, and write a description. Use phrases from the box.

It's got ...	on the floor	There's a ...	in the corner	There are ...	on the wall
big	nice	large	comfortable	small	

a ....

b ....

B Phrases

Links

north, south	⮕37
near, not far from	⮕12A

Flats and houses

It's a nice flat.

It's got **three rooms** and a **big balcony**.

It's **on the third floor**.

It **faces south**, so it's sunny.

It's got **a view of** the park.

It's **on** a quiet side road.

It's **near** the shops.

It's **not far from** the city centre.

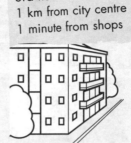

FLAT TO LET
3rd floor
1 km from city centre
1 minute from shops

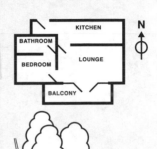

It's on the	top third ground	floor.		It's got a view of	the park. the city. the sea.		It faces	north. south.

It's got	three rooms. a balcony.		It's on	a main road. a side road.		It's	near not far from	the centre. a station. the shops.

Links

so, but	⮕98
quite	⮕25B

3 Complete the sentences with phrases from the box.

a The balcony _faces east_____, so it's sunny in the morning.

b It's _____, but there's a lift.

c It's got _____ the river, so you can sit and watch the boats.

d It's got _____ and a kitchen.

e It's _____, so it's quite noisy.

f It's _____, so you can get to the town centre quite quickly.

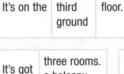

a view of
near a station
on a main road
on the top floor
✓ faces east
four large rooms

4 Write some sentences about your own flat or house.

....
....
....

Write in your language

Are there carpets and curtains in the flat?

In the kitchen, there's only a cooker and a sink.

The living room has a lovely view of the river.

A Vocabulary — Things in the home

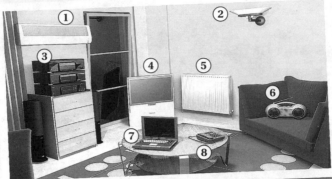

1 air conditioning unit
2 light
3 stereo *or* hi-fi
4 television *or* TV
5 radiator
6 radio
7 computer
8 telephone *or* phone

9 iron
10 washing machine
11 vacuum cleaner
12 microwave
13 cooker
14 dishwasher
15 refrigerator *or* fridge

We can also say:
Our flat has central heating (= radiators in every room)
Our house has air conditioning (= air conditioning units in every room)

Links

wash, cook, do
the ironing   ➲35
use ... to   ➲64A
quickly, slowly ➲26

1 Match the things in the pictures with the sentences.

a _14_ You use this to wash plates and cups.
b _____ You use this to wash clothes.
c _____ This keeps the room warm ...
d _____ ... and this keeps the room cool.
e _____ You can send e-mails with this.
f _____ This cooks things very quickly ...
g _____ ... and this cooks things more slowly.
h _____ You use this to do the ironing.

i _____ You can watch the news on this.
j _____ You can listen to the news on this.
k _____ You can use this to clean the carpets.
l _____ You use this to keep food cold.
m _____ You use this to play CDs.
n _____ You can talk to people on this.
o _____ You use this when it's dark.

2 Which of the things do you have at home? Write **three** lists.

We have more than one:	We have one:	We don't have one:

B Phrases — *turn it on/off*

Link

➜RU1 **Phrasal verbs**

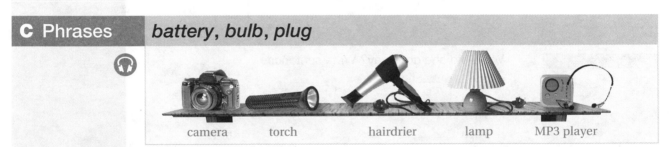

switch turn	the light the TV the radio	on off

| turn | the radio the music the radiator | up down |

Links

Let's…, Why don't we …? ➜75A

Would/Could you… ? ➜74A

3 Add words from the boxes to these sentences.

switch	on
turn	off
	up
	down

       switch   off

a Please⟍the lights⟍when you go to bed .

b It's cold. Let's the radiator a bit .

c The music's too loud. Could you the radio ?

d It's getting dark. Let's the light .

e Why don't we the radio ? It's time for the news .

f I can't hear what you're saying. Could you the TV ?

C Phrases — *battery, bulb, plug*

| camera | torch | hairdrier | lamp | MP3 player |

4 Which of these things have
   – a bulb?
   – a battery or batteries?
   – a plug?
   Complete the table.

	bulb	battery	plug
camera	✓	✓	–
torch			
hairdrier			
lamp			
MP3 player			

Link

put ➜56A

5 Match the sentences with the things.

   a Put a bulb in it, plug it in, and switch it on.   *Lamp*
   b Put a bulb in, put some batteries in, and switch it on.
   c Put a battery in, switch it on, then press the button.
   d Put some batteries in, switch it on, and listen to music.
   e Plug it in, switch it on, and turn it to 'hot' or 'cold'.

Write in your language

Have you switched the lights off?

Could you turn the radio down, please?

My torch needs new batteries.

35

Housework

A Vocabulary — *cleans, cooks, washes …*

This woman works for a rich family in London.

Link
➲34   **Electricity**

She cleans the house …

she cooks the meals …

she washes up … washes the dishes …

she washes the clothes …

she irons the sheets …

and she makes the beds.

clean	the house
	the floors
	the kitchen

cook	the meals
	dinner

make	the beds

wash	the clothes
	the dishes
	up

iron	the clothes
	the sheets

Present	Past
clean	cleaned
cook	cooked
wash	washed
iron	ironed
make	made

Link
past simple   ➲85A

1   What did she do today? Write sentences.

a   She _cleaned the bathroom_ .

b   Then she _____ .

c   Then _____ .

d   Then _____ .

e   Then _____ .

f   Then _____ .

TODAY'S JOBS

Bathroom	✓
Beds	✓
Lunch	✓
Dishes	✓
Shirts	✓
Kitchen windows	✓

B Phrases — *do the …-ing*

Link
do   ➲63C

I wash the clothes every Monday. ⟹ I do the washing every Monday.

NOT
~~I do the washing the clothes.~~

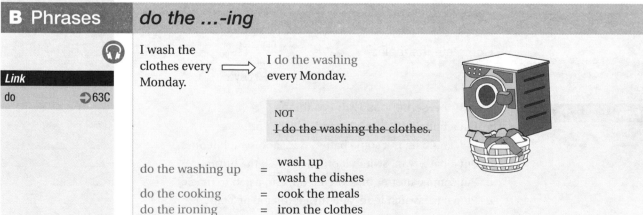

do the washing up	=	wash up / wash the dishes
do the cooking	=	cook the meals
do the ironing	=	iron the clothes
do the cleaning	=	clean the house
do the shopping	=	buy food
do the gardening	=	work in the garden
do the housework	=	cook + clean + wash …

2 Five friends are living in the same flat: Alex, Bill, Chris, David and Ed. Read the conversation. Who *didn't* do any housework today?

....

Now write sentences. Use words from the table.

"That was a wonderful meal, Alex," said Ed. "Thanks. Who's doing the washing up?"

"Not me," said Bill. "I did it this morning."

"Well, I cleaned the kitchen – and the bathroom," said Chris. "I think David should do the washing up."

"I bought the food," said David. "And I washed the clothes."

"Well, I ironed the sheets," said Bill. "What about you, Ed …?"

a <u>David did the washing.</u>
b ....
c ....
d ....
e ....
f ....

	✓washing
	washing up
did the	cleaning
	ironing
	shopping
	cooking

3 Who usually does the housework in your home? Write two or three sentences.

....
....
....
....
....

I usually do the gardening. My brother usually does the shopping, but my mother always does the cooking.

Links

| verb (+ -s) | ➲81A |
| usually | ➲9A |

C Vocabulary   *tidy, untidy …*

Links

| always, hardly ever | ➲9A |
| every morning, twice a year | ➲10 |

A
I keep my room very tidy. I always put things away, and I tidy the room up every morning.

B
My room's always very untidy. I hardly ever clear things away. I probably tidy the room about twice a year.

Adjectives

| a tidy | room |
| an untidy | |

Verbs

| tidy …. (up) | clear | … away |
| | put | |

Link

tidy … up, put … away, clear … away ➲RU1

4 Complete the remarks. Which go with Picture A, and which go with Picture B?

a <u>B</u> 'You really should <u>tidy</u> your room some time.'
b ...... 'I'll just .... my clothes away, and then you can sit down.'
c ...... 'Come in. I've just .... my room.'
d ...... 'Your room is so .... ! Why don't you .... all these things away?'
e ...... 'His room is really .... He always .... everything away.'

tidy
tidied
untidy
put
puts
clear

Write in your language

I'll cook, and you can wash the dishes.

I don't usually do the shopping.

Why don't you tidy your room?

36 In the street

A Vocabulary — Things in the street

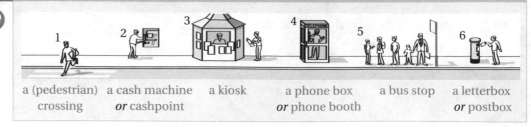

| 1 | 2 | 3 | 4 | 5 | 6 |

a (pedestrian) crossing   a cash machine *or* cashpoint   a kiosk   a phone box *or* phone booth   a bus stop   a letterbox *or* postbox

Links

make	➲63
across	➲23
is (wait)ing	➲82

1 Find these people in the picture. Write numbers.

a __6__ He's posting a letter.   d _____ He's getting some money.

b _____ He's waiting for a bus.   e _____ He's making a phone call.

c _____ He's crossing the road.   f _____ He's buying a newspaper.

> cross the road
> = go across the road.

2 Write **one** word in each gap.

a I need to _get_ some money at a _____ machine.

b Could you _____ this letter for me? There's a _____ next to the _____ stop.

c Be careful when you _____ the road – always use the pedestrian _____ .

d If you want to _____ a phone call, there's a phone _____ in the station.

3 Think about a street near you where you go shopping. Which things in A are there?

_____

_____

_____

> There's a phone box, a post box, and a bus stop, and there are two cashpoints. There isn't a kiosk or a pedestrian crossing.

B Phrases — Questions in the street

> Excuse me. Is there **a cash machine** near here?

> Excuse me. Where's the nearest **cash machine**?

> Excuse me. Where can I **buy a paper** near here?

> Excuse me. Is there anywhere I can **buy a paper** near here?

> Yes, there's one in Queen Street, next to the cinema.

> There's one just along there.

> There's a kiosk just down that road.

> Not near here, no, but there's a kiosk by the station.

4 Write questions like these. Use the blue expressions in the bubbles.

a (post box?) _Is there a post box near here?_

b (get a cup of coffee?) _____

c (phone box?) _____

d (buy stamps?) _____

e (toilet?) _____

5 Choose **two** of the questions in Ex. 4. Write true answers.

a _____

b _____

> (– Excuse me, is there a toilet near here?)
> – Yes, there's one at the bus station.
>   It's just along this road.

C Phrases

Street directions

Read these directions and find the three places on the map.

traffic lights

a crossroads

a turning

STOP

a main road

YOU ARE HERE

A Go along here and turn left at the main road. Then carry on until you come to some traffic lights. You'll see the Shiva Restaurant on the right.

B Go down this road, cross the main road, and carry on until you come to a crossroads – you'll see a café on the corner. That's the Café Noir.

C Go along this road and turn right. Then take the second turning on the left, and carry on. You'll see the school on the left – it's a big grey building.

Go along here Go down this road Carry on	until you come to	the main road. some traffic lights.	Turn	left right	at the café. at the main road.

You'll see	a big building a café	on your right. on the left. on the corner.	Take the	first second	turning on the	left. right.

Links

until	7A
along, down	23
You'll (see)	78

6 Look at the map again and write the numbers next to the names.

a the Shiva Restaurant _____ b the Café Noir _____ c the school _____

Now write directions to the other two places.

d _Go along this road_ _____

_____

e _____

_____

Write in your language

Excuse me. Is there a cash machine near here?

Carry on until you come to a crossroads.

You'll see the café on the left.

37

The world

A Vocabulary Continents, oceans and regions

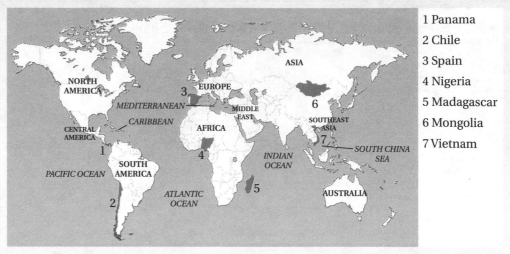

1 Panama
2 Chile
3 Spain
4 Nigeria
5 Madagascar
6 Mongolia
7 Vietnam

1 Write words from the map in three lists.

Continents	Regions	Oceans and seas
Asia	the Middle East	the Caribbean

> **We say:**
> the Atlantic (Ocean)
> the Mediterranean
> but:
> Europe, Asia
> NOT
> ~~the Europe~~
> ~~the Asia~~

2 Find these countries on the map. Write their names.

a   Madagascar   is a large island in the Indian Ocean, near the coast of Africa.

b _____ is a European country with a coast on the Atlantic and on the Mediterranean.

c _____ is a small country in Central America.

d _____ is a country in Southeast Asia, on the South China Sea.

e _____ is a long, thin country in South America, on the Pacific Ocean.

f _____ is a large country in Central Asia, not on the sea.

g _____ is a West African country on the Atlantic Ocean.

Continents	
Noun	**Adjective**
Africa	African
America	American
Asia	Asian
Australia	Australian
Europe	European

3 Write about your own country.

_____

_____

_____

_____

Places in a country

Link

➲38 **Countries and languages**

Link

near, not far from, 100 km south of ➲12

Lille is in northern **France,** not far from the border with **Belgium.**
Strasbourg is in eastern **France,** on the German border.
Bordeaux is in the southwest of **France,** near the west coast.
Nice is in the south of **France,** on the Mediterranean.
Orléans is in the centre of **France,** about 100 kilometres south of Paris.

in the	north southwest centre	of France	in	northern southwestern central	France	on near not far from	the border with Germany the German border the west coast

4 Write sentences from the notes.

a Kabul / east / border / Pakistan   *Kabul is in the east of Afghanistan, not far from the border with Pakistan.*

b Herat / northwest / border / Iran

c Kandahar / 500 km / southwest / Kabul

d Lagos / southwest / south coast

e Ibadan / 100 km / northeast / Lagos

f Kano / north / border / Niger

5 Write a sentence about a town or city in your own country, saying where it is.

Write in your language

It's a small country in southeast Europe.

They live on the west coast of America.

We're in northern Italy, near the French border.

38 Countries and languages

A Vocabulary Countries and nationalities

He's Russian   She's Mexican   She's Chinese   He's Iraqi

Link

→ 37   **The world**

1 What about these people? Complete the table.

-ian	He's from Russia.	She's from Italy.	We're from Egypt.
	He's Russian.	*She's Italian.*	
-an	She's from Mexico.	They're from South Africa.	He's from Korea.
	She's Mexican.		
-ese	They're from China.	I'm from Japan.	She's from Vietnam.
	They're Chinese.		
-i	He's from Iraq.	They're from Israel.	She's from Pakistan.
	He's Iraqi.		

B Vocabulary Irregular forms

Most irregular nationalities are in Europe.

Swiss Greek Spanish
Finnish Scottish
Turkish NORWEGIAN
Dutch German Danish
Polish English Irish
Swedish French Belgian
Portuguese

2 Match the countries and the nationalities. Complete the table.

I'm from …	I'm …	I'm from …	I'm …	I'm from …	I'm …
England	English	Finland		Belgium	
Scotland		Poland		Portugal	
Ireland		Spain		Greece	
Denmark		Turkey		Switzerland	
Sweden		France		The Netherlands	
Norway		Germany			

Note these other irregular forms: Thailand – Thai; Lebanon – Lebanese; Peru – Peruvian

3 Change the phrases in *italics*.

a We aren't *from England* – I'm *from Scotland* and he's *from Ireland*.

English _____   _____   _____

b On the language course, I met students *from China, Vietnam and Korea*.

_____ students

c I like food *from Italy, Greece and Turkey*.

_____ food

d They sell cheese *from France, the Netherlands and Switzerland*.

_____ cheese

e Is he *from Norway or from Sweden*? Or is he *from Denmark*?

_____   _____

f There were people *from Mexico, Colombia and Venezuela* at the meeting.

_____ people

Links

well, (fluent)ly	26
a bit	14A
a few	15A

C Phrases — Languages

What languages do you speak?

	0	1	2	3	4
English			✓		
French				✓	
Spanish	✓				
Chinese	✓				
Arabic					✓
Others:					
Japanese		✓			

0 = I don't speak it at all.
1 = I speak a few words of it.
2 = I speak it a bit, but not very well.
3 = I speak it quite well.
4 = I speak it fluently.

I speak English	fluently. / quite well.	I speak	a bit of / a few words of	English.	I don't speak English	very well. / at all.

4 Look at the questionnaire and the woman's answers. Are these sentences correct?

a She speaks Arabic fluently. Yes.

b She speaks a bit of Spanish. No. She doesn't speak Spanish at all.

c She speaks Japanese quite well. _____

d She doesn't speak English. _____

e She speaks French fluently. _____

f She speaks Chinese quite well. _____

5 Write a few sentences about yourself. Begin **I speak…** or **I don't speak…** .

_____

_____

_____

Write in your language

She's Italian, and her husband is Scottish.

Are they Swedish or Norwegian?

She speaks Japanese quite well.

39 Places to stay

A Phrases

On holiday

Links

for	⮌7A
round	⮌23A
I'm + (stay)ing, we're + (go)ing	⮌82
then, after that	⮌100A
this/next week	⮌5A

A
We're on holiday in Malaysia for two weeks. This week we're staying in a hotel in the centre of Kuala Lumpur, and next week we're going down to the south coast. We'll probably travel by bus.

B
We're going on holiday next week. We're staying with friends in London on Saturday, then we're staying in a cottage in Scotland for a week. After that, we're going to travel around and see other places.

C
I've decided to take a holiday! I'm travelling round Mexico for two weeks, and then I'm staying in a friend's apartment in Miami.

D
I've got a week's holiday, but I'm not going anywhere – I'm just staying at home.

1 Match the emails with the pictures.

2 Find expressions, and add them to the lists:

holiday	**stay**	**travel**
be on holiday	stay in a hotel	travel around

3 Write complete sentences from the notes.

a I'm going / holiday / Italy next week   I'm going on holiday to Italy next week.

b He's staying / uncle / Berlin / two weeks

c They're staying / friend's house / Hawaii

d I'm travelling / China / three weeks

e I'm / holiday / Egypt / a week

Asking about rooms

A tourist is talking to a hotel receptionist.

Links

has got	➲66
at the front, at the back	➲22
with	➲24

1 Have you got any rooms free?

2 Do you want a double room or a single room?

3 Have you got a single room with a shower?

4 How many nights are you staying?

5 Has the room got a balcony?

6 Is it at the front or at the back?

7 How much is the room?

8 Can I see the room?

| a room with | a shower |
| | a balcony |

| a room | at the front |
| | at the back |

of the hotel

a single room
a double room
a twin room

4 Look at the questions. Who asks them, the tourist or the receptionist? Write **T** or **R**.

1 _T_   2 _____   3 _____   4 _____   5 _____   6 _____   7 _____   8 _____

5 Write the questions.

a – Has the room got a balcony?
– Yes, a small one.

b – _____
– No, it's at the front.

c – _____
– Yes, I'll show it to you now.

d – _____
– Three nights - till Friday.

e – _____
– A TV? No, it hasn't.

f – _____
– €70 a night.

Renting a flat

Links

| hers | ➲20A |
| pay | ➲47 |

This woman owns a flat. (= it's hers)
She wants to let it out (or rent it out).
Her flat is to let.
The man wants to rent the flat.
The rent is £100 per month. The man has to pay £100 rent.

Can I see the flat?

Flat to let
Sitting room, bedroom, kitchen.
£100 per month

6 Complete the sentences with words from the box.

a We needed some money, so we decided to _let out_ our second bedroom.

b I saw in the paper that you've got a flat to _____ .

c We don't _____ this flat – we just _____ it.

d Can you lend me some money? I need to _____ my _____ .

e They _____ three apartments. They live in one and _____ the others.

| pay |
| own |
| rent |
| let (out) |

Write in your language

She's on holiday for two weeks.

Have you got a double room with a balcony?

He pays $50 rent a week.

40 Transport

A Phrases — *go by bus, take a taxi*

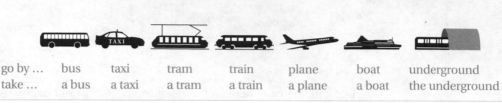

Excuse me. How can I get to the airport?

You can go by bus, you can take a taxi or you can take the underground.

buses to the airport

T — airport taxis

U

Madison hotel

| go by … | bus | taxi | tram | train | plane | boat | underground |
| take … | a bus | a taxi | a tram | a train | a plane | a boat | the underground |

1 Look at the maps and complete the answers.

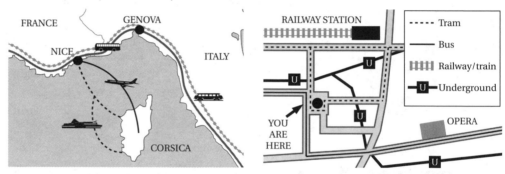

	Tram
	Bus
	Railway/train
U	Underground

FRANCE · GENOVA · NICE · ITALY · CORSICA

RAILWAY STATION · YOU ARE HERE · OPERA

a How can I get from Nice to Corsica? *You can take a plane or you can*

b How can I get from Nice to Genova? _____ or _____

c How can I get to the railway station? _____ or _____

d How can I get to the Opera House? _____ or _____

B Vocabulary — *cycle, drive, fly*

drive = go by car   cycle = go by bicycle   fly = go by plane or helicopter

2 Write verbs from the table.

Present	Past
drive	drove
cycle	cycled
fly	flew

a It's raining. I'll have to *drive* to work.

b They got married in the afternoon, and in the evening they

_____ to the Caribbean.

c We _____ across Europe last summer.

d Did you _____ ___ to Edinburgh or did you _____ ?

e He _____ ___ to the station, and left his car in the car park.

Journeys

Links

cost ➲47A

have to, don't have to
➲72

There aren't any direct trains to Ainsworth from London, so you'll have to change at Manchester. The trains to Ainsworth leave from platform 2. I think there's one every hour. The journey takes about 5 hours, and it costs about £70 single or £120 return. Have a good trip!

| single A ——> B | A ——> C a direct train to C (You don't have to change.) | The train leaves | at 2.00. from platform 2. |
| return A ⇄ B | A ——> B ——> C (You have to change at B.) | The journey | takes 5 hours. costs £120. |

3 Look at the information on the right, and complete the sentences.

a The train _leaves Warsaw at_ 9.30.

b The journey _____ 3 hours.

c A _____ ticket _____ 80 euros.

d You have to _____ in Poznań.

e The train _____ Platform 4.

f There isn't a _____ train from Warsaw to Konin.

Your travel itinerary
Warsaw - Konin, 5th Sept.

0930	Leaves Warsaw	platform 3
1115	Arrives Poznań	
1145	Leaves Poznań	platform 4
12.30	Arrives Konin	

Cost: €80 (single)

4 A passenger is asking questions. Write them in the conversation below.

Link

How long …? ➲7B

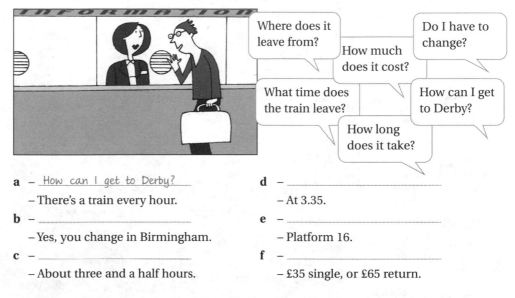

Where does it leave from?

How much does it cost?

Do I have to change?

What time does the train leave?

How can I get to Derby?

How long does it take?

a – _How can I get to Derby?_
  – There's a train every hour.

b – _____
  – Yes, you change in Birmingham.

c – _____
  – About three and a half hours.

d – _____
  – At 3.35.

e – _____
  – Platform 16.

f – _____
  – £35 single, or £65 return.

Write in your language

You can drive or you can take the underground.

It costs about €60 return.

How long does the journey take?

41 Sport

A Vocabulary — TV sports

Links

like (watch)ing ➔67
often, sometimes ➔9
I've never (watched) ➔92B

> I like watching sport on TV. I often watch football, tennis and athletics, and I sometimes watch snooker and horse-racing. I don't watch basketball or boxing, though – I don't like them. I've never watched ice-hockey, but people say it's interesting.

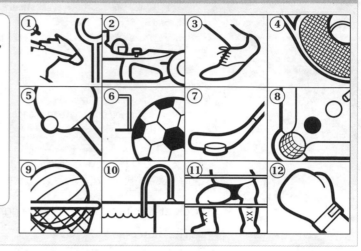

1 Find the sports in the pictures. Write numbers.

  a The man often watches these: _6_ , _____ , _____
  b He sometimes watches these: _8_ , _____
  c He doesn't watch these: _9_ , _____
  d He's never watched this: _____

  Now match these sports with the other four pictures:

  e _11_ wrestling   **f** _____ table tennis   **g** _____ swimming   **h** _____ motor-racing

2 Write sentences about yourself.

  a I often watch _____ .
  b I sometimes watch _____ .
  c I don't watch _____ .
  d I've never watched _____ .

B Vocabulary — *win, lose, beat ...*

Links

have (lost), has (won) ➔90
I expect, I hope ➔70
too many ➔29C
not enough ➔30

FOOTBALL
'We're losing too many matches,' said Smith. 'We're a good team, and we have some very good players, but unfortunately we aren't scoring enough goals.'

MOTOR RACING
'I expect it will be a hard race,' said Alonso yesterday, 'but I hope I can win it.'

TENNIS
Roger Federer has won the US Open. He beat Andy Roddick 6-4, 6-3, 6-3. 'It was a very exciting match,' said Federer.

FOOTBALL
If Chelsea lose to Arsenal tonight, Arsenal will be top, with 24 points. But Chelsea have only lost one game this year.

Points	
Chelsea	23
Arsenal	21
Man United	20

score	points a goal

win lose	a race a game a match

beat lose to	(someone)

a good	player team

Verb	Past	Past Participle
win	won	won
lose	lost	lost
beat	beat	beaten

3 Write the answers in the diagram.

1 Ten horses are running in the next ____. ▶

2 Manchester United have 20 _____. ▶ | P | O | I | N | T | S |

3 Are you going to the tennis _____ tomorrow? ▶

4 He's won 9 games this year, and he's only ____ one. ▶

5 I expect Chelsea will ___ Arsenal at the weekend. ▶

6 I think The Eagles are the best basketball ____ in the country. ▶

7 Who do you think is going to ___ the next World Cup? ▶

8 Boca Juniors need to _____ a goal soon ... ▶

9 ... or they will ____ the match! ▶

Now complete the sentence:

10 ▼ I really like _____ , especially the 100 metres and the long jump.

C Vocabulary · **Sportsmen and sportswomen**

Here are three well-known sportsmen and sportswomen:

Thierry Henry, French footballer

Wang Hao, Chinese table tennis player

Catherine Ndereba, Kenyan athlete

If you're well-known or famous, many people know about you.

4 Write words in the lists.

+ -er	... + *player*	*others*
footballer	table tennis player	athlete
skier		

✓skier
cyclist
basketball player
tennis player
swimmer
boxer
racing driver

Links

best/most + adjective
➔28

5 Who are the best-known sportsmen/women in your country?

The best-known footballer in England is David Beckham.
The most famous cyclist in the USA is Lance Armstrong.

Write in your language

I've never watched boxing on TV.

They've won three games, and they've lost one.

Who's the best-known athlete in your country?

42

Work

A Vocabulary · Jobs

1 nurse	7 pilot
2 factory worker	8 farmer
3 lorry driver	9 actor
4 mechanic	10 manager
5 cleaner	11 journalist
6 postman/woman	12 architect

To talk about jobs, we can use
– a noun, to say what you are: I'm a nurse.   NOT ~~I'm nurse.~~

– a verb, to say what you do: I work at St. Peter's House. I look after old people.

Link

make   ➲63

1 Match the sentences with the jobs.

a _11_ I write for *The Times* newspaper.   **g** _____ I clean hotel bedrooms.

b _____ I deliver letters.   **h** _____ I work for Air France.

c _____ I do a lot of work for television.   **i** _____ I deliver furniture around Europe.

d _____ I design office buildings and shops.   **j** _____ I work in a garage.

e _____ I make parts for washing machines.   **k** _____ I grow rice.

f _____ I run a small business.

2 Complete these sentences. Use verbs or phrases from Exercise 1.

a He's a gardener. He _looks after_ the gardens round the hospital.

b She's a writer. She _____ stories for children.

c She's a hotel manager. She _____ a large hotel in Singapore.

d I'm a clothes designer. I _____ my own clothes, and I also _____ Calvin Klein.

e He's a bank manager. He _____ the Bank of Saudi Arabia.

f She's a computer programmer. She _____ computer games.

B Phrases · Good and bad jobs

Link

a lot, not much ➲14B

It's not a very interesting job. It's quite difficult, but it's quite well paid.

It's a very easy job, but I don't earn much, and I work very long hours.

It's hard work, but it's very interesting, and I earn a lot of money.

| It's
It isn't | interesting.
well paid.
difficult. |
|---|---|

| It's
It isn't	hard work.

I earn a lot (of money).
I don't earn much (money).

I (don't) work long hours.

Links

have to ⮕72

a very …, quite a …
⮕25B

3 Match the jobs with the descriptions.

| 1 hairdresser | 2 gardener | 3 film actor | 4 factory worker |

a ⎯⎯ It's a very boring job, I have to work long hours, and it isn't very well paid.

b ⎯⎯ It's quite a difficult job, but it's always interesting, and I earn a lot of money.

c ⎯⎯ I don't earn very much, and it's hard work, but I enjoy being outside.

d ⎯⎯ I work quite long hours, but I meet new people all the time, so it's quite an interesting job.

4 Think about your job (or a friend's). What's the job like?

⎯⎯

⎯⎯

C Phrases

I'm looking for a job

Links

going to ⮕79

lose, find ⮕58A

get, got ⮕57A

closed, found, got
⮕85

haven't got ⮕66A

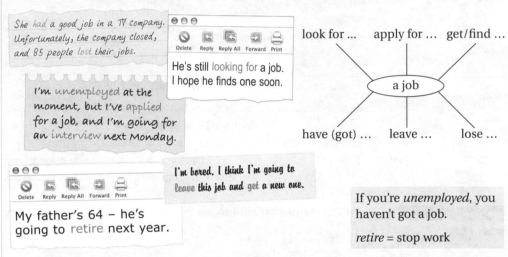

She had a good job in a TV company. Unfortunately, the company closed, and 85 people lost their jobs.

He's still looking for a job. I hope he finds one soon.

I'm unemployed at the moment, but I've applied for a job, and I'm going for an interview next Monday.

look for … apply for … get/find …

a job

have (got) … leave … lose …

I'm bored. I think I'm going to leave this job and get a new one.

My father's 64 – he's going to retire next year.

If you're *unemployed*, you haven't got a job.

retire = stop work

5 Read this story about a man's life, and fill the gaps with words from the box.

He left school when he was 16, and started to (a) _look for_ a job. He (b) ⎯⎯⎯⎯⎯ a job washing up in a hotel kitchen. He didn't like hotel work, so he (c) ⎯⎯⎯⎯⎯ his job and (d) ⎯⎯⎯⎯⎯ a job in a factory. A year later the factory closed down and he (e) ⎯⎯⎯⎯⎯ his job. Unfortunately, he couldn't (f) ⎯⎯⎯⎯⎯ another job. He (g) ⎯⎯⎯⎯⎯ lots of jobs, and went for several (h) ⎯⎯⎯⎯⎯, but nobody wanted him, and he was (i) ⎯⎯⎯⎯⎯ for two years. In the end, he (j) ⎯⎯⎯⎯⎯ a job in a hospital, and worked there for the next 40 years. He (k) ⎯⎯⎯⎯⎯ two years ago, when he was 65.

find	unemployed
found	retired
got	interviews
got	applied for
left	✓look for
lost	

Write in your language

He's a lorry driver, and his son is a hairdresser.

It's not a very interesting job, but it's well paid.

She lost her job, but she soon found a new one.

43

Everyday activities

A Phrases Sleeping and waking

I went to
sleep at
11.00 …

… slept for
8 hours …

… and
woke up
at 7.00.

He's asleep.
She's awake.

I woke him
up …

… but he fell
asleep again.

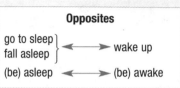

Opposites		**Present**	**Past**
go to sleep ⎤		sleep	slept
fall asleep ⎦ ⟶ wake up		fall	fell
		go	went
(be) asleep ⟷ (be) awake		wake	woke

1 Read about this person's bad night, and fill the gaps.

I (a) __slept__ really badly last night. I was (b) _____ by 11 o'clock, but a lorry
(c) _____ me up at 1.00. I tried to (d) _____ again, but I couldn't,
so I turned on the light and read a book. Eventually, I think I (e) _____ at about
5.00. I (f) _____ at 7.00 this morning with the book in my hand. So I was
(g) _____ for most of the night!

Link

usually, often ➲9

2 Write one or two sentences about yourself. Use expressions from A.

_____

_____

_____

_____

> I usually go to sleep at 11.30.
> I don't often sleep in the
> afternoons.

B Phrases *In the morning*

Links

get dressed ➲57C

your, his, my ➲20A

wash your
face

wash your
hands

wash your
hair

clean
brush your teeth

brush
your hair

put on your
make-up

have
a bath

have
a shower

have breakfast

get up

get dressed

shave

make coffee
(or tea)

clean, wash, brush, put on + my, your, his …

You should clean your teeth.	She washed her hands.	NOT ~~clean the teeth~~
He's cleaning his teeth.	They're washing their hands.	~~wash the hands~~
I cleaned my teeth.	I'll wash my hands.	

3 Complete these sentences. Add verbs and **my**, **your**, **his**, etc.

a He _cleans his_ teeth three times a day.

b She always _____ make-up before she goes out.

c After you go to the toilet, you should always _____ hands.

d Wait a minute. I just need to _____ hair, then we can go.

e I can't come out this evening. I need to _____ hair.

f Tell the children to _____ teeth before we go out.

Links

had, got, put ⮞85B
then ⮞100

4 What did you do this morning? In what order? Write true sentences.

_____

_____

_____

_____

_____

_____

Present	Past
have	had
get	got
put	put
make	made
wash	washed
clean	cleaned
brush	brushed
shave	shaved

C Phrases — Going out

Link

film, exhibition, play
⮞54

MON	Sue + Dave 8.00 Film
TUE	Cambridge (Uncle Joe) Clara (Bistro Roma 7.30)
WED	in London
THUR	in London
FRI	–

I had a very busy week …
On Monday I met some friends and we went to see a film. Then on Tuesday I visited my uncle in Cambridge. In the evening, I went out for a meal with an old schoolfriend. On Wednesday and Thursday, I stayed with some friends in London. We went to a Matisse exhibition, and then we went to see a play. On Friday, I did nothing. I just stayed at home and read a book.

go out	for lunch for a meal	with a friend	stay	at home with friends	visit meet	a friend	go to see	a film a play

Link

she's (meet)ing
⮞82B

5 What is the person doing next week? Complete the sentences.

a At 8.00 on Tuesday, _she's meeting_ some friends at the station. They're _____ a film at the Apollo Cinema.

b _____ her parents on Friday afternoon.

c On Wednesday evening, _____ a drink with some friends.

d On Monday evening, _____ and watching tennis on TV.

e At the weekend, _____ friends in Glasgow.

Sat-Sun 18 May
Kate - 19 Comptons Road, Glasgow

TUESDAY
Station 8.00
Apollo Cinema

Mum + Dad's house Friday p.m.

John + Flo
Drink 8.00 p.m. Wed.

MONDAY 7.30 - 9.30
TENNIS (CHANNEL 1)

Write in your language

He's asleep – don't wake him up.

I got up, had a shower and cleaned my teeth.

I stayed with some friends in London.

Family and friends

A Vocabulary Relatives

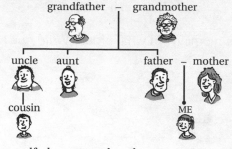

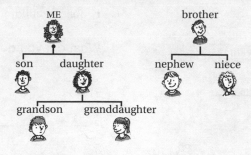

grandfather + grandmother = grandparents
grandson + granddaughter = grandchildren

All these people are your relatives
or relations.

Link

(my father)'s ➜20

1 Look at the two family trees, and complete the sentences.

a my father's father = _my grandfather_
b my father's mother = ...
c my father's sister = ...
d my father's brother = ...
e my uncle's son = ...

f my son's son = ...
g my son's daughter = ...
h my brother's son = ...
i my brother's daughter = ...
j my children's children = ...

2 How far away do your relatives live? Write some sentences.

....
....
....
....
....

> My uncle and aunt live in Brazil.
> I've got a cousin in Australia.
> My grandmother lives in the next
> street.

B Vocabulary meet, get engaged ...

Charles and Diana met in 1978, when she was 16. They got engaged
in February 1981, and got married later that year. Seven years later
they got divorced. Then Diana met Dodi al Fayed. They started going
out together, and fell in love. On 31 August 1997, they had dinner at
the Ritz Hotel in Paris. Some people think
they got engaged during dinner.
Later that evening, they both died in a
car crash.

Link

➜45   **Life events**

Links

get engaged, get
married   ➜57C

started + (go)ing
            ➜65C

got   ➜85B

meet

go out together

fall in love

get engaged

get married

get divorced

> She goes out with him, and he
> goes out with her.
> = They go out together.

3 Put the events in the right order.

   a They *got married* in 1990, and *met* a year later, but they only *got engaged* in 2001.
   They met in 1990, and

   b We *got married* at a party. We *met* immediately, and *fell in love* a year later.

   c They first *got married* at university. They *got divorced*, but five years later they *met*.

Links

a month ago, a few
weeks ago ➲5C

mine ➲20

C Vocabulary Friends

This is Sue. She's a friend of mine. And that's her boyfriend …

This is my brother with his fiancée …

These are our neighbours, Mr and Mrs Green …

… and this is me with some colleagues at work.

my *boyfriend/girlfriend*	= we go out together
my *fiancé(e)*	= we're engaged
my *neighbour*	= he/she lives next to us, or near us
a *colleague*	= we work in the same company

Male	Female
	friend
boyfriend	girlfriend
fiancé	fiancée
neighbour	
colleague	

4 Complete the sentences with words from the table.

   a I don't like our new ____neighbour____ . He plays loud music all the time.

   b I'm going out with a _____ from the office tonight.

   c Peter's a very old _____ of mine. We were at school together.

   d This is my _____ , Bob. We got engaged a few weeks ago.

   e He's got a new _____ . He started going out with her last weekend.

5 Write sentences about you or your relatives. Use words from **A**, **B** or **C**.

   _____

   _____

   _____

   _____

> I met my wife in Spain in 2002.
>
> My grandparents got married in 1930.

Write in your language

My grandparents got married in 1945.

This is my fiancée. We got engaged last week.

He isn't her boyfriend – he's just a friend of hers.

45 Life events

A Phrases — Early life

Link

⟳ 2   **Years and centuries**

Links

was (born)   ⟳ 94

started + verb + -ing   ⟳ 65

grew up   ⟳ RU1

Mozart was born in 1756 in Salzburg, Austria. He grew up in a small family, with just his parents and one sister. He started writing music when he was 5 years old, and wrote his first symphony when he was 8. When he was 11, the family moved to Vienna …

Louis Armstrong was born in 1901, and grew up in a poor part of New Orleans. As a child, he sang on street corners to earn money, and when he was a teenager he started playing and singing in New Orleans jazz clubs. In 1924, he went to live in New York City …

| He | was born / grew up | in … |

| He started | writing |

| He | moved to … / went to live in … |

1 Complete the sentences about these musicians. Use phrases from the tables.

Igor Stravinsky
Russian composer

Igor Stravinsky (a) __was born__ near St. Petersburg in Russia in 1882.

He (b) _____ music when he was a student. In 1914, he (c) _____ to Switzerland, and then (d) _____ in Paris.

Oum Koulthoum
Egyptian singer

Oum Koulthoum (e) _____ in 1904, and (f) _____ in a small village in the north of Egypt. Her father and brother were singers, and she (g) _____ when she was still a small child. She travelled with her family around the countryside until 1923, and then (h) _____ in Cairo.

B Phrases — School, study and work

Links

After …   ⟳ 100

got   ⟳ 57

get a job, work for   ⟳ 42

1987 – 1996	Brunton High School, Glasgow
1996 – 1997	Secretary, HSBC Bank
1997 – 1999	Bristol University (Russian)
1999 – 2001	Teacher, Anglia School, Moscow
2001 – 2002	Brighton College (Business Studies)
2002 –	IBM, London

After I left school, I worked as a secretary at HSBC Bank. Then I went to Bristol University, where I studied Russian. After I left university, I got a job as a teacher at a school in Moscow. In 2001, I did a course in Business Studies at Brighton College. In 2002, I started working for IBM in London, and I became a sales manager in 2004.

2 Look at the verbs and phrases in blue. Put them in two lists:

School, college, university:

left (school)

Work:

worked as (a secretary)

3 Write some sentences about yourself. Use verbs and phrases from the lists.

_____

_____

C Vocabulary — Exams

Links

| if | ➲78B |
| might, probably | ➲71 |

These teenagers are taking exams in their last year at school. If they pass (their exams), they might go to university or college. If they fail (their exams), they will probably leave school and look for a job.

Present	Past
take	took
pass	passed
fail	failed

Links

| only | ➲6C |
| both, all | ➲18 |

4 Look at the results and complete the sentences.

a Only one person _passed_ maths.

b Tim and Bob _____ the French exam.

c Only one person _____ the music exam.

d Tim only _____ one exam.

e Zoe was best: she _____ all her exams.

f Bob only _____ two exams, and he _____ both of them.

EXAM RESULTS (40%+ = Pass)				
	Maths	English	French	Music
Eva	29	61	48	–
Tim	38	42	30	–
Zoe	62	75	44	72
Bob	34	–	36	–

D Phrases — How did they die?

Links

was, (kill)ed	➲94
(plane) crash	➲50
1893, 1937	➲2A

Mao Zedong, Chinese leader, 1893–1976

Buddy Holly, rock singer, 1937–1959

Indira Gandhi, Prime Minister of India 1917–1984

Mao Zedong died in 1976, at the age of 82.

Buddy Holly was killed in a plane crash in 1959.

Indira Gandhi was shot in Delhi in 1984.

He She	died was killed was shot	in (1959) in (Delhi). at the age of (82).

shot is the past participle form of _shoot_.

5 How did these people die? Make sentences from the notes.

a Yassir Arafat – Paris – 2004 _Yassir Arafat died in Paris in 2004._

b Elvis Presley – Memphis, Tennessee – 42 _____

c John Kennedy – shot – Dallas – 1963 _____

d Princess Diana – car crash – 36 _____

e Che Guevara – killed – Bolivia – 1967 _____

Write in your language

She was born in 1950 and grew up in London.	
After I left school, I got a job in a bank.	
He was killed in a plane crash.	

A Vocabulary — Feelings

Links

| quite, very | ➲25B |
| a bit | ➲14A |

I felt quite sad when the President died. I thought he was a good leader.

'I'm very happy that you're getting married,' she said.

The film was much too long. I was really bored.

I think I'll pass my English exam tomorrow, but I feel a bit nervous.

My daughter's very excited about going to Mexico, but I'm a bit worried about her. I hope she's going to be all right.

Chelsea lost 3–1 to AC Milan last night. 'We're very disappointed', the manager said.

At a factory in London, 6,000 workers will lose their jobs. 'We feel really angry about it', said one of the workers.

I was very frightened when I heard a strange noise in the night, but I tried to be calm.

Present	am/is/are feel	happy sad	**Past**	was/were felt	happy sad

1 Match the sentences with the notes in the box, and write them out correctly.

was / everyone / frightened / really	he / about / excited / very / feels / it
really / them / worried / I'm / about	✓it / about / nervous / feel / quite / I
it / angry / was / I / about / really	really / I'm / disappointed

a I'm taking my driving test tomorrow.   *I feel quite nervous about it.*

b I've just failed my driving test.

c It's my son's fifth birthday on Saturday.

d It's after midnight, and they still haven't phoned.

e Someone hit my car and then drove away.

f The plane suddenly started to fall.

B Phrases — *interested in, afraid of ...*

Link

| verb + -ing | ➲RU3 |

He's interested in football.

He's afraid of (*or* frightened of) spiders.

She's worried about money.

He's keen on cooking. (= He enjoys it.)

After these phrases, we can use a noun or verb + *-ing*:

He's interested in	football. reading about football.

NOT ~~interested about~~

He's keen on	food. cooking.

2 Which phrases go best in these sentences? Choose **two** for each sentence.

  a He's ... old cars.   _interested in_   *or* _keen on_

  b She's ... her children's schoolwork.   *or*

  c He's ... being alone at night.   *or*

  d He's ... 19th century novels.   *or*

  e I was ... breaking my leg.   *or*

C Vocabulary   *friendly, clever, lazy ...*

My colleagues at work:

She's very quiet. She doesn't say much.

He's very friendly. He always smiles and says 'Hello.'

She's quite clever. intelligent. She learns things very quickly.

She's very hard-working. She comes to work early, goes home late, and often doesn't stop for lunch.

He's very lazy. He never does any work.

He's really nervous when he meets new people.

She's very unfriendly. She never says 'Hello'.

Link

always, often

➲9

3 Write sentences describing these people:

  a She often talks to people on the bus.   _She's friendly._

  b She never smiles at anyone.

  c He gets up at 12.00 on Saturdays.

  d He doesn't like big parties.

  e She knows what $e = mc^2$ means.

  f He often works 11 or 12 hours a day.

  g Sometimes he says nothing all evening.

4 Choose three words that describe you. Write sentences.

> I think I'm quite a friendly person. I'm not very intelligent, but I'm hard-working.

Write in your language

I'm a bit nervous about my exams.

She's interested in learning languages.

He isn't very clever, but he's very hard-working.

47 Money

A Vocabulary — *It cost €1,000*

I bought an old car last year. It was very cheap. I paid €1,000 for it. Unfortunately, it was expensive to drive. In one month, I spent €600 on petrol. Then it broke down, so I took it to the garage. It cost me €1,500 to repair it.

Present	Past
pay	paid
cost	cost
spend	spent
buy	bought

Links

bought ➲85

cheap, expensive ➲28A

We can say:

I bought it (for €1000).
It cost (me) €1000.
I paid €1000 for it.
I spent €1000 (on it).

FOR SALE

1992 VOLVO XM
€1,000
Tel: 02341 6540569

1 Add **on** or **for** to these sentences.

a I bought a new coat ⟍only $30. *for*

b How much did you pay those shoes?

c He loves music – he spends all his money CDs.

d We had to pay €50 the hotel room, and €140 the evening meal.

e I spend quite a lot food, but not much clothes.

f Do you want to sell your computer? I'll pay you $50 it.

Link

over, almost, nearly ➲1C

2 Look at the receipts, and complete the sentences. Use verbs from the table.

a I ___spent___ over €24 on food at the supermarket.

b Two cups of coffee at Café Dolce _____ us €8.50.

c We _____ almost €60.00 for the meal.

d I _____ some petrol at the garage.

e I _____ nearly €200 for my new glasses at Optika.

f The petrol _____ €65.30.

ALPHA STATION
♦♦♦♦♦♦♦♦♦♦♦♦♦♦♦♦
Petrol   65.30
TOTAL   65.30

OPTIKA
👁
Lens   145.00
Frames   49.00
TOTAL   194.00

CAFÉ DOLCE ☕
2 Espresso   8.50
TOTAL   8.50
Thank you

SAVECO £ £ £
Milk   2.90
Eggs   3.20
Chicken   7.80
Pasta   3.30
Yoghurt   2.50
Apples   4.60
TOTAL   24.30

L'ESCARGOT RESTAURANT
Meals   52.90
Service   5.30
TOTAL   58.20

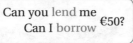

She lends him €50. He borrows €50 from her. He gives/pays back the money.

Links

give ➔56A

enough ➔30

3 Complete the sentences with words from the table.

Present	Past
lend	lent
borrow	borrowed
give	gave
pay	paid

a I _lent_ _____ him £50 last year, but he never _____ it back.

b I haven't got any money. Can you _____ me some?

c To start her business, she _____ $20,000 from the bank.

d I'll _____ you enough money for the bus. _____ it back tomorrow.

e Can I _____ your dictionary? I want to look up a word.

f You look cold. Do you want to _____ a coat?

C Phrases **Using money**

a credit card a cheque a bill a ticket a receipt a note change
or bank card (money *or* cash)

Links

Can I ...? ➔74

4 Match the questions with the dialogues.

Do you have any change? Can I have a receipt, please? Can we have the bill, please? Can I pay by credit card?

a – That's €55.00, please.
– _____
– Sorry. We only take cash or cheques.

b – More coffee, madam?
– No thanks. _____
– Yes, of course.

c – Here's your ticket. That's $10.20, please.
– OK. _____
– Yes. Here you are.

d – _____ I want to use the coffee machine.
– Sorry. I've only got a €10 note.

Write in your language

We paid €15 for two coffees!	
Could you lend me £10?	
Can I pay by cheque?	

48 Health and illness

Link

→49 **Accidents and problems**

Links

I've got →66

better, worse →27A

take (medicine) →56B

A Phrases — Feeling ill

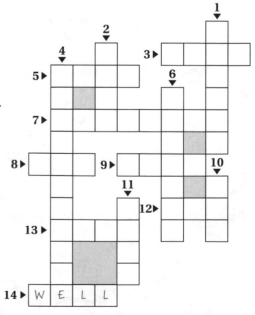

I don't feel very well, so I'm staying at home today. I think I've got a cold.

I'm really ill. I've got a temperature (39º) – I think I've got flu.

I felt even worse this morning, so I went to see the doctor. He said I've got flu. I'm sleeping a lot and I'm taking some medicine and lots of vitamin C.

I feel a lot better today. I'm still at home, but I hope I'll be back at work tomorrow.

be	well									
feel	ill									

have	a cold
have got	flu
	a temperature

take	medicine
	vitamin C

feel	better
	worse

Present	**Past**
feel	felt
take	took

Link

should →75C

1 Fill the gaps, and write the answers in the crossword.

– I don't feel very _ _ _ _ [14▶]. I think I'll _ _ _ _ [9▶] at home today.

– OK. I hope you feel _ _ _ _ _ _ [1▼] soon.

– You look hot. Have you got a _ _ _ _ _ _ _ _ _ _ _ [4▼]?

– No – I've just got a _ _ _ _ [2▼]. I'll be fine.

– Well, I think you should go to bed and _ _ _ _ [13▶] lots of _ _ _ _ _ _ _ [6▼] C!

– I feel really _ _ _ [12▶]. I think I've got _ _ _ [10▼].

– Perhaps you should _ _ _ [8▶] the doctor. She'll probably give you some _ _ _ _ _ _ _ [7▶].

– When I woke up this morning, I _ _ _ _ [11▼] really ill. I _ _ _ _ [5▶] some medicine after breakfast, but it didn't help. Now I _ _ _ _ [3▶] even worse!

Crossword grid with numbered clues 1–14; 14▶ filled in as W E L L

hurt, *ache*, *pain*

What's the matter?

My back aches.

I've got a pain in my chest .

My stomach hurts.

I've got an ache in my shoulders.

Verbs

My back	hurts. aches.

Nouns

I've got	a pain an ache	in my back.

An *ache* is a pain which is not very strong. We say:
a head*ache*
a stomach *ache*
a back*ache*
tooth*ache*

---

2 Look at the bubbles. Which person …

a .... has just carried something heavy?
b .... has eaten some bad food?
c .... has got flu?
d .... has just climbed a mountain?

1 I've got a stomach ache.

2 My chest hurts, I've got a headache, and my neck aches.

3 My feet hurt and my legs ache.

4 I've got a backache, and my shoulders ache, and my arms hurt.

---

3 Find words for parts of the body in Exercise 2. Match them with the picture.

a _head_
b ....
c ....
d ....
e ....
f ....
g ....
h ....
i ....

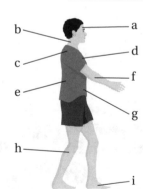

---

4 Complete these sentences. Use one word from each box (A and B).

a My (A) _neck_ (B) _hurts_ when I turn my head.
b These shoes are too small. My (A) .... (B) ....
c I can't walk. I've got a (B) .... in my left (A) ....
d I never eat ice-cream. It gives me a (A) .... (B) ....
e Could you carry the suitcase? My (A) .... (B) ....

A	B
leg	ache
feet	aches
arm	pain
neck	hurt
stomach	hurts

Write in your language

I don't feel very well.

My back hurts, and I've got a temperature.

I've got a stomach ache.

49 Accidents and problems

A Vocabulary Accidents

Link

my/her + part of
the body   ➲43B

| break | cut | burn | slip | fall (off) | fall (over) |

I was riding my bike, and I fell off.
I broke my arm.

NOT ~~I broke the arm.~~

Present	Past
break	broke
cut	cut
burn	burned
slip	slipped
fall	fell

Links

past simple   ➲82
was + verb + -ing
                   ➲87
arm, leg   ➲48B

1 What happened? Make sentences using verbs from the table.

a She was cutting meat, and the knife slipped.
  She cut her finger.

b He was taking a pizza out of the oven, and
  he slipped. _____

c She was climbing a ladder, and she slipped
  and fell off. _____

d He was shaving, and his hand slipped.

  _____

e He stepped on a broken bottle on the beach.

  _____

f She was skiing, and she fell over.

  _____

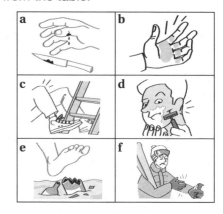

B Phrases Problems

The carpet's dirty, the window doesn't open, the
door of the wardrobe won't close, the armchair is
broken, and the lamp doesn't work …

| It | doesn't
won't | open.
close. | It doesn't work. | It's | dirty.
broken. |

2 What's wrong with the things in this room? Complete the sentences.

a The window _is broken_ .   **d** The table _____ .
b The TV _____ .   **e** The drawer _____ .
c The fridge _____ .   **f** The cooker _____ .

It needs mending

They need mending.   We should repair them.   I need to paint it.   It needs painting.

I / We	need to / should	repair them. / mend them. / paint it.

They need / It needs	painting. / mending. / repairing.

Links

clean, wash	⮩35A
mend	⮩64A
too + adjective	⮩29

3 Add a sentence, using **should**, **need to** or **need** + **-ing**. Use verbs from the box.

a The car won't start. It _needs repairing_ .
b My shoes are dirty. I _____ .
c The computer doesn't work. It _____ .
d These jeans are really dirty. They _____ .
e The bedroom walls are too dark. We _____ .
f My hair's too long. It _____ .

clean
cut
mend
paint
✓repair
wash

4 What needs doing in your house or flat? Write sentences.

_____
_____
_____
_____

My front door needs painting.
The fridge needs repairing.

Write in your language

I've cut my finger.

All the windows are broken.

The fridge needs repairing. It doesn't work.

50 Disasters and emergencies

A Vocabulary Disasters

| a fire | a flood *or* floods | a hurricane | an earthquake | a plane crash |

1 Here are some sentences from newspaper reports. What are they about?

a On the coast of Florida, the winds were over 150 kilometres an hour. _a hurricane_

b The water was three metres deep in some parts of the town. ....

c More than 3,000 people lost their homes, and are now living in tents outside the town. ....

d It started in the kitchen, while the family were asleep upstairs. ....

e The Boeing 737 was taking off from Milano Airport when smoke started coming from one of the engines. ....

B Vocabulary *were killed, were injured ...*

Link

were (killed) ⤳ 95

> An earthquake hit the town of Bazgan on Monday. Many buildings in the town centre were damaged, and some houses in the old part of the town were completely destroyed. At least 200 people were killed, and many more were injured. Yesterday, more than 60 people were rescued from buildings in the town.

People ...

... were killed   ... were injured   ... were rescued   ... were damaged   ... were destroyed

Buildings ...

Links

There was, there were
⤳ 84

hundreds of,
thousands of ⤳ 1D

2 Complete the sentences. Use words from the boxes.

There was a train (a) _crash_ near Paris last night. Fortunately, no-one was (b) ...., but 8 people were (c) .... and were taken to hospital. The train was badly (d) .... in the accident.

floods
✓crash
fires
damaged
destroyed
killed
injured
rescued

After months of dry weather, there were (e) .... across parts of north-east Australia last week. Many forests were (f) ...., and thousands of animals were (g) ....

There were (h) .... again in Mozambique last week. Many villages were under water, and hundreds of people were (i) .... from their homes by helicopter.

Emergencies

Links

got, put, took	➲85B
later	➲100B

A fire

'A fire started across the road last night. I saw it, and called the fire brigade. Ten minutes later, a fire engine arrived, and several firemen got out. They quickly put out the fire.'

An accident

'There was an accident in the High Street yesterday, and a woman was badly injured. Someone called an ambulance, and they took her to hospital.'

A robbery

'Some thieves broke into a shop last night and stole some money. Someone called the police. A few minutes later, four policemen arrived in two police cars. They caught the thieves and took them away.'

Verbs		People		Vehicles
call (an ambulance)	steal (money)	policeman/woman	the police	police car
put out (a fire)	catch (a thief)	fireman/woman	the fire brigade	fire engine
break into (a shop)		thief (*plural* thieves)		ambulance

3 Look at the pictures. What words go with the letters?

a _firemen_ **b** _____ **c** _____

d _____ **e** _____ **f** _____

4 Write the answers in the crossword.

1 Go away or I'll call the _ _ _ _ _ _!

2 The firemen quickly _ _ _ the fire out.

3 They broke _ _ _ _ a bank and took £1 million.

4 The _ _ _ _ _ took my wallet and ran away.

5 He ran down the road, but the police _ _ _ _ _ _ him.

6 People who steal things.

7 We think the fire _ _ _ _ _ _ _ in the kitchen.

8 The injured people were taken to _ _ _ _ _ _ _ _.

9 10 minutes later, a fire _ _ _ _ _ _ arrived.

10 Quick! Call the _ _ _ _ brigade!

11 A man _ _ _ killed in the accident.

12 The thief _ _ _ _ _ my watch and all of my money.

13 Someone saw the accident and _ _ _ _ _ _ an ambulance.

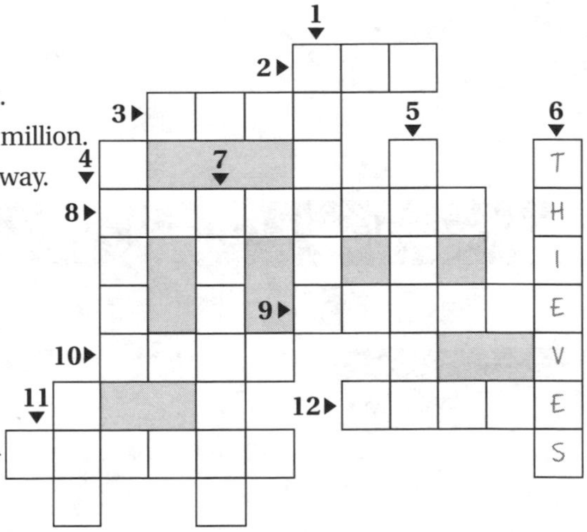

(Crossword grid with across clues 2, 3, 8, 9, 10, 12, 13 and down clues 1, 4, 5, 6, 7, 11. Column 6 spells vertically: T H I E V E S)

Write in your language

Many buildings were destroyed in the earthquake.

No-one was killed, but 20 people were injured.

Call the police! Call an ambulance!

51 Clothes

A Vocabulary — *I wore a jacket*

Link
wore ➲ 85

At my father's 70th birthday party, some people wore formal clothes and some people wore casual clothes. I wore a jacket, trousers and a shirt. My father wore a suit and tie. My sister wore a new dress, but her husband wore jeans and an old jumper. My daughter wore a skirt and a top, and my son wore jeans and a T-shirt.

Present	Past
wear	wore

1. Read the text. Find these people in the picture:

   a <u>3</u> the speaker   **b** ___ his father   **c** ___ his sister

   d ___ her husband   **e** ___ his daughter   **f** ___ his son

2. Which clothes in the text do you think are more formal? Which are more casual? Write them in the box.

FORMAL	FORMAL OR CASUAL	CASUAL
tie	trousers	

B Vocabulary — Materials

Link
➲ 25   **Adjectives**

 leather gloves
(They're made of leather.)

 a cotton shirt
(It's made of cotton.)

 a woollen scarf
(It's made of wool.)

 silk pyjamas
(They're made of silk.)

Link
made of ➲ 52

3. Which of these is normal? Which is unusual? Which is very unusual? Write ✓ (= normal), ? (= unusual) or ?! (= very unusual)

   a a cotton shirt ✓   **b** a leather shirt ?!   **c** a woollen hat

   d leather shoes   **e** woollen shoes   **f** a cotton jacket

   g a leather jacket   **h** leather trousers   **i** a silk tie

4. Write about a time you went out. What did you wear?

   _____

   _____

   _____

   > I went to the theatre on Saturday. I wore a black leather jacket, a white shirt, a red silk tie, and black trousers.

C Phrases — *a pair of trousers*

boots   shoes   trainers   sandals   socks   trousers   jeans   shorts   glasses   sunglasses

a shoe | shoes *or* a pair of **shoes** | two **pairs** of **shoes** | trousers *or* a pair of trousers | two pairs of trousers

NOT ~~a trouser~~
~~a jean~~

5 A man is going on holiday. Complete the description. Add **pair(s) of** if necessary.

He's taking (a) ___five T-shirts___ , (b) ___two pairs of trousers___ ,

(c) _____ , (d) _____ ,

(e) _____ , (f) _____ ,

(g) _____ , (h) _____ ,

and (i) _____ .

> **PACKING LIST**
> | T-shirts 5 | socks 7 |
> | trousers 2 | brown shoes |
> | shorts 2 | black shoes |
> | shirts 3 | sandals |
> | jumpers 2 | jacket |

D Phrases — In a clothes shop

Links

try … on, put … on
➲ RU1

too + adjective ➲ 29

1 Can I try it on? **2** What size is it? **3** It fits very well. **4** It doesn't fit me. **5** It really suits you.

6 Look at the sentences in the bubbles. Match them with the meanings.

a __4__ It's too big (or too small).   **d** ____ Can I put it on to see if I like it?

b ____ Is it large, medium or small?   **e** ____ It's the right size.

c ____ It looks good on you.

7 Fill the gaps in the conversations. Use words and phrases from the bubbles.

a
– What ___size___ is this coat?
– It's 38.
– Can I _____ ?
– Yes, of course.

b
– That's a nice jumper. Why don't you _____ ?
– OK. … What do you think?
– Yes. It _____ you.

c
– Do you like those shoes?
– No. They're too big. They don't _____ .
– _____ are they?
– 46. I'm 42.

Write in your language

I wore a red silk shirt and a brown leather jacket.	
He's got five pairs of trainers.	
Can I try on these trousers?	

52

Containers and materials

A Vocabulary *a jar of jam*

Link

oil, orange juice

⮕13

I went to the supermarket today. I bought …

some oil,	a bottle of oil,
some jam,	a jar of jam,
some spaghetti,	a packet of spaghetti,
some potatoes,	a bag of potatoes,
some orange juice,	a carton of orange juice,
some lemonade	a can of lemonade
and some chocolates	and a box of chocolates.

We can buy things in …

bottles   packets   cartons   jars

bags   boxes   cans *or* tins

1 What are these?

a <u>a bag of sweets</u>
b ....
c ....
d ....
e ....
f ....
g ....
h ....

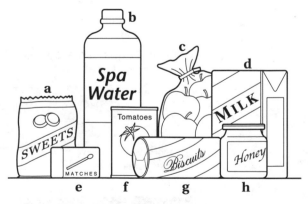

Link

(I've) bought   ⮕90

2 What have you bought in the past week?
Look at the example, and write a list.

<u>In the past week, I've bought</u>
....
....
....
....

In the past week, I've bought
– a bottle of mineral water
– a packet of cigarettes
– a packet of sweets
– a can of tomatoes
– a box of tissues

It's made of ...

Link

made ➲63B, 93B

GLASS 1
METAL 2
PLASTIC 3
PAPER + CARDBOARD 4
W O O D 5

Bottles are made of glass or plastic. Boxes are made of wood or cardboard.
Cans are made of metal. Bags are made of plastic or paper.

3 Where would you put these things, and why?

		Where?	Why?
a	an empty shoe box	4	It's made of cardboard.
b	bags from the supermarket		
c	a wine bottle		
d	some old magazines		
e	an empty can of tomatoes		
f	an empty box of oranges		

C Vocabulary *a cardboard box*

This is a box. It's made of cardboard.
→ It's a cardboard box.

| a | paper plastic | bag | a | cardboard wooden | box | a | glass plastic | bottle | a | paper cardboard plastic | carton |

Link

usually ➲9A

4 Look at the examples. Then write about your country.
Complete the sentences.

a You usually buy milk ....
b You usually buy peas ....
c You usually buy orange juice ....
d You usually buy yoghurt ....
e You usually buy lemonade ....

You usually buy milk in a plastic bottle or a cardboard carton.

Write in your language

I'd like a carton of milk, please.

These shoes are made of plastic.

Have you got a cardboard box?

53 Communicating

A Phrases

Links

start up, shut
down, print out ➲RU1

forgot to,
remember to ➲69

Using a computer

Using a computer to write a letter:

| start (up) the computer | open a new document (or file) | type the document | save the document | print (out) the document | shut down the computer |

1 Complete the sentences.

a He can't __type__ very well. He only uses two fingers.

b 'How do you _____ a file?' 'Press *Ctrl-O.*'

c I forgot to _____ the document, and now I've lost everything I wrote.

d Remember to _____ the computer before you go home.

e I'll _____ the document and post it to you.

f I get to work at 8.00, _____ the computer and then make a cup of coffee.

B Phrases

Link

by ➲24B

Contacting people

You can contact people …

by email

by phone

by post

| = you email them / send them an email | = you call them / phone them | = you write to them / send them a letter |

2 Look at these phrases. Which are about sending emails? Which are about phoning? Which are about sending a letter? Write **E, P** or **L**.

P put the phone down	post it	write the address	pick up the phone
type in the message	click 'Send'	type in the address	put a stamp on it
put it in an envelope	talk to the person	dial the number	write the letter
start a new email			

Now write the phrases in the right order.

a Sending an email: First you __start a new email__. Then you _____ and _____. And then you _____.

b Phoning someone: You _____ and _____. Then you _____. When you've finished, you _____.

c Sending a letter: First you _____ and _____. Then you _____ and _____. And then you _____.

Links

| use | ➲64 |
| visit | ➲43C |

A beginner's guide to the Internet

Google
You can use Google to *search for* websites. Just *type in* words, and Google will show you a list of sites. For example, if you want to know about theatres in London, type in 'London' and 'theatres', and then click the 'Search' button.

eBay
You can visit this website if you want to buy or sell something over the Internet: furniture, clothes, cars, computers – almost anything.

eBay's web address is ebay.com (ebay dot com).

Outlook Express
You *use* this program to *write* emails to people. Then you can *connect to* the Internet and *send* them. You can also *receive* emails and *reply to* them.

OpenMG Jukebox
This is a music website. You can find all your favourite songs, and *download* them onto your hard disk.

amazon.com
Visit this website if you want to buy books or CDs – it's an online bookshop.

Link

the same, similar, different ➲31A

3 Look at the words in blue. Are they the same in your language? Write three lists:

The same ....

Similar ....

Different ....

4 Which verbs go in the gaps? Find them in the texts above. (They're in *italics*.)

a You _write_ an email.
reply to
....

b You .... programs, songs and pictures from the Internet.

c You .... programs.

d You .... the Internet.

e You .... a website.

f You .... words.

5 Write the answers in the diagram.

Click this button to send and .... emails. **1▶** R E C E I V E

How do I .... to the Internet? **2▶**

Just .... in your name and click 'OK'. **3▶**

Which program do you .... to write emails? **4▶**

Save the file onto your .... disk. **5▶**

Do I have to pay to .... songs? **6▶**

I'm sorry I didn't .... to your email. **7▶**

eBay and amazon.com are .... **8▶**

Now complete the sentence:

9 If you're online, you're using the ....

Write in your language

When you've finished, you save the file.	
Don't forget to put a stamp on the envelope.	
How do I download things from the Internet?	

A Vocabulary *theatre, cinema ...*

Links

| by | ➲24 |
| most (famous) | ➲28 |

On Monday, an exhibition of paintings by young Australian artists opens at the Dimarco Art Gallery.

CAMEO CINEMA
After Midnight
Mon. 18.00, 20.30
A new film by Mexican director Juan Sandovar. Stars Carlos Mendoza, one of Mexico's most famous actors.

FREE CONCERT!!
The Koots, Britain's most exciting new band, with singer Michaela, playing music from their new CD.

A new play, 'Smoke' by Alex Greenman, starts at the Kings Theatre on Friday. The actors, who are all under 21, are students at Oxford Drama School.

The next concert will be at the Webb Concert Hall on Saturday, 14th April. The National Radio Orchestra will play music by Mozart and Schubert.

An *orchestra* plays at a classical concert.
A *band* plays at a *pop concert* or a *rock concert*.

1 Complete the table with blue words from the texts.

Where?	theatre	....	art gallery	concert hall
What?	....	*film*	....	....
			paintings	
Who?	....	....	....	orchestra

2 Look at the advertisements. What do you think the people and places are?

a The Morgs are probably a *band* .
b The Usher Hall is a ....
c *Under the Moon* is a ....
d John Manolo and Julia Finch are ....
e There is an .... at the Bond Gallery.
f Max Klein is an ....
g *Richard II* is a .... by Shakespeare.

NEW THEATRE
RICHARD II
BY
WILLIAM SHAKESPEARE

USHER HALL
THE MORGS
IN CONCERT

BOND GALLERY
PAINTINGS BY
MAX KLEIN

ADELPHI CINEMA
UNDER THE MOON
starring
JOHN MANOLO
JULIA FINCH

What's on …?

Link

What …?   ➔95

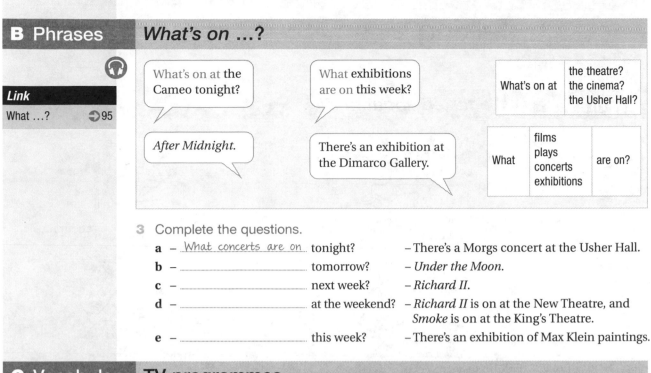

What's on at **the** Cameo tonight?

After Midnight.

What **exhibitions are on** this week?

There's an exhibition at the Dimarco Gallery.

What's on at	the theatre?
	the cinema?
	the Usher Hall?

What	films	are on?
	plays	
	concerts	
	exhibitions	

3 Complete the questions.

a – ___What concerts are on___ tonight?   – There's a Morgs concert at the Usher Hall.

b – _____ tomorrow?   – *Under the Moon.*

c – _____ next week?   – *Richard II.*

d – _____ at the weekend?   – *Richard II* is on at the New Theatre, and *Smoke* is on at the King's Theatre.

e – _____ this week?   – There's an exhibition of Max Klein paintings.

TV programmes

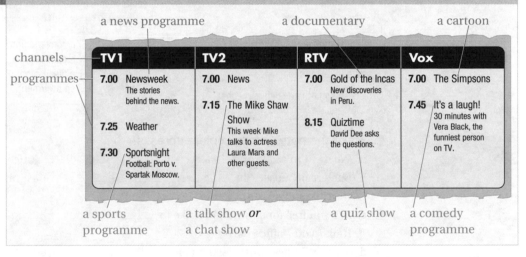

a news programme   a documentary   a cartoon

channels

programmes

TV1	**TV2**	**RTV**	**Vox**
7.00 Newsweek The stories behind the news.	**7.00** News	**7.00** Gold of the Incas New discoveries in Peru.	**7.00** The Simpsons
	7.15 The Mike Shaw Show This week Mike talks to actress Laura Mars and other guests.		**7.45** It's a laugh! 30 minutes with Vera Black, the funniest person on TV.
7.25 Weather		**8.15** Quiztime David Dee asks the questions.	
7.30 Sportsnight Football: Porto v. Spartak Moscow.			

a sports programme   a talk show *or* a chat show   a quiz show   a comedy programme

Links

favourite   ➔67B

What …? Which …?   ➔95

4 Think about TV in your country. Answer these questions.

a Which is your favourite TV channel? _____

b What kind of programme do you watch most often? _____

c How many times a week do you watch:

sports programmes? _____   documentaries? _____   talk shows? _____

comedy programmes? _____   news programmes? _____   quiz shows? _____

d What is your favourite TV programme? _____

Write in your language

There's a new exhibition on at the art gallery.	
What's on at the cinema this evening?	
I like watching talk shows and documentaries.	

55 Talking

A Phrases — We talked about music

We chatted / had a chat about the weather.

We talked / had a conversation about music.

We discussed / had a discussion about the new road.

We argued / had an argument about money.

Verbs

talk (to someone)	
chat (to someone)	about something
argue (with someone)	
discuss something (with someone)	

Phrases with *have*

have	a conversation	with someone
	a chat	about something
	a discussion	
	an argument	

1 Make the notes into complete phrases.

a We went to a café and _had a nice chat about holidays_ . (nice / chat / holidays)

b She's really upset. She _____ last night. (terrible / argument / father)

c Are you free for a minute? I'd like to _____ . (talk / you / office party)

d I met a Chinese businessman on the plane. We _____ . (interesting / conversation / China)

e The meeting went on for hours. We _____ . (long / discussion / the new sports centre)

f I never _____ . (discuss / money / my parents)

B Grammar — Reported speech

Links

was, were	⮌83
past simple	⮌85
past continuous	⮌87

I live in Canada, but I'm staying with friends in London.

I was talking to someone on the train. He told me he lived in Canada, but he was staying with friends in London.

This is my first time on a plane. I feel quite nervous.

The man next to me told me it was his first time on a plane. He said he felt quite nervous.

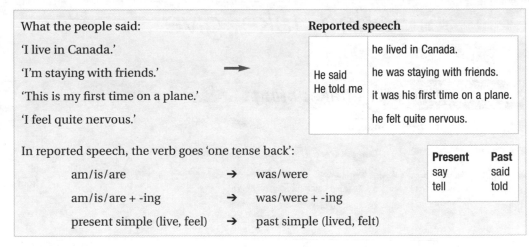

What the people said:		Reported speech
'I live in Canada.'		he lived in Canada.
'I'm staying with friends.'	He said / He told me	he was staying with friends.
'This is my first time on a plane.'		it was his first time on a plane.
'I feel quite nervous.'		he felt quite nervous.

In reported speech, the verb goes 'one tense back':

Present	Past
say	said
tell	told

am/is/are	→	was/were
am/is/are + -ing	→	was/were + -ing
present simple (live, feel)	→	past simple (lived, felt)

2 Here are some other things the Canadian said. Write them as reported speech. Begin **He said …** or **He told me ….**

   a 'I like England.' — *He told me he liked England.*

   b 'I'm having a good time here.'

   c 'I have a lot of friends in London.'

   d 'I'm going back to Canada in June.'

   e 'I need to earn some money.'

   f 'I'm starting university in September.'

Link

I'll …   ⟳77A

3 Look at the examples. Then continue the replies, using the words in brackets.

   a – Hurry up. The film starts at 9.00.
      – 9.00? You said *it started at 9.30* . (9.30)

   b – Let's watch the match.
      – You told me _____ . (not like / football)

   c – He's studying French.
      – Really? He told me _____ . (Arabic)

   d – That's Magda's husband.
      – She told me _____ . (not married)

   e – They're leaving today.
      – Today? They said _____ . (on Sunday)

   f – That's their house.
      – But they told me _____ . (live / flat)

Write in your language

We had a long conversation about the weather.	
He told me he was staying with friends.	
They said they were going to buy a new car.	

56 *bring, take, give ...*

A Vocabulary *put, take, bring ...*

Links

out of, into, on, off ⟳ 23

get ⟳ 57

take, put

Don't forget the cake. Please take it out of the oven at 3.30 and put it on a plate to cool down.

TAKE PUT

take it	out of ... off ... from ...
put it	in(to) ... on(to) ...

bring, take, get, fetch

I'm taking Bill to the airport. See you later.

I'm fetching the children from school. Back soon.
Pam

We've only got $10. Can you go and get some money from the bank?

Come and see us tomorrow. Bring something to drink!
Joe

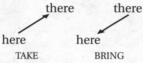

there   there

here   here
TAKE   BRING

FETCH or GET

take ... to ...	(go and)	get fetch	... from ...

give, take

Give me the money!

Here you are. Take it.

GIVE   TAKE

Links

got, put, took ⟳ 85B

I've/You've + past participle ⟳ 90

1 Complete the sentences. Use verbs from the box.

a Wait a minute. I'll just go and __fetch__ my coat from the bedroom.

b I think you _____ my book yesterday. Could you _____ it back, please?

c He _____ me 25 euros, but I only spent 10.

d He _____ a gun out of his pocket, and _____ it on the table. 'I hope you've _____ the money,' he said.

e I've _____ the car to the garage. I need to go and _____ it tomorrow.

Present	Past	Past Participle
take	took	taken
put	put	put
bring	brought	brought
get	got	got
fetch	fetched	fetched
give	gave	given

Phrases with *take*

| take a bus | take sugar | take a photo (of) | take medicine | take an exam | take a driving test |

2 Answer these questions. Answer with a word or phrase.

a If you go into town, how often do you take a bus or train? _Twice a week._

b Who takes the best photos in your family? (You? Or someone else?) _____

c What do you usually take photos of? (People? Buildings? Views?) _____

d When was the last time you took medicine? _____

e When was the last time you took an exam or test? Did you pass or fail? _____

f Do you take sugar in tea or coffee? _____

Now choose three of your answers. Write sentences.

a _____

b _____

c _____

> *I take a bus into town about twice a week.*
>
> *I take sugar in coffee, but not in tea.*

I bought her some flowers

I got my mother some flowers.

I bought her some flowers.

I'm giving her some flowers.

NOT ~~I'm giving to her some flowers.~~

| verb → person → thing |

I got these flowers for my mother.

I bought them for my mother.

I'm giving them to my mother.

NOT ~~I'm giving them my mother.~~

| verb → thing → *to/for* + person |

3 Are these sentences correct? Write **for, to** or **– (nothing)** in the gaps.

a I haven't got much money. Can you give _–_ me 10 euros?

b I've brought blankets _for_ everyone. It might be cold tonight.

c I've got plenty of money. Let me buy _____ you lunch.

d If you don't want those shoes, give them _____ someone else.

e I gave my concert ticket _____ a friend.

f Look. I've bought _____ you a birthday present.

g She always buys chocolate _____ the children.

Present	buy
Past	bought
Past participle	bought

Write in your language

We need to get some money from the bank.

She takes very good photos.

I bought him a present for his birthday.

57 get

A Vocabulary · get

Link

bring, take ⤳56

> At 5.45, I got a text on my mobile. It said, 'I'm working late. Please get some food for this evening. M.'
> The shops closed at 6.00, so I had to hurry. I got my bike from the garage, and cycled quickly down to the shops.
> I got to the shops at exactly 5.58. Then I remembered: I didn't have my wallet with me.

(*get* = receive)
(*get* = buy)

(*get* = take, bring)

(*get to* = arrive at)

Present	Past
get	got

you *get* or *receive* a present, an email, a letter = someone gives or sends it to you

1 Look at these sentences. What does **get** mean in each one?

  a How much milk shall I get? = buy

  b Could you get my coat from the car? ....

  c She always gets lots of birthday cards. ....

  d Did you get my text message? ....

  e I forgot to get any sugar. ....

  f He didn't get to work until 9.30. ....

2 Write sentences about yourself, using **get** or **got**.

....

....

....

I need to get a chicken from the market.

On Saturday, I got a new T-shirt.

I got to work late this morning.

B Phrases · get dark, get ready ...

Links

is + verb + -ing	⤳82A
dark, wet	⤳25A
pain, ill	⤳48
better, worse	⤳27A

It's getting dark.

(= It will be dark soon.)

Wait a minute. I'm just getting ready.

(= I'll be ready in a minute.)

I'm getting fat.

(= He's fatter now than before.)

***get* + adjective**	get	dark ready fat

3 When might you say these things? Match the sentences with the situations.

1	'The pain's getting worse.'	**a**	You're driving along a motorway.
2	'Hurry up! Your food will get cold.'	**b**	A friend of yours is ill.
3	'I hope he gets better soon.'	**c**	You've just cooked a meal.
4	'My feet are getting wet.'	**d**	You're visiting friends.
5	'Let's stop for a bit. I'm getting tired.'	**e**	You're walking in the rain.
6	'We ought to go home soon. It's getting late.'	**f**	You have a headache.

get lost, get married ...

Link
get engaged,
get married ➔44B

Link
➔51   Clothes

get stuck   get lost   get engaged   get married   get dressed   get undressed   get changed

4 Complete the sentences. Use phrases with **get** or **got**.

   a We tried to move the piano, but it _got stuck_____ on the stairs.

   b I'll be ready in 10 minutes. I just need to have a shower and _____ .

   c They _____ last week, and they're going to _____ in July.

   d I was tired, so I _____ and went to bed.

   e I think you should _____ . You can't go to the party in those jeans.

   f Don't go too far into the forest on your own. It's very easy to _____ .

D Phrases

get on, get off ...

Link
➔40   Transport

get on a bus   get off a bus   get in(to) a car   get out of a car

5 When do we use **on/off**? When do we use **in(to)/out of**? Read the sentences, and write words in the lists.

   a We got off the bikes and walked the rest of the way.

   b Quick! Get on the train. It's leaving!

   c I saw her again yesterday. She was just getting out of a white taxi.

   d I can't ride at all. I don't even know how to get on a horse.

   e Finally, two hours later, we got on the plane and took off.

   f He finds it difficult to get out of bed in the morning.

get on/off ...	get in(to)/out of ...
a bus	a car
a bike	

Write in your language

Did you get my text?	
Let's go. It's getting late.	
We got lost, so we bought a street map.	

58 find, lose, keep ...

Link

(I've) lost ➡90

A Phrases   lose, find

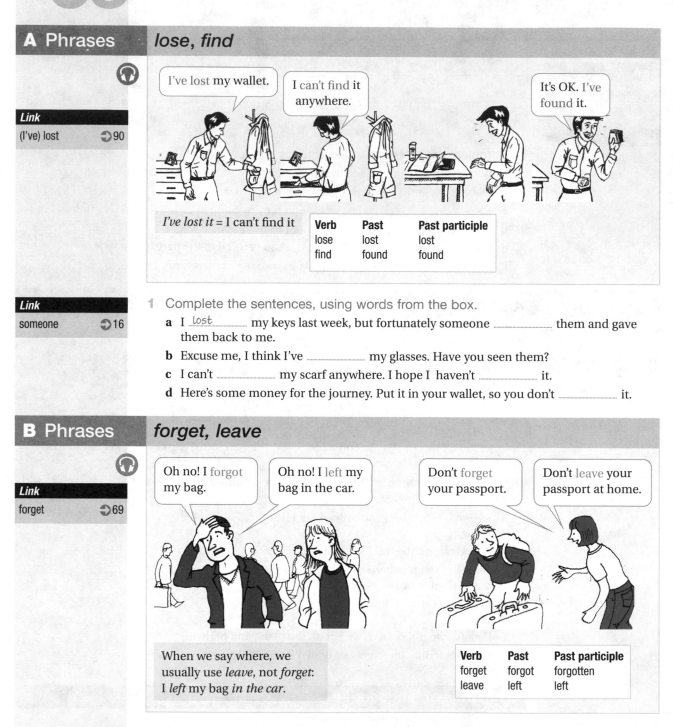

I've lost my wallet.

I can't find it anywhere.

It's OK. I've found it.

I've lost it = I can't find it

Verb	Past	Past participle
lose	lost	lost
find	found	found

Link

someone ➡16

1 Complete the sentences, using words from the box.

a I __lost__ my keys last week, but fortunately someone _____ them and gave them back to me.

b Excuse me, I think I've _____ my glasses. Have you seen them?

c I can't _____ my scarf anywhere. I hope I haven't _____ it.

d Here's some money for the journey. Put it in your wallet, so you don't _____ it.

B Phrases   forget, leave

Link

forget ➡69

Oh no! I forgot my bag.

Oh no! I left my bag in the car.

Don't forget your passport.

Don't leave your passport at home.

When we say where, we usually use *leave*, not *forget*: I *left* my bag *in the car*.

Verb	Past	Past participle
forget	forgot	forgotten
leave	left	left

2 Choose the correct verb.

a He often *leaves* / *forgets* his umbrella on the train.

b Excuse me, I think you've *left* / *forgotten* your hat.

c I think I *left* / *forgot* my coat in the restaurant.

d Have you *left* / *forgotten* the tickets?

e They *left* / *forgot* their towels on the beach, but when they went back they were still there.

f Don't *leave* / *forget* your glasses. You'll need them.

keep

You can keep things …

| in a cupboard | in your wallet | in the attic |
| in a drawer | in a box | in the cellar |

      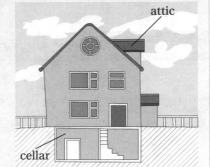

on a shelf   in your pocket

attic

cellar

3 Choose five things from the box. Where do you keep them?

a _I/we keep suitcases in the attic._

b _____

c _____

d _____

e _____

money	car
suitcases	bike
potatoes	socks
vegetables	keys
old books	biscuits

keep, throw away …

Links

throw away, give away	⟳RU1
would, I'd	➲80
too	➲29

Imagine you have an old TV …

| Would you keep it? | Would you throw it away? | Would you sell it? | Or would you give it away? |

4 Look at the situations. What would you do?

a You have some shoes that are too small.   I'd _____

b You have some old children's toys. _____

c You have some old chairs. They're broken. _____

d You have an old carpet. It's too big for your flat. _____

e You have a box of old books. _____

f You find some old CDs. You don't want to listen to them. _____

Write in your language

I can't find my wallet. I think I've lost it.

She left her coat on the bus.

Do you want to keep this or throw it away?

A Vocabulary · stand, sit, lie, walk, run

Links

She's (walk)ing ⮕ 82

along, across ⮕ 23

1 She's walking along the path.
2 They're running across the grass.
3 She's sitting on a bench.
4 He's standing by the gate.
5 They're lying on the grass.

1 Find these people, and complete the sentences.

a __7__ He's _sitting_ _____ under a tree.
b ____ She's _____ along a wall.
c ____ She's _____ under a tree.
d ____ They're _____ on a wall.
e ____ She's _____ by the pond.
f ____ He's _____ along the road.

B Phrases · stand up, get up, sit down, lie down

Links

worried, frightened ⮕ 46

then, after ⮕ 100

stand up, sit down, lie down ⮕ RU1

I was tired. I lay down on the sofa and closed my eyes. Just then, the doorbell rang. I got up, went to the door and opened it. It was my sister. She came into the room and sat down at the table. She looked worried. After a few seconds, she stood up again and looked through the window. 'I'm frightened,' she said. 'I think someone is following me.'

| *stand up* or *get up* | *sit down* | *stand up* or *get up* | *lie down* |

Present	Past
stand up	stood up
get up	got up
sit down	sat down
lie down	lay down

2 Complete the sentences with verbs from the table.

a She _sat down_ _____ at her desk and turned on the computer.
b I got undressed, _____ and fell asleep.
c He looked at his watch and _____ . 'Time to go,' he said.
d 'Please take off your shirt and _____ on the bed,' the doctor said.
e 'Let's have some tea,' he said. He _____ and went into the kitchen.
f We found a free table, _____ and looked at the menu.

went, drove, ran ...

Link

➲85 **Past simple (1)**

Links

get in, get on, get out
➲57
drive away, take off
➲RU1
get in(to) ➲RU7

She got in her car ... ... and drove away. off.

He stopped ... ... and got out (of the car).

He got on his bike ... ... and rode away. off.

The plane took off. The plane landed.

He walked down the road ... ... and I followed him.

They ran away ... off ... ... and I chased them.

I stood at the bus stop ... ... and waited for the bus.

They came out of the building ... ... and went across the road.

Irregular verbs	
Present	**Past**
get	got
drive	drove
ride	rode
take	took
run	ran
stand	stood
come	came
go	went

3 Complete the sentences with verbs from the boxes. Use the past simple tense.

a They ___ran___ out of the bank, _____ on their horses and _____ away. I _____ them, but they were too fast for me.

get	✓run
ride	chase

b He _____ out of the house and _____ down the road. I _____ him, but he _____ into a car and _____ away.

drive	walk	come
follow	get	

c She _____ me down the road. I _____ at the corner and _____ for her.

follow	stop	wait

d The plane _____ off from London at 6.00, and _____ in Moscow four hours later. We _____ off the plane, _____ out of the airport, and _____ for a taxi.

get	go	wait
take	land	

Write in your language

They're lying on the grass.

She got up, then she sat down again.

He got in his car and drove away.

60 Moving things

A Vocabulary — *pull, push, move …*

Link
pick up, put down
→RU1

These people are moving furniture from one room to another.

He's picking up a table.   They're carrying a sofa.   She's putting down a chair.

He's pushing a piano.   She's pulling a piano.

| move (from A to B) | carry | push | pull | pick up (a box) pick (a box) up | put down (a box) put (a box) down |

Link
was/were (carry)ing →87

1 Choose the **two** best answers.

a He was carrying *a suitcase* / ~~*a motorbike*~~ / *a baby*.

b They were pushing *a car* / *their bikes* / *a newspaper* along the road.

c Could you move *your car* / *these books* / *the room* , please?

d He picked all the *clothes* / *carpets* / *magazines* up off the floor.

e Put the *suitcases* / *washing machines* / *bags* down over there.

2 Complete the sentences with verbs from the box.

Link
(open)ed, went →85

a She _pulled_ me by the arm. 'Come quickly,' she said.

b She couldn't walk, so we _____ her upstairs.

c John _____ his jacket _____ from the chair. 'Goodbye,' he said.

d I _____ the door and it opened. I went in.

e She _____ her suitcases _____ on the floor, and sat down.

f He _____ his chair closer to the window, and looked out.

put … down
pushed
moved
✓ pulled
picked … up
carried

B Phrases — *It won't move*

– The window won't open.
  I think it's locked.
– Mm. Can you see a key?

– What's the problem?
– I can't turn the handle. It's stuck.

| I can't | open close move turn | it. | It won't | open. close. move. turn. | It's | locked. stuck. | (It's stuck. = It won't move.) |

Link

too →29

3 Complete the remarks. Use words from the box.

a This suitcase is too full. I _can't_ _close_ it.

b The door ____ ____ . Have you got a key?

c I ____ the drawer. It's ____ .

d The wardrobe ____ ____ . It's too heavy.

e The key's in the door, but it ____ ____ . It's ____ .

stuck	open
locked	close
can't	move
turn	won't

C Vocabulary *throw*, *kick*, *hit* ...

Link

score, goal, lost, match →41B

'Riveiro kicks the ball ...   ... Koku tries to catch it ...   ... but he misses it – and Riveiro has scored a goal!'

'Gomez hits the ball ...   ... Alexi catches it ...   ... and throws it to Barton ...   ... but Barton drops it!   And that means they've lost the match.'

Link

going to →79

4 What are these people going to do? Complete the sentences.

catch   drop   hit   kick   miss   ✓throw

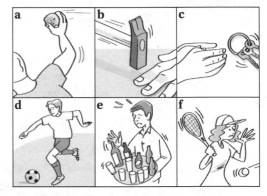

a _He's going to throw_ a stone.

b ____ his hand.

c ____ the keys.

d ____ the ball.

e ____ the drinks.

f ____ the ball.

Write in your language

She picked the paper up from the table.

The window won't open – it's stuck.

He tried to catch the ball, but he dropped it.

129

61 see, hear ...

A Phrases

Links

were (watch)ing	➲87
(look)ed, saw	➲85

see, look, watch

I looked through the window.

I saw two people in the room.

They were watching television.

see (past: **saw**)
I was in town this afternoon when I saw an old friend of mine.
Turn the light on. I can't see anything.

look (past: **looked**)
Look at this. It's a photo of my grandfather.
I looked through the telescope and saw hundreds of stars.

watch (past: **watched**)
The police watched the house all day, but nobody went in.
The children were playing football. I stood and watched them.

at someone	at a picture
LOOK	
over a wall	**through** a window

television	a DVD
WATCH	
a football match	a video

1 Here is part of a story. Choose the best verb.

I sat in my car all morning, and (a) *looked at / watched* __watched__ the house. At around 12.30 I (b) *saw / looked at* _____ Marlene. She was walking quickly along the street, and she was (c) *seeing / looking* _____ down, so she didn't (d) *see / watch* _____ me. She went into the house and closed the door.

Quietly, I went up to the house and (e) *saw / looked* _____ through the study window. I (f) *saw / looked at* _____ Marlene at her desk. She was (g) *looking at / watching* _____ some photos, but I couldn't (h) *see / watch* _____ them clearly. I stood by the window and (i) *saw / watched* _____ .

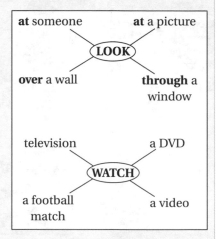

hear, listen

Link

carefully ➲ 26A

2 Complete each sentence in **two** ways. Choose phrases from the box.

a When I drive to work, I usually listen to ___music___ .

_____ .

b I woke in the night. I could hear _____ .

_____ .

c Listen _____ . I need to tell you something.

_____ .

to me
✓ music
someone in the street
the news
carefully
the wind

C Phrases *I saw her go into the house*

Link

infinitive ➲ RU2

She went into the house. I saw her. → I saw her go into the house.

She said 'Hello'. I heard her. → I heard her say 'Hello'.

NOT ~~I saw her to go~~
~~I saw her went~~

I	saw heard	her	+ infinitive

3 Here is some more of the story in exercise A1. Rewrite the words in *italics* using **saw** or **heard**.

Behind me, (a) *a car stopped outside the house*. I looked round. (b) *Two men got out of the car*, and went up to the house. (c) *They rang the bell*. (d) *One of them said, 'I know she's there'*. I looked through the window again. (e) *Marlene put the photos in a drawer*. Then (f) *she got up* and (g) *ran out of the room*.

a I heard a car stop outside the house.
b I saw two men get out of the car.
c _____
d _____
e _____
f _____
g _____

Write in your language

Look at this picture! It's beautiful.	
I saw them get into a taxi.	
I can hear someone in the next room.	

62 look, sound ...

Link

➲25 Adjectives

Link

see, hear ➲61

A Vocabulary · It looks lovely

It **looks** lovely.   It **sounds** awful.   It **tastes** delicious.   They **smell** lovely.   It **feels** nice.

I can	see it. ◁	→	It looks	
	hear it.		It sounds	
	taste it.		It tastes	+ adjective
	smell it.		It smells	
	feel it.		It feels	

It's delicious.
= It tastes (or smells) very good.

1 Complete the sentences. Use a verb from the table + a word from the box.

a I hate the new airport building. I think it _looks ugly_ .

b I think there's something bad in the fridge. It _____ !

c – My daughter is studying Chinese medicine.

– Really? That _____ .

d I think Peter works too hard. He _____ .

e Try this chocolate. It _____ .

f Don't put on this shirt. It _____ .

| awful |
| delicious |
| interesting |
| tired |
| ✓ugly |
| damp |

B Phrases · It sounds like Vivaldi

Links

like ➲31D

meat, fish, lamb ➲32

What's the music?

I'm not sure. It sounds like Vivaldi.

Are you sure this is meat? It tastes like fish to me.

		looks		
		sounds		
It		tastes	like	+ noun
		smells		
		feels		

2 Rewrite the sentences in *italics*. Use words from the table.

a What kind of tea is this? *I think it's Assam.*   It _tastes like_ Assam tea.

b I can hear someone in the next room.   It _____ your father.
I think it's your father.

c What kind of meat is this? *I think it's lamb.*   It _____ lamb.

d What are you cooking? *I think it's cabbage.*   It _____ cabbage.

e Who's that baby in the photo? *I think it's you.*   It _____ you.

f I like this tie. *I think it's made of silk.*   It _____ silk.

C Phrases — *What does it taste like?*

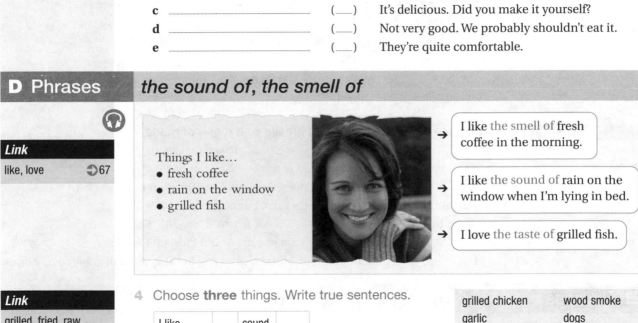

> What does it taste like?

> Not bad. It needs more salt.

3 Look at the replies below. What is each person talking about? Write **1–5**.

1 a cake   **2** a pair of shoes   **3** a fish   **4** a singer   **5** a new building

Now write the questions.

a	What does it look like?	(5)	Terrible. I think it's really ugly.
b	....	(......)	Awful. She can't sing at all.
c	....	(......)	It's delicious. Did you make it yourself?
d	....	(......)	Not very good. We probably shouldn't eat it.
e	....	(......)	They're quite comfortable.

D Phrases — *the sound of, the smell of*

Link

like, love   ➔ 67

Things I like…
- fresh coffee
- rain on the window
- grilled fish

→ I like the smell of fresh coffee in the morning.

→ I like the sound of rain on the window when I'm lying in bed.

→ I love the taste of grilled fish.

Link

grilled, fried, raw   ➔ 32B

4 Choose **three** things. Write true sentences.

I like		sound	
I love	the	smell	of …
I don't like		taste	

grilled chicken	wood smoke
garlic	dogs
fried onions	raw fish
the sea	motorbikes

a ....

b ....

c ....

Write in your language

It sounds very interesting.

That looks like your brother's car.

It smells of garlic here.

63 *make and do*

A Phrases *make*

make a cake · make tea · make dinner · make a salad · make a list

make a phone call · make a note (of) · make a decision · make a mistake · make an appointment

Link

I think I'll …,
I'm going to … ➲77

1 Complete the sentences. Use phrases with **make** or **made**.

a I feel ill. I think I'll _make an appointment_ to see the doctor.

b Can I borrow your mobile? I need to ....

c He .... of my phone number and put it in his pocket.

d Buy some tomatoes, lettuce and onions. I want to ....

e Sorry, I .... His name isn't 'Kosta', it's 'Kolya'.

f .... of the food you need, and I'll get it for you.

g I .... for his birthday last year, but this year I'm going to buy one.

Present	Past
make	made

B Phrases *made by, made in, made of*

Links

is/are made	➲93B
Japanese, Turkish, Swiss	➲38
plastic, paper	➲52B

100% PURE WOOL
BRUNTONS of London

It's made of wool.

It's made by Bruntons.

It's made in England.

2 What about these things?

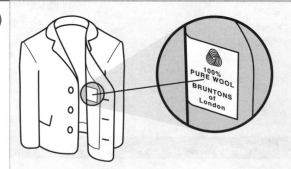

a a Nokia phone _It's made by Nokia._   f Esprit jeans ....

b a plastic bag ....   g gold earrings ....

c a Japanese car ....   h Gucci shoes ....

d a Mercedes lorry ....   i a paper cup ....

e Swiss chocolate ....   j Turkish carpets ....

do

Links

do the housework,
do the cleaning
🔗35B

a lot of 🔗14B

We use do to talk about :

work:	do the housework	do the cleaning (= clean the rooms)	
	do (a lot of) work	do the washing (= wash the clothes)	
	do your homework	do the shopping (= buy things)	
activities:	do sport	do a lot of reading (= read a lot)	
	do exercise	do a lot of travelling (= travel a lot)	
	do yoga		

housework = work in the house, e.g. cleaning, washing

homework = work for school that you do at home

3 Are these sentences correct? Correct them if necessary, using words from the table.

Present	Past	Past Participle
do/does	did	done
make	made	made

a She does a lot of work for UNICEF. ✓

     did

b He ~~made~~ a lot of reading on holiday. ✗

c Have you made your homework yet?

d They did all the shopping for us.

e He doesn't make much sport.

f Have a rest. I'll do the cooking today.

g What do we need? I'll do a list.

h I've made a fruit salad for lunch.

i He does lots of mistakes when he writes.

j I've done an appointment to see Mr Chan.

Questions with *do*

Links

What do you …?
🔗81C

What are you
(do)ing? 🔗82C

What did you …?
🔗86C

What are you doing?
I'm sending an email.

What shall we do?
Let's go for a walk.

What are you doing this evening?
We're going to the cinema.

What do you do?
I'm a teacher.

What did you do at the weekend?
I just stayed at home.

4 Make questions for these answers.

a – What do you do?
   – I work in a bank.

b – ....
   – I'm trying to open this box.

c – ....
   – I'm going to a party.

d – ....
   – Well, on Saturday I went to the theatre.

e – ....
   – I don't know. Shall we have something to eat?

f – ....
   – I'm a student at Cairo University.

Write in your language

Make a list of the things you need.	
These shoes are made in Spain.	
He does a lot of sport at school.	

A Grammar — *You use it to/for …*

Link
⮕ 89   **used to**

Links
is (used)   ⮕ 93
-ing forms   ⮕ RU3

Link
boil, fry   ⮕ 32

You use it to kill / for killing flies.

It is used to kill / for killing flies.

a fly swat

| use + to + verb | use + for + -ing form |

1 Match the pictures with the sentences, then complete the sentences. Write **You use it to**, **You use it for**, **It is used to** or **It is used for**.

a	5	It is used to	buy things.
b	4	You use it for	catching fish.
c			boil water.
d			light a fire.
e			frying eggs.
f			taking photos.
g			make cakes.

B Vocabulary — **Things and their uses**

cut	paint	clean	stick	tie	mend

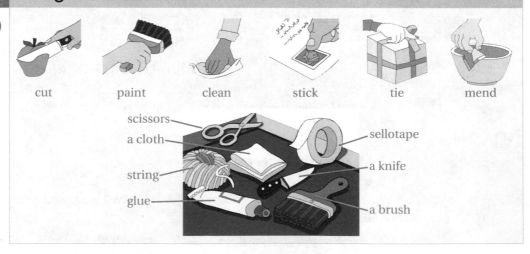

scissors
a cloth
string
glue
sellotape
a knife
a brush

2 Which nouns go with which verbs? Complete the list on the right.

You want to …

a … stick two pieces of paper together.
b … cut an onion.
c … cut a piece of paper.
d … tie some flowers together.
e … paint a wall.
f … clean the windows.
g … mend a chair.

You could use …

glue or sellotape

3 Look at the example. Complete these sentences in the same way.

I need a knife for cutting vegetables.

Link

paper, wood, metal
➲52

a I need a small brush *for painting* _____ wood.
b I'd like a pair of scissors _____ hair.
c I need some strong glue _____ wood and metal.
d Have you got any string _____ parcels?
e I'd like a cloth _____ mirrors.
f Have you got a knife _____ plastic?

C Vocabulary *useful, useless*

Links

would ➲80
the most, the least
➲28

Imagine you are alone on a desert island.

A knife would be very useful.
(= you could use it for lots of things)
A computer would be (completely) useless.
(= you couldn't use it for anything)

4 Which of these things would be:
– very useful?   – quite useful?   – not very useful?   – completely useless?

a a mobile phone

completely useless

e a bottle of water

b a box of matches

f a tent

c a fishing line

g a pen

d a newspaper

DAILY TIMES

h a camera

Which do you think would be:
– the most useful? _____   – the least useful? _____

Write in your language

It's used for killing flies.

Have you got any sellotape?

This knife is completely useless.

65 *start* and *finish*

A Vocabulary — *start, begin, end, finish*

Link

on 25th May, in July

➔4

The festival begins on 25th May.
It ends in June.

The concert starts at 9.00.
It finishes at midnight.

	starts begins	at …
The festival The concert It		in … on …
	finishes ends	

BATH MUSIC FESTIVAL
25 MAY – 14 JUNE

NICK CAVE CONCERT

Sat 9 June

9.00 – 12.00

Tickets £25

1 Complete the sentences.

   a The meeting _starts at_ 2.30 p.m.
   b *Newsnight* _____ 10.30.
   c The English lesson _____ 11.00.
   d The school holidays _____ 16th July.
   e *Music at Midnight* _____ 2.00 a.m.
   f The Film Festival _____ Saturday.

LESSONS
9:00   10:00   11:00
MON   Music   English

MEETING:
Fri 10th April
2:30 – 4.30

16th July – 18th August HOLIDAY

10:30 Newsnight
12:00 Music at midnight
2:00   Film: Sisters of Seattle

FILM FESTIVAL
Mon 10 May – Sat 15 May

B Phrases — *at the beginning, in the middle, at the end*

KUMIKO SATO   APRIL

Berlin   Paris   Shanghai   Caracas   Buenos Aires

1 2 3 4 5 6 7 8 9 10 11 12 13 14 15 16 17 18 19 20 21 22 23 24 25 26 27 28 29 30

London   Tokyo   São Paolo

CONCERT TOUR

She'll be in Europe at the beginning of April.
She'll be in East Asia in the middle of April.
She'll be in South America at the end of April.

at	the beginning the end	of

in the middle	of

2 Complete the sentences with **at the beginning of**, **in the middle of** or **at the end of**.

   a There's a useful index _at the end of_ the book.
   b Most people have a holiday _____ December.
   c I'm arriving _____ October – probably the 16th or 17th.
   d He was born in Warsaw in 1945, _____ the second World War.
   e I had to leave _____ the film, so I don't know how it ended.
   f _____ the 20th century, there were very few cars on the roads.

start playing, start to play, stop playing

Links

| to + verb | ⮌ RU2 |
| verb + -ing | ⮌ RU3 |

I stayed at a cheap hotel in the town centre, but I didn't sleep much.

I went to bed at 11.00. At 11.30 the people in the next room began playing music, and in another room a baby started to cry.

At around 2.00, the people in the next room stopped playing music and the baby stopped crying. I started to fall asleep, but then a dog started barking in the street outside the hotel.

At about 4.00, the dog stopped barking, and everything was quiet. But then it was morning. The sun began to shine through the window, and the first trams started going along the street.

start/begin + -ing or *start/begin + to*

start begin	playing crying barking

start begin	to	play cry bark

stop + -ing

stop	playing crying barking

NOT ~~stop to play~~

3   Complete the sentences with a verb from the box. Add **to** or change the verb to an -ing form.

| rain | arrive | ✓ talk | read |
| think | ring | write | read |

a   This is a library. Would you please stop _talking_ ?

b   The party was at 9.00, but the first people started _____ at 8.30.

c   He picked up his pen and began _____ on a sheet of paper.

d   You don't need your umbrella. It stopped _____ half an hour ago.

e   I'm very worried about Richard. I can't stop _____ about him.

f   I opened my book and began _____ . Five minutes later, the phone started _____ , so I stopped _____ and went downstairs to answer it.

Write in your language

The film starts at 8.00 and finishes at 9.30.

The library is at the end of the road.

Could you stop talking, please?

66 *have got*

A Grammar · *have* and *have got*

> These are the Gold Coast Beach Apartments, near Brisbane, Australia. Our building is on the left. It's got 50 floors, and we've got an apartment right at the top. The apartment has got two very small rooms, but both of them have got balconies, so there's a great view of the sea.

have and *have got* mean the same. We can say:

It has 20 floors. *or* It's got 20 floors.
We have an apartment. *or* We've got an apartment.
The apartment has two rooms. *or* The apartment has got two rooms.
Both of them have balconies. *or* Both of them have got balconies.

have got: full forms

I / We / You / They	have got	He / She / It	has got

have got: short forms

I've got / We've got / You've got / They've got	He's got / She's got / It's got

he's got = he has got
NOT ~~he is got~~

1 Write these sentences with forms of **have got**.

  a He has two sisters. — *He's got two sisters.*
  b Ten million people in Britain have a car. — ....
  c I have two tickets for the film. — ....
  d All the rooms have satellite TV. — ....
  e I hope you have enough money with you. — ....
  f My computer has a 250GB hard disk. — ....

B Grammar · *haven't got, hasn't got*

Link
not much ➔ 14

I haven't got a key.

The house hasn't got any electricity.

Come on. We haven't got much time.

Positive			Negative	
I've / They've / He's	got		I haven't / They haven't / He hasn't	got

Link

have to ➔72

2 Complete the sentences. Use **haven't got** or **hasn't got**, and phrases from the box.

a I can't pay the bill. I _haven't got any money_ .

b We'll have to use the stairs. The hotel _____ .

c I'll have to write him a letter. He _____ .

d They can't go abroad. They _____ .

e You'll have to have black coffee. We _____ .

f She can't come to the concert. She _____ .

g You can have a shower, but we _____ .

a ticket
✓ any money
much hot water
an email address
passports
any milk
a lift

C Grammar

Have you got ...? Has it got ...?

TICKETS €2

Have you got two euros?

Yes, I think I have … Here you are.

HOTEL ROMA ROOMS

Has the room got a shower?

No, it hasn't. It's got a washbasin and a toilet.

Question

Have	you they	got …?

Short answer

Yes,	I	have.
No,	we they	haven't.

Question

Has	he she it	got …?

Short answer

Yes,	he	has.
No,	she it	hasn't.

Link

headache, stomach, hurt ➔48B

3 Complete the questions.

a – _Have they got_ any children?

  – I think they've got a boy and a girl.

b – _____ a pen?

  – Yes, I have. Here you are.

c – _____ my mobile number?

  – Yes. I gave it to her yesterday.

d – I've got a headache and my stomach hurts.

  – Oh dear. _____ a temperature?

e – _____ a watch?

  – Yes, but he never wears it.

f – This is my new car.

  – It's lovely. _____ air conditioning?

4 Read these questions, and give true short answers.

a Have you got *Language Links 2*? _Yes, I have._

b Have you got any children? _____

c Have your neighbours got a dog? _____

d Has your house or flat got air conditioning? _____

e Has your kitchen got a TV in it? _____

f Have you got a mobile phone? _____

Write in your language

Our neighbours have got an apartment in Miami.

He hasn't got a ticket.

Have you got any money?

67 I like …

A Phrases *like, love, hate, enjoy*

Link

verb + -ing ➲RU3

Things I like …
I like big cities. I love living in London – I think it's got a great atmosphere.

Things I don't like …
I don't like the winter much. I hate getting up early in the winter, when it's still dark.

What about work?
I really enjoy my work. I enjoy making films, but I enjoy working in the theatre, too.

| 🙂 | love
like
don't like
hate | + noun
+ verb + -ing |
| 🙁 | | |

| I | like
love | London.
living in London. |

| I | don't like
hate | the winter.
getting up in the winter. |

| I enjoy | my work.
making films. | (*I enjoy something* =
I feel good when I do it) |

Link

cook, do the
ironing ➲35

1 Write sentences, using like, don't like, love, hate or enjoy.

a I drive to work, but I don't like it.   I don't like driving to work.
b I often sit in cafés. I love it.
c Chocolate is wonderful!
d I do the ironing, but I hate it.
e I get up late on Saturdays. I like that.
f I never drink milk. I don't like it.
g I cook. I really enjoy it!

2 Write sentences about yourself. Use ideas from the box. Add -ing if necessary.

| chocolate | watch football | dogs | get up early | hot weather | cook | be ill | dance |

B Phrases — *my favourite …*

Links

her, my, your	➲20A
painter, actor	➲54

That's her favourite chair. She always sits there.

I love Matisse. He's one of my favourite painters.

What's your favourite colour?

Yellow.

my favourite = the one I like best

3 Complete the sentences. Choose phrases from all three boxes.

my	our	her		drinks	city	writers
your	their		favourite	room	films	sport

a I've seen *Casablanca* five times. It's one of <u>my favourite films</u> .

b – What's _____ ?   – I'm not sure. I like Paris – or maybe New York.

c This is _____ . We always sit here in the evenings.

d She loves playing tennis. It's _____ .

e I really like fresh lemonade. It's one of _____ .

f My parents have got all her books. She's one of _____ .

4 Read the examples, and write about yourself.

_____
_____
_____
_____

> My favourite vegetable is aubergine.
> Brad Pitt is one of my favourite actors.

C Grammar — *I like* and *I'd like*

Links

would	➲80
Would you like …?	➲74

I like coffee.
I like drinking coffee.
(= I think coffee is nice.)
– Do you like coffee?
  – Yes, I do. – No, I don't.

I'd like some coffee.
I'd like to have some coffee.
(= I want some coffee.)
– Would you like some coffee?
  – Yes, please. – No, thank you.

I'd like = I *would* like

5 Choose the correct form.

a *I like* / (*I'd like*) a cup of coffee, please.

b *He likes* / *He'd like* books – he reads a lot.

c – *Do you like* / *Would you like* a drink?
  – Not now, thanks.

d They like *walk* / *walking* in the mountains.

e *I like* / *I'd like* to get a new television.

f *Do you like* / *Would you like* swimming?

g I'd like *to pay* / *paying* the bill, please.

Write in your language

I hate getting up early.	
He's one of my favourite writers.	
I'd like to go now.	

143

68 know

A Phrases | know

Links

already ➲ 6A
(near)est ➲ 28

Do you know that the Earth is 150 million km from the Sun?

Yes, I know.

I knew that already.

Did you know that the nearest planet to the Sun is Mercury?

Really? I didn't know that.

Do you Did you	know (that) …?

I know.
I knew that (already).
I didn't know that.

Present	Past
know	knew

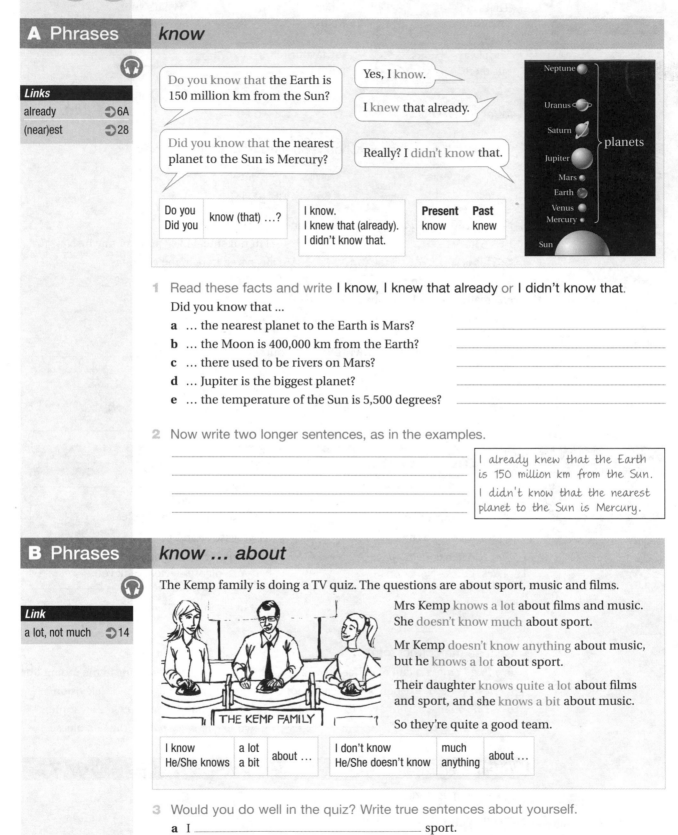

Neptune
Uranus
Saturn
Jupiter
Mars
Earth
Venus
Mercury
planets
Sun

1 Read these facts and write **I know, I knew that already** or **I didn't know that.**

Did you know that …

a … the nearest planet to the Earth is Mars? ....

b … the Moon is 400,000 km from the Earth? ....

c … there used to be rivers on Mars? ....

d … Jupiter is the biggest planet? ....

e … the temperature of the Sun is 5,500 degrees? ....

2 Now write two longer sentences, as in the examples.

....

....

....

....

> I already knew that the Earth is 150 million km from the Sun.
> I didn't know that the nearest planet to the Sun is Mercury.

B Phrases | know … about

Link

a lot, not much ➲ 14

The Kemp family is doing a TV quiz. The questions are about sport, music and films.

Mrs Kemp knows a lot about films and music. She doesn't know much about sport.

Mr Kemp doesn't know anything about music, but he knows a lot about sport.

Their daughter knows quite a lot about films and sport, and she knows a bit about music.

So they're quite a good team.

THE KEMP FAMILY

I know He/She knows	a lot a bit	about …

I don't know He/She doesn't know	much anything	about …

3 Would you do well in the quiz? Write true sentences about yourself.

a I .... sport.

b I .... music.

c I .... films.

C Phrases   *know what, know how ...*

The police are looking for a man, but they don't know much about him.

| Age: | 30–35 (?) |
| Address: | ? |

They know what he looks like.

They're not sure how old he is.

They don't know
They have no idea   where he lives.

4   What else do they know or not know?
Make sentences from the table.

		tall he is.
They know	what	his friends are.
They're not sure	where	his name is.
They don't know	how	languages he speaks.
They have no idea	who	he comes from.
		his job is.

a   They know what his name is.
b
c
d
e
f

Name: Joe Cook
Drives a lorry? (or a bus?)
Nationality: ?
Speaks English, Spanish
Friends??
About 1.80–1.85m tall?

D Phrases   Knowing people

Link

well   ➲26A

How well do you know your neighbours?

I know **them** very well.

I know **them** quite well.

I don't know **them** very well.

I don't know **them** at all.

I know **them** by sight.   (= I know who they are when I see them)

5   Add the remarks in the bubbles to these sentences.

a   I don't know them at all   . I've never seen them.
b   . We're really good friends.
c   , but I don't speak to them.
d   . We say 'Hello', but I don't often talk to them.
e   . We sometimes have coffee together.

Write in your language

Did you know that Jupiter has four moons?

My brother knows a lot about computers.

We don't know our neighbours very well.

69 remember and forget

A Phrases

Links

He's got	⮑66A
I've (forgotten)	⮑90
forget	⮑58B

memory, remember, forget

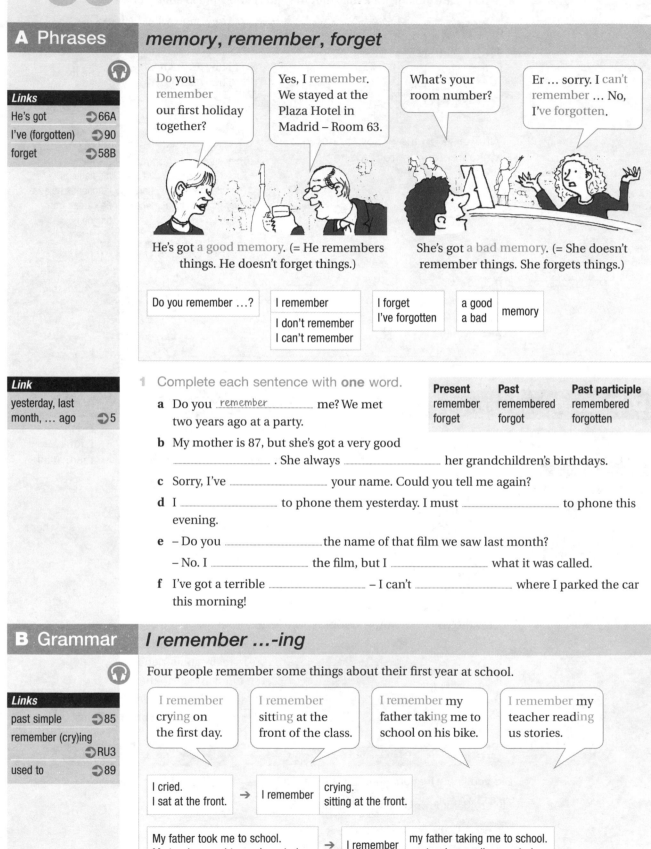

> Do you remember our first holiday together?

> Yes, I remember. We stayed at the Plaza Hotel in Madrid – Room 63.

> What's your room number?

> Er … sorry. I can't remember … No, I've forgotten.

He's got a good memory. (= He remembers things. He doesn't forget things.)

She's got a bad memory. (= She doesn't remember things. She forgets things.)

Do you remember …?	I remember I don't remember I can't remember	I forget I've forgotten	a good a bad	memory

Link

yesterday, last
month, … ago   ⮑5

1 Complete each sentence with **one** word.

Present	Past	Past participle
remember	remembered	remembered
forget	forgot	forgotten

a Do you _remember_ me? We met two years ago at a party.

b My mother is 87, but she's got a very good _____. She always _____ her grandchildren's birthdays.

c Sorry, I've _____ your name. Could you tell me again?

d I _____ to phone them yesterday. I must _____ to phone this evening.

e – Do you _____ the name of that film we saw last month?

– No. I _____ the film, but I _____ what it was called.

f I've got a terrible _____ – I can't _____ where I parked the car this morning!

B Grammar

Links

past simple	⮑85
remember (cry)ing	⮑RU3
used to	⮑89

I remember …-ing

Four people remember some things about their first year at school.

> I remember crying on the first day.

> I remember sitting at the front of the class.

> I remember my father taking me to school on his bike.

> I remember my teacher reading us stories.

I cried. I sat at the front.	→	I remember	crying. sitting at the front.

My father took me to school. My teacher used to read us stories.	→	I remember	my father taking me to school. my teacher reading us stories.

2 Here are some other things they remember. Rewrite them using **I remember + -ing**.

   a I used to wear a blue uniform.   *I remember wearing a blue uniform.*

   b The other children looked at me.

   c I arrived at school late one day.

   d I used to play football at lunchtime.

   e My grandmother met me after school.

   f My teacher fell off her desk.

3 What do you remember about your first year at school? Use **remember + -ing**.
   Write one or two sentences.

C Phrases

remember to, don't forget to

Link

cooker, iron, radiators
➲34A

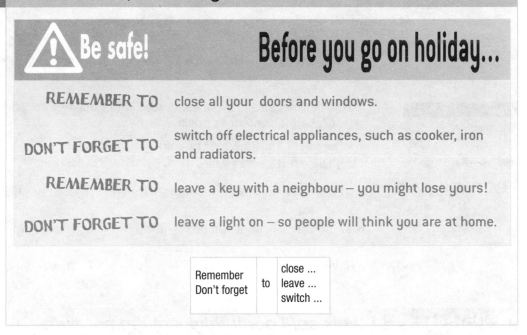

⚠ **Be safe!**   **Before you go on holiday...**

REMEMBER TO   close all your doors and windows.

DON'T FORGET TO   switch off electrical appliances, such as cooker, iron and radiators.

REMEMBER TO   leave a key with a neighbour – you might lose yours!

DON'T FORGET TO   leave a light on – so people will think you are at home.

Remember Don't forget	to	close ... leave ... switch ...

Links

I'm + verb + -ing
➲82A

I'll   ➲78A

verb + to ➲RU2

4 Write replies. Begin **Remember to ...** or **Don't forget to ....**. Use words from both
   boxes.

ask for	write	your passport	the date	a key
buy	take	some flowers	some bread	a receipt

a – It's her birthday on Saturday.   **d** – I'm going shopping.
     – *Don't forget to buy some flowers.*   –

b – I'm leaving for the airport now.   **e** – I'm getting a taxi to the meeting.
     –   –

c – I'll be home very late tonight.   **f** – I'll write you a cheque.
     –   –

Write in your language

He's got a very good memory.

I remember going to school by bike.

Don't forget to turn the cooker off.

70 *think, expect, hope ...*

A Grammar · *I'm sure, I think*

Link

→71 probably, perhaps

Links

was, wasn't →83

I think, I don't think →77

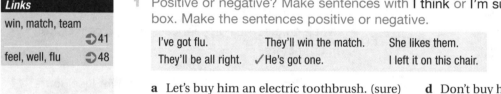

| What kind of car was it? | I'm sure it was a Mercedes. | I don't think it was a Mercedes. I think it was a Volvo. | I'm sure it wasn't a Mercedes. It was too small. |

| YES ↑ ↓ NO | I'm sure … I think … I don't think … I'm sure + not … | **Positive** I'm sure it was … I think it was … | **Negative** I'm sure it wasn't … I don't think it was … | NOT ~~I think it wasn't …~~ |

Links

win, match, team →41

feel, well, flu →48

1 Positive or negative? Make sentences with **I think** or **I'm sure** using items from the box. Make the sentences positive or negative.

| I've got flu. | They'll win the match. | She likes them. |
| They'll be all right. | ✓ He's got one. | I left it on this chair. |

a Let's buy him an electric toothbrush. (sure)
   I'm sure he hasn't got one.

b Don't worry about the children. (sure)

c I don't feel very well. (think)

d Don't buy her flowers. (think)

e Where's my jacket? (sure)

f They're not a very good team. (think)

B Phrases · *I think so, I don't think so, I'm not sure*

| Was it a Mercedes? | Yes, I think so. | I'm not sure. | No, I don't think so. | YES ↑ ↓ NO I think so. I'm not sure. I don't think so. |

Link

Europe, Asian, Indian Ocean →37

2 Answer these questions. Write **Yes**, **No**, **I think so**, **I don't think so** or **I'm not sure**.

a Is Timbuktu in Australia?

b Was there a US President called Edgar Wallace?

c Is the Japanese flag red and white?

d Is 'knifes' the plural of *knife*?

e Were the 2000 Olympic Games in Europe?

f Is Madagascar in the Indian Ocean?

g Has an Asian country ever won the football World Cup?

C Grammar — I expect, I hope

Links

probably ➲71A

will ➲78A

ELECTION 10th OF SEPTEMBER

Vote FPU

Manning Vote PLP

Vote DSP

> It's very close – they both have about 35%. But I expect the PLP will win.

> I don't expect the DSP will get many votes.

> I hope Manning wins. I think he'd be a good leader.

> I hope the FPU don't win. I hate them!

(*I expect* … = This will probably happen.)   (*I hope* … = I want this to happen.)

I expect + will   **I hope + present simple**

I expect I don't expect	they will win.

I hope	they win. they don't win.

NOT ~~I don't hope they win~~

Link

get + adjective ➲57

3 Write sentences with I hope, I expect, or I don't expect, using the notes.

a She's taking her driving test. (hope / she / pass) _I hope she passes._ .

b It's starting to rain. (hope / we / not / get wet) _____ .

c I haven't seen her for years. (not / expect / she / remember me) _____ .

d They don't know London. (expect / they / get lost) _____ .

e He's lost his wallet. (hope / he / find it) _____ .

f The traffic is terrible this evening. (expect / they / late) _____ .

D Phrases — I think so, I expect so, I hope so

> Do you think the PLP will win?

> I expect so.

> I don't expect so.

> I hope so.

> I hope not.

4 Write **two** answers for these questions: one with **expect** and one with **hope**.

In five years from now …

a Do you think you'll have a job? _____ _____

b Do you think you'll be married? _____ _____

c Do you think you'll live in a different town? _____ _____

d Do you think the world will be a better place? _____ _____

Write in your language

I don't think we stayed at that hotel.

– Are they English? – Yes, I think so.

I hope the bus isn't late.

71 *probably, perhaps ...*

A Grammar — *definitely, certainly, probably*

Link

→ 70 **think, expect, hope ...**

Link

was → 83

The Empire State Building, NY, 1963
What was in the sky?
Was it a flying saucer?

Loch Ness, Scotland, 1934
What's in the water?
Is it the Loch Ness Monster?

It was definitely a flying saucer. My grandfather was there, and he saw it.

It certainly wasn't a flying saucer – it was probably a plane, or a parachute.

There's certainly something in the water, but it probably isn't a monster. It's probably a big fish, or a piece of wood.

Positive

is was will have	certainly ... definitely ... probably ...

Negative

certainly definitely probably	isn't ... wasn't ... won't ... haven't ...

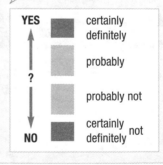

YES ↑ ? ↓ NO		
	■	certainly definitely
	■	probably
	■	probably not
	■	certainly definitely not

Link

will, won't → 78

1 What do you think? Choose a sentence, and add **definitely**, **certainly** or **probably**.

a There *is/isn't* water on Mars.   *There is definitely water on Mars.*

b There *is/isn't* life on other planets.

c We *will/won't* travel to other planets.

d We *are/aren't* the most intelligent animals on Earth.

e The world *will/won't* get warmer over the next century.

f There *is/isn't* a monster in Loch Ness.

perhaps, maybe

Links

or	➲98A
have gone	➲90

The lights are off in his flat.

Perhaps / Maybe he isn't at home, or perhaps / maybe he's gone to bed.

2 Write sentences with **maybe/perhaps** and **or**. Choose **two** sentences from the box.

a His hair is wet. _Perhaps he's been for a swim or_
....

b He isn't answering his mobile. ....
....

c He didn't say 'Hello'. ....
....

> He didn't see you.
> He didn't switch it on.
> He doesn't like you.
> ✓ He's been for a swim.
> He left it at home.
> He's just had a shower.

may, might

Link

may, might	➲RU5

> I've phoned Robert several times, but he isn't at home. I'm not sure where he is – he might be on holiday. I know he wanted to go to Berlin, so perhaps he's there now.
> We may be away this weekend ourselves, so we might not come to the meeting. I'll phone you tomorrow and tell you what we're doing.
> We'll be here next week, so we may see you at the concert on Friday.

may and *might* are modal verbs. They mean the same here.

I We He	may might	(not)	be come see	He might be on holiday.	=	Maybe he is on holiday.
				We might not come.	=	Perhaps we won't come.
				We may see you.	=	Perhaps we'll see you.

3 Write sentences with **may** or **might**.

a _He might be at home._ = Maybe he's at home.
b _I may not go to the party._ = Perhaps I won't go to the party.
c .... = Maybe we'll go out tomorrow.
d .... = Perhaps John will phone this evening.
e .... = Maybe I won't stay very late.
f .... = Take a coat – maybe you'll be cold.
g .... = Perhaps you'll need some money.

Write in your language

He probably isn't at home.	
Perhaps they're on holiday.	
I might see you next Sunday.	

72 *must* and *have to*

A Grammar — *I must go*

> It's 10 o'clock. I must go home now.

> We must buy some petrol.

must + infinitive

I		go home now.
We	must	buy some petrol.

NOT ~~I must to go~~

1 Add a sentence. Use **must** and a phrase from the box.

  a I don't have any money. _I must go to the bank._

  b It's his birthday tomorrow. _____

  c I'm really tired. _____

  d We're going to the theatre on Saturday. _____

  e I'm really dirty. _____

  f We don't have much food. _____

> have a shower
> ✓ go to the bank
> go shopping
> buy him a present
> go to bed
> buy the tickets

B Grammar — *must, mustn't*

SILENCE
NO TALKING

This sign means:

You must be quiet.
You mustn't talk.

This sign means:

You must take off your shoes.
You mustn't wear shoes.

You must	be quiet. take off your shoes.

You mustn't	talk. wear shoes.

mustn't = must not

2 Look at these signs. Where could you find them?

  1 _e_ in an art gallery
  2 _____ on a coat or dress
  3 _____ in a hotel
  4 _____ on a plane
  5 _____ in a park
  6 _____ at an airport

a PASSPORTS

b (football crossed out)

c FASTEN SEATBELTS

d NO MUSIC AFTER 11 p.m.

e (drink and bin crossed out)

f (washing machine crossed out)

What do the signs mean? Write **You must** or **You mustn't**.

  a _You must_ show your passport.

  b _____ play football.

  c _____ fasten your seat belt.

  d _____ play music after 11.00 pm.

  e _____ eat or drink.

  f _____ put it in a washing machine.

Links

| must | ➲ RU5 |
| infinitive | ➲ RU2 |

Link
buy, pay, cost ⮕47

DIGIVIEW 35 FREE TV CHANNELS!

Buy our Digiview digital receiver

for only £80!

With Digiview, you have to buy a receiver, but you don't have to pay for the TV channels.

SATVIEW
Get a FREE Satview digital receiver!

50 TV channels
for only £20 a month!

With Satview, you don't have to pay for the receiver, but you have to pay for the TV channels.

| You | have to | buy a receiver. |
| | don't have to | pay for the TV channels. |

You don't have to pay.
= It's free. It costs nothing.

Link
Internet, online ⮕53

3 Complete the text with **have to** or **don't have to**.

I like shopping on the Internet. You (a) _don't have to_ drive to the supermarket, you (b) _____ park the car, and you (c) _____ bring the shopping home. You just buy it online, and wait for the delivery. Of course, you (d) _____ have a computer, and you (e) _____ be at home when the food arrives, but you (f) _____ pay for the delivery – it's free.

Are you on the Internet?
Do your shopping at home with

SAVECO Online

We deliver the food to your door – free!

Links
it's got, it hasn't got ⮕66
same, different ⮕31

You have to / must carry it.
(It hasn't got wheels.)

You don't have to carry it.
(It's got wheels.
You can pull it.)

You mustn't carry it.
(It's very heavy.
You'll hurt your back.)

Have to and *must* mean the same. *Don't have to* and *mustn't* have different meanings.

4 Choose the best answers.

a I start work at 11.30 in the morning. I *have to* / (*don't have to*) get up early.

b I can't see you tomorrow. I *have to* / *don't have to* go to work.

c We're leaving at 10.30 tomorrow morning. You *mustn't* / *don't have to* be late.

d We *have to* / *don't have to* walk. We can go by taxi.

e I'm feeling ill. I *must* / *mustn't* see a doctor.

f I'm sorry – you *mustn't* / *don't have to* use your mobile phone on the plane.

Write in your language

I must go to the bank and get some money.

We don't have to go to work tomorrow.

Sorry – you mustn't smoke in here.

73 *can, could, know how to ...*

A Grammar **could, couldn't**

Five years ago, I got a job as an English teacher in Japan.

When I first arrived, I couldn't speak Japanese and I couldn't understand anything.

After a few months, things got better. I could say a few things, and I could read and write a few easy words.

And now I can speak and read quite well.

Links

| can, can't, could, couldn't | ➲RU5 |
| infinitive | ➲RU2 |

Present: *can/can't* + infinitive

| I He They | can can't | speak ... |

Past: *could/couldn't* + infinitive

| I He They | could couldn't | speak ... |

NOT ~~I could to speak~~

1 What other things do you think he could do after a few months? Write **could** or **couldn't**.

a He _could_ ask for things in shops.
b He .... read Japanese newspapers.
c He .... say 'Hello' in Japanese.
d He .... write his name in Japanese.
e He .... write business letters in Japanese.
f He .... read a few Japanese shop signs.

B Phrases **know how to**

Take 1,000 adults in Britain, aged 18–60. Out of those 1,000 people ...

❑ 150 people know how to play the piano.
❑ one person knows how to fly a plane.
❑ 50 people don't know how to read.
❑ 75 people don't know how to swim.

I *know how to* read. = I can do it. I've learned it.

Link

➲68   **know**

2 Guess the answers. Complete the sentences with **know how to** or **don't know how to**.

Out of 1000 people ...

a 780 people _know how to_ drive a car.
b 40 people .... ride a bike.
c 60 people .... juggle.
d 20 people .... ride a unicycle.
e 90 people .... use a computer.
f 5 people .... speak Japanese.

Links

verb + -ing	➲RU3
well	➲26A
has (written)	➲90

JOHN KNOWLES		CLASS 5C	
ENGLISH	*He has written some good stories this year. His work is generally very good.*	He's good at writing stories. (= He writes stories well.) He's good at English.
MUSIC	*He sings quite well. Guitar: He has learnt a new piece. Quite good, but he needs to practise more.*	He's quite good at singing and playing the guitar.
SPORT	*He played football this year, but he wasn't in the school team.*	He's not very good at football.

very good good quite good not very good	at	football singing writing stories English

NOT ~~good in (football)~~

Link

| team, basketball | ➲41 |

3 Write about these people.

a He can only swim five metres. *He's not very good at swimming.*

b She makes wonderful meals.

c He plays basketball for the college team.

d He had five accidents in his car last year.

e I can only play one song on the guitar.

f She always listens to people's problems.

g She speaks French fluently.

4 Read the examples, then choose three activities from this unit. Write sentences about yourself.

I can play the piano, but I don't know how to play the guitar.

I'm quite good at cooking.

I know how to juggle, but I'm not very good at it.

Write in your language

Pope John Paul II could speak lots of languages.

I don't know how to fly a plane.

He's quite good at cooking.

74 Requests and offers

A Phrases — *Would you mind ...?*

Links

can, could, would ➲RU5

verb + -ing ➲RU3

> Can you go to the baker's? We need some bread …

> …and could you get some potatoes?

> And would you mind taking this parcel to the post office?

Can Could	you	go … get … take …	Would you mind	going …? getting …? taking …?

→ more formal

Links

move ➲60

lend ➲47B

1 Write requests in **two** ways. Use phrases from the box.

a You need to get up early tomorrow.

Could you wake me up tomorrow?

Would you mind waking me up tomorrow?

b You need 50 euros to get some food.

....

....

c You're at home, and your train leaves in 20 minutes.

....

....

d Someone has parked their car in front of your garage.

....

....

> move
> lend me
> drive me
> ✓ wake me up

B Phrases — Offers

Links

would like ➲67C

shall ➲75, RU5

> Do you want some more coffee?

> Would you like another drink?

> Would you like me to bring your bill?

> Shall I get your coat?

> Can I call a taxi?

Offering things

Do you want	another drink?
Would you like	some more coffee?

Offering to do things

Shall I	
Can I	
Do you want me to	get your coat?
Would you like me to	call a taxi?

2 The pictures show a business trip. What do you think the people said?

At the airport:	On the plane:	At the airport:
a window seat?	**b** cold drink?	**c** carry / suitcase? **d** get / taxi?

At the hotel:

e room / balcony?   **f** show you / room?

a Would you like a window seat?   **d** ....

b ....   **e** ....

c ....   **f** ....

C Phrases

Help

Asking for help

Can you help me?

Would you help me with the shopping?

Could you help me take the shopping in?

Offering help

Do you need any help?

Would you like me to help you?

Can I help you with the shopping?

Shall I help you take the shopping in?

help	me	with + noun
	you	+ verb

3 Put the words in the right order to make questions.

a you help me could ? Could you help me?

b help you do any need ? ....

c for the flat I shall you clean ? ....

d my homework with me help you can ? ....

e would these suitcases me help you with ? ....

f you like you would me to help ? ....

Write in your language

Would you mind going to the supermarket?

Do you mind if I borrow your computer?

Would you like me to move my car?

75 Suggestions

A Phrases

Why don't we ...? Let's ...

– What shall we do this evening?
– Let's go and see a film. We could see 'Terminus'.
– No – I've already seen it. Why don't we go bowling?
– Yes, that's a good idea. Where shall we go?
– How about going to City Bowl? It's cheaper there.
– OK. Let's do that, then.

Links

| verb + -ing | ➲RU3 |
| shall, could | ➲RU5 |

Questions	Suggestions		Replies
Where shall we go?	Let's ...	How about ...-ing?	That's a good idea.
What shall we do?	We could ...		Let's do that.
	Why don't we... ?		

Link

theatre, What's on ...?
➲54

1 Complete the sentences with expressions from the tables.

a – _Let's_ go out this afternoon.
– That's _____ . Where _____ go?

b – _____ going out for a meal tonight?
– I'm a bit tired. _____ just eat at home.

c – _____ go to the theatre tonight?
– _____ a good idea. _____ do that.

d – What _____ this weekend?
– I don't know. We _____ see what's on at the cinema.

B Phrases

Why don't you ...? You could ...

○○○
⊘ ⤺ ⤺ ⤻ 🖨
Delete Reply Reply All Forward Print

We've rented a house near the sea, and we're there for most of the summer. Why don't you and Barbara come down for a few days?

In fact, how about staying next weekend, if you're free then? It would be wonderful to see you. There are plenty of trains – or you could come by car.

Suggestions

| Why don't you ... ? |
| You could ... |

| How about ...-ing? |

Links

trainers, T-shirt ➲51
try on, put on, throw
away, turn on ➲RU1

2 Complete the sentences with suggestions. Use ideas from the box.

a If you're cold, why <u>don't you put on a jumper?</u>
b It's my birthday! How _____
c Maybe this T-shirt will fit you. Why _____
d I'll drive you home if you like. Or you _____
e It's getting a bit dark. How _____
f Those trainers are really old. Why _____

throw them away
sleep on the sofa
buy me dinner
turn the lights on
✓ put on a jumper
try it on

should, ought to

Links

infinitive ⮌RU2

should, shouldn't ⮌RU5

> I feel tired all the time. Maybe I should see a doctor.

> You shouldn't go to bed so late.

> You ought to sleep more.

> You ought not to work so hard.

***should / ought to* + infinitive**

I You He/She	should ought to	sleep more.

NOT ~~should to sleep~~ …

***shouldn't / ought not to* + infinitive**

I You He/She	shouldn't ought not to	work so hard.

NOT ~~shouldn't to work~~ …

Link

hurts, ache ⮌48B

3 Find two replies to each problem. Write **should(n't)** or **ought (not) to** in the gaps.

1 I never have any money. **2** My chest hurts. **3** I'm bored! **4** My eyes ache.

a You *should* or *ought to* go out more.   3
b You _____ smoke so much.
c You _____ buy so many clothes.
d You _____ go and lie down.
e You _____ eat in expensive restaurants.
f You _____ work at the computer so much.
g You _____ get some new glasses.
h You _____ stay at home all the time.

4 Correct the mistakes.

a It's getting late. How about ~~we get~~ *getting* a taxi home?

b I'm busy today, but you could to call me tomorrow morning.

c You don't ought to work so hard.

d If you're feeling hungry, why you don't have some chocolate?

e I think he should to get a new job.

f – What shall we do this afternoon? – Let's playing tennis.

Write in your language

– Let's go to the theatre. – That's a good idea.	
Why don't you come and see us next week?	
You shouldn't work so hard.	

A Phrases — Saying sorry

Link
very, really ⮕ 25B

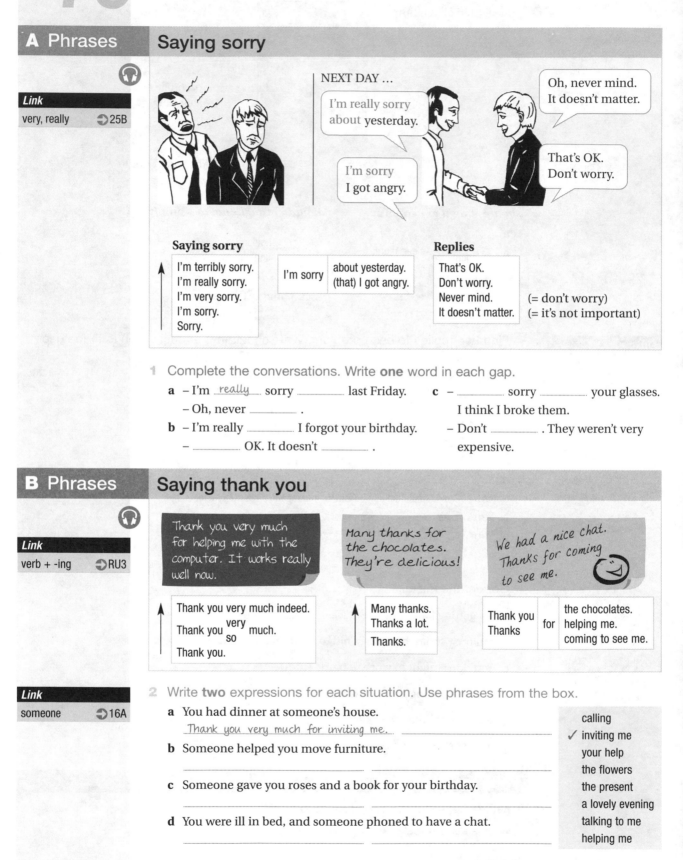

NEXT DAY …

I'm really sorry about yesterday.

I'm sorry I got angry.

Oh, never mind. It doesn't matter.

That's OK. Don't worry.

Saying sorry			**Replies**	
I'm terribly sorry.	I'm sorry	about yesterday.	That's OK.	
I'm really sorry.		(that) I got angry.	Don't worry.	
I'm very sorry.			Never mind.	(= don't worry)
I'm sorry.			It doesn't matter.	(= it's not important)
Sorry.				

1 Complete the conversations. Write **one** word in each gap.

a – I'm _really_ sorry _____ last Friday.
– Oh, never _____ .

b – I'm really _____ I forgot your birthday.
– _____ OK. It doesn't _____ .

c – _____ sorry _____ your glasses. I think I broke them.
– Don't _____ . They weren't very expensive.

B Phrases — Saying thank you

Link
verb + -ing ⮕ RU3

Thank you very much for helping me with the computer. It works really well now.

Many thanks for the chocolates. They're delicious!

We had a nice chat. Thanks for coming to see me.

Thank you very much indeed.	
Thank you very / so much.	
Thank you.	

Many thanks.
Thanks a lot.
Thanks.

Thank you / Thanks	for	the chocolates. / helping me. / coming to see me.

Link
someone ⮕ 16A

2 Write **two** expressions for each situation. Use phrases from the box.

a You had dinner at someone's house.
Thank you very much for inviting me. _____

b Someone helped you move furniture.
_____ _____

c Someone gave you roses and a book for your birthday.
_____ _____

d You were ill in bed, and someone phoned to have a chat.
_____ _____

calling
✓ inviting me
your help
the flowers
the present
a lovely evening
talking to me
helping me

Link

(just) about to ➜ 6B

3 What could you say in each of these situations? Choose either **one** or **two** phrases.

   a It's your father's sixtieth birthday. _Congratulations! Happy birthday!_

   b A friend is about to drive across the Sahara Desert. _____

   c Your daughter has just got a Grade A in all her exams. _____

   d Your son is just about to sing in a school concert. _____

   e You're in a car. The driver is just about to go through a red light. _____

D Phrases

Replies

- ... We had a lovely holiday.
- Oh, good. I'm glad to hear that. ...

- ... John's got a new girlfriend.
- Oh, really? That's interesting.
- Yes. She's really nice.
- Oh, that's great.
- But he lost his job last week.
- Oh, I'm sorry to hear that.

- ... My mother's in hospital.
- Oh, dear. That's a pity.
- Yes. She fell and broke her leg.
- Oh, that's terrible.

| Oh, | good.
dear.
really? | That's | great.
terrible.
a pity.
interesting. | I'm | glad
sorry | to hear that. |

4 Write the phrases in **three** lists:

Good news: _Oh, good._ _____

Bad news: _Oh, dear._ _____

Interesting news: _____

5 Write replies. Use **two** phrases in each reply.

   a 'My son is ill.'
      Oh, dear. That's a pity.

   b 'My daughter's getting married.'
      _____

   c 'This building is nearly 300 years old.'
      _____

   d 'They lost all their money.'
      _____

Write in your language

I'm really sorry about yesterday.

– Thanks for coming. – That's all right.

Oh dear. I'm sorry to hear that.

77 *will* and *going to* (1): decisions

A Grammar *I'll, I won't*

Links

I think, I don't think
➲70

I'll have a fresh orange juice.

I won't have a drink. I'm not thirsty.

I don't think I'll have a cold drink. I think I'll have coffee.

FRESH ORANGE JUICE

| I'll
I won't | have a drink. |

| I think I'll
I don't think I'll | have a drink. |

NOT ~~I think I won't ...~~

1 Add a sentence, using a phrase from the box, and **(I think) I'll, I don't think I'll** or **I won't**.

a I feel terribly tired. *I don't think I'll go out tonight.*

b I feel really hungry. ....

c The water's cold. ....

d I don't want to wait for a bus. ....

e That's an interesting article. ....

f The food wasn't very good at that restaurant. ....

....

> eat there again
> get a taxi home
> go for a swim
> print it out
> have a sandwich
> ✓ go out tonight

B Phrases *decided to, decided not to*

Link

infinitive   ➲RU2

I feel terrible. I don't think I'll go to work today. I think I'll stay in bed.

NEXT DAY ...

When I woke up, I felt terrible. I decided not to go to work. I decided to stay in bed.

| decide | to
not to | + infinitive |

2 Look at Exercise 1, and write what happened. Use **decided (not) to**.

a *I decided not to go out.*

b ....

c ....

d ....

e ....

f ....

I'll, I'm going to

Links

going to ➔79

this year, next month ➔5A

I think I'll have a birthday party this year ...

LATER ...

It's my 30th birthday next month. I'm going to have a party. Do you want to come?

(I think) I'll ... =
he's deciding now

I'm going to ... =
he has already decided

Links

clean, paint ➔64B

make ➔63A

3 Look at the pictures. What are the people going to do? Make sentences with **going to** + words from the table.

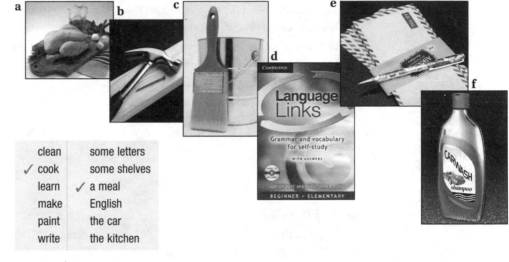

clean	some letters
✓ cook	some shelves
learn	✓ a meal
make	English
paint	the car
write	the kitchen

a They *'re going to cook a meal.*   **d** She _____

b He _____   **e** He _____

c They _____   **f** She _____

4 **will** or **going to**? Choose the best form.

a She's got a place at university. *She'll / She's going to* study psychology.

b Those bananas look nice. *I'll / I'm going to* have a kilo, please.

c – Have some water. – No, *I won't / I'm not going to*, thanks. I'm not thirsty.

d It's a lovely day. Maybe *I'll / I'm going to* go for a walk.

e We've got some good news. *We'll / We're going to* get married.

f – Why have you bought so much cheese? – *I'll / I'm going to* make a pizza.

Links

she's got, we've got ➔66

Write in your language

I don't think I'll go out tonight.

They decided not to get married.

I'm going to write some letters.

78 *will* and *going to* (2): the future

A Grammar | *will, won't*

Links

probably	➡71A
beat, win, match, score	➡41B

Baker is a strong player, so she will beat Marco quite easily. Then she'll play Gassi. That won't be an easy match, but Baker will probably win if she plays well. But she probably won't beat Stankova in the final – Stankova is a better player.

Today: Baker v. Marco

She	will (probably) (probably) won't	win.

Who will Baker probably beat? _____
Who will probably beat Baker? _____

Link

retire, interview ➡42C

1 Complete the sentences with **will probably** or **probably won't**.

a My father is over 60, so he _will probably_ retire quite soon.

b United are playing well at the moment, so they _____ win the match.

c I'm very busy on Saturday, so I _____ come to the party.

d I was very nervous in the interview, so they _____ give me the job.

e The school holidays start tomorrow, so the roads _____ be very busy.

f It's a very small place, so you _____ find it on your road map.

2 Write sentences that are true for you.

> It won't rain tonight.
> I'll probably go to the bank this week.

a It / rain tonight. _____

b I / go to the bank this week. _____

c I / have fish for lunch tomorrow. _____

d I / have a good weekend. _____

e I / buy a new car next year. _____

B Grammar | *if, when*

Links

might, might not	➡71C
present simple	➡81

OK. If I'm free tonight, I'll call you.

OK. I'll call you when I get home.

(*if* = this might happen, or it might not. I don't know.)

(*when* = I know this will happen.)

After *if* and *when*, we use the present simple:

If I'm free, When I get home,	I'll call you.	*or*	I'll call you	if I'm free. when I get home.	NOT ~~if I will be free~~ ~~when I'll get home~~

3 if or **when**?

a I'll tell him _..when.._ he comes home.

b _____ you leave me, I'll kill myself.

c _____ she arrives, she'll probably be quite tired.

d I'll turn off the TV _____ the programme finishes.

e _____ you don't stir it, it'll burn!

f _____ it doesn't rain, we'll probably go for a walk.

4 Complete the sentences from this email. Use **if** or **when** + present tense.

```
●●●
⊘  ◤  ◥  ↩  🖨
Delete  Reply  Reply All  Forward  Print
Hi Jan and Peta,
It'll be great to see you tomorrow.
```

a _If you leave early_ , the journey will only take 2 or 3 hours. (you / leave early)

b _When_ _____ , you'll see a factory on your left. (you / leave the motorway)

c We might not be at home _____ . (you / arrive)

d _____ , we'll leave a key under the mat. (we / be out)

e We'll tell you all our news _____ ! (we / see you)

f _____ , we'll have dinner by the river. (the weather / be nice)

```
See you tomorrow – Paul
```

C Grammar *going to*

Link

➲79   **going to**

'Tomorrow will be cloudy. It will rain in some places.'

'Look at those clouds. I think it's going to rain.'

(= I can see it coming.)

'Don't eat too much. You'll be sick.'

'Oh dear. I think I'm going to be sick.'

(= I can feel it.)

5 Look at the pictures. What is going to happen? Use verbs from the box.

have	✓ fall	fall asleep
get wet	break	crash

a He's _going to fall_ _____ .

b The cars _____ .

c The clothes _____ .

d The rope _____ .

e The woman _____ a baby.

f The man _____ .

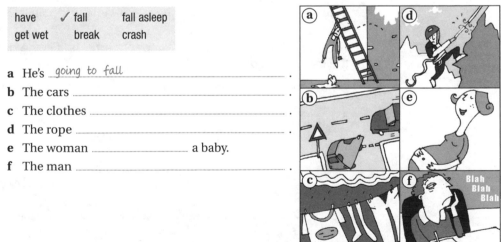

Write in your language

I'll come, but I probably won't stay long.

If I don't see you, I'll call you this evening.

It's going to rain.

79 *going to*

Link
→77 will & going to (1): decisions

Link
apply for / get / find a job →42C
infinitive →RU2

A Grammar — *going to, not going to*

Here is part of a magazine article.

After university...

We asked students in London about their plans for the future.

Julia, 21, is studying business

'I'm going to have a long summer holiday, and then I'm going to start applying for jobs in the London area. I'm going to stay in London if I can – all my friends are here.'

Paula, 22, is studying Arabic

'I'm going to go to Cairo to practise my Arabic. My boyfriend lives there already, and he's going to help me find a job there as an English teacher.'

Juan, 20, is studying music

'I'm not going to get a job just yet. I'm going to stay with friends in Singapore, and then we're going to travel round Thailand together.'

Positive			Negative		
I'm We're/You're/They're He's/She's/It's	going to	+ infinitive	I'm not We aren't/We're not He isn't/He's not	going to	+ infinitive

1 Complete these sentences.

a Paula *is going to* live in Egypt.
b Paula _____ teach English.
c Julia _____ leave London.
d Julia _____ start work in the summer.
e Paula and Juan _____ stay in England.
f Julia and Juan _____ go on holiday.

Link
got engaged, get married →44

2 Read these sentences from newspaper articles. Fill the gaps using the words in the box + **(not) going to**.

| build | leave | get married | save | stay | ✓meet | not / retire | not / spend |

a The Prime Ministers of India and Pakistan *are going to meet* next month to discuss Kashmir and other problems.

b Prince Michael and Lady Margaret Downing got engaged on Saturday. They _____ in early September.

c Lucia, a 30-year-old taxi driver from Madrid, has won €5 million on the Spanish lottery. 'I _____ it,' she said last night. 'I _____ it for my old age.'

d 'We _____ 15 new hospitals in the next three years,' said the Prime Minister.

e Salma Rahman _____ her job as director of internet company Klick.com. 'I _____ until the summer,' she said last night, 'but then I want to do something different.'

f Nick Formby, manager of Derby Football Club, is 65, but he says he _____ for at least three more years.

Questions

Link

Where …? What …?
➲95

'We're going to spend the summer in Greece this year. We're going to stay in Athens for a few days, and then we're going to visit Naxos and some of the other Greek islands …'

> Where are you going to stay in Athens?

> What are you going to do there?

> Are you going to see the Acropolis?

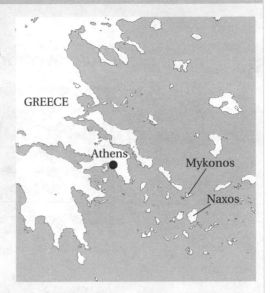

GREECE

Athens

Mykonos

Naxos

Yes/no questions

Are you Are they Is he/she	going to … ?

Wh- questions

What Where When	are you are they is he/she	going to …?

3 Ask yes/no and Wh- questions. Use ideas from the box.

a *How long are you going to stay in Greece?*
b ....
c ....
d ....
e ....
f ....

stay in Greece?
hire a car?
get to Naxos?
go by boat?
visit Mykonos?
come back?

Links

the day after tomorrow, this/next Saturday
➲5A

have/has (bought)
➲90

4 Ask questions. Use going to.

a – It's my husband's 40th birthday next week.
   – Is it? What *are you going to give him?* ?
b – They're going to the theatre the day after tomorrow.
   – That's nice. What .... ?
c – I've bought some chicken for dinner.
   – Oh good. How .... ?
d – I'm going to a very formal party this Saturday.
   – Are you? What .... ?
e – He's lost his job.
   – Oh dear. What .... ?
f – She's left home and gone to London.
   – Really? Where .... ?

cook
see
wear
✓give
do
live

Write in your language

We're going to stay with some friends.	
He isn't going to leave his job.	
How are you going to get to the airport?	

A Grammar — *would*, *wouldn't*

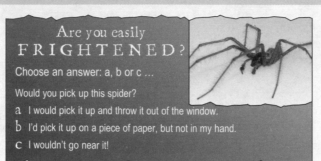

Are you easily FRIGHTENED?

Choose an answer: a, b or c ...

Would you pick up this spider?

a I would pick it up and throw it out of the window.

b I'd pick it up on a piece of paper, but not in my hand.

c I wouldn't go near it!

We use *would* to talk about a situation that isn't real.

(There isn't really a spider – it's just a photo.)

Full form		Short form		Negative		Question		
I He They	would go	I'd He'd They'd	go	I He They	wouldn't go	Would	I he they	go ?

Links

certainly, probably ➔ 71A

alone, on my own ➔ 21D

1 Here are some more questions and answers. Fill the gaps with **'d**, **would** or **wouldn't**. Then choose answers!

___Would___ you go bungee jumping?

a Yes. I ___would___ do it. It looks really exciting!

b I ___would___ do it once, but I ___would___ be quite frightened.

c No, thanks! I certainly ___wouldn't___ do it!

___would___ you stay the night alone in this cottage?

a Yes, I ___would___ stay there. I ___would___ take a good book to read.

b I ___would___ stay there, but I probably ___wouldn't___ sleep much.

c No. I ___would___ be too frightened on my own.

B Grammar — *... would ... if ...*

Links

was, wasn't ➔ 83A

had, didnt have ➔ 86A

if ➔ 78B

I'm sorry. Mr Smith can't see you ...

Mr Smith would see you ...

... He isn't free.

... He's busy.

... You don't have an appointment.

... He has a meeting this morning.

... if he was free.

... if he wasn't busy.

... if you had an appointment.

... if he didn't have a meeting.

We use the past tense because the situation isn't real: Mr Smith *isn't* free. He *is* busy.

After *if*, we can also use *were* with the singular, e.g. He would see you if he *were* free.

2 Positive or negative? Choose the correct form.

a If I (*had*) *didn't have* a passport, I'd come to Italy with you.

b She'd write to you if she *knew* / *didn't know* your address.

c If the shops *were* / *weren't* closed, I'd buy some food.

d If they *lived* / *didn't live* in Australia, we'd visit them more often.

e I'd ask you to stay if we *had* / *didn't have* a bed.

f I'd come to the party if I *was* / *wasn't* ill.

3 What's the man thinking? Complete each sentence twice, using **I would** or **I'd** and ideas from the bubbles.

a If I had more money, I'd _____

_____

b If I had more free time, _____

_____

... go home by taxi

... get some exercise

... clean my flat

... buy a new mobile

4 What would you do if you had more money and more free time? Write two sentences with *If* ...

If _____

_____

C Grammar

... if it wasn't so expensive

Links

| cheaper, more (comfortable) | ➲27 |
| so (expensive) | ➲25C |

I'd go in if it wasn't so expensive.

PICASSO EXHIBITION
Adults €30.
Children €20

I'd go in if it was cheaper.

| if ... | was/were (cheaper) |
| | wasn't/weren't so (expensive) |

5 Complete these sentences. Use ideas from the box.

a I'd buy these armchairs <u>if they were more comfortable</u> .

b I'd learn Arabic <u>if it wasn't so difficult</u> .

c I'd go to his lessons <u>if wasn't so far</u> .

d I'd read that book <u>if they're not very interesting</u>

e I'd go for a swim <u>if the water's not very warm</u>

f I'd go to work by bike <u>if isn't too far</u> .

They're not very
✓comfortable.

It's too long.

✓It's very difficult

It's too far.

The water's not very warm.

They're not very interesting.

Write in your language

I wouldn't pick up a spider.

If I had more free time, I'd learn Japanese.

I'd go by bike if it wasn't so cold.

A Grammar

Positive and negative

- Over 100,000 people visit the old Inca city of Machu Picchu every year.
- There is no road to Machu Picchu, so most people go there by train, or they walk.
- The train stops at the village of Aguas Calientes, in the valley below Machu Picchu.
- About 2,000 people live in Aguas Calientes. Almost everyone in the village earns money from tourists.

Juanita Mendes:
"We have a stall by the railway station. We don't sell anything in the morning. I open the stall at 1 o'clock, just before the train arrives. My son Pedro waits at the station. It often rains here, and many tourists don't bring raincoats. So he sells them plastic sheets to put over their shoulders. He doesn't earn much money – but it's better than nothing."

We use the present simple:

1 to talk about things that are always/usually true:

> About 2,000 people *live* in Aguas Calientes. (= all the time)
> We *have* a stall by the railway station.

2 to talk about things that often/usually happen:

> Over 100,000 people *visit* Machu Picchu every year.
> My son *waits* at the station. (= usually, every day)

Positive forms

I We You They	live … go …	He She It	lives … goes …

Negative forms

I We You They	don't	live … go …	He She It	doesn't	live … go …

NOT ~~doesn't lives, doesn't goes~~

Link
often, usually ⤳9

Link
infinitive ⤳RU2

1 Complete the sentences. Use verbs from the box. Make them positive or negative.

a A bus _takes_ tourists from Aguas Calientes up the hill to Machu Picchu.

b Some people _____ to Machu Picchu by helicopter, but it _____ about $150.

c – Pedro is my only child. I _____ any other children.

d – I _____ a lot of T-shirts, and some tourists also _____ rugs and carpets.

e – We _____ much money, but it's enough to live on.

f – My brother _____ in a factory in Lima. He _____ us money every month.

buy
cost
earn
fly
have
sell
send
✓take
work

B Grammar   *yes/no* questions

Sentence			Question		
I You We They	speak … go …		Do	I you we they	speak …? go …?

Sentence		Question		
He She It	speaks … goes …	Does	he she it	speak …? go …?

NOT ~~Does he speaks …?~~

Link

too   ➲98B

2 Complete the questions.

a I know they eat chicken, but <u>do they eat</u> lamb?

b I hear you like Beethoven. _____ Mozart too?

c I know he takes milk in his coffee, but _____ sugar?

d I see you play the piano. _____ the guitar too?

e I know she works on Saturdays. _____ on Sundays too?

f I know they sell computers – but _____ fax machines?

C Grammar   *Wh-* questions

Link

How much …?   ➲14

**Kate Moore –
Company director**

Kate Moore, director of IFX
46 years old.
Earns ???   ➤ How much does **she** earn?
Married to actor Tim Cullen
They have ??? children   ➤ How many **children** do **they** have?
They live in ???   ➤ Where do **they** live?

Links

How many …?   ➲15

What kind of …?
Which …?   ➲95

3 Write questions from the notes. Use these question words.

What …?   What kind of …?   How many …?   Where …?   Which …?

a Their children go to ??? school.   <u>Which school do their children go to?</u>

b They spend the summer in ???   _____

c She speaks ??? languages.   _____

d In the evenings, she ???   _____

e She owns ??? houses.   _____

f She drives a ???   _____

Write in your language

She doesn't eat lamb, but she likes chicken.	
I don't usually work on Saturdays.	
Where does this bus go?	

Present continuous

now and around now

We use the present continuous tense to talk about:

1 **now**

(She's on the balcony now – you can see her.)

2 **around now**

(She's studying a lot – but not exactly now.)

... No, it's OK. I'm not working at the moment. I'm sitting on the balcony and I'm having a cup of coffee ...

... John's working a lot in the evenings and I'm studying for my exams, so we aren't going out very much at the moment ...

Positive			**Negative**			
I'm We're/You're/They're He's/She's/It's	working		I'm not We aren't/We're not He isn't/He's not	working		at the moment = **now** or **around now**

1 Look at these sentences. Are they about **now** or **around now**? Write **N** or **AN**.

a ___AN___ I'm reading a lot.

b _____ They're watching TV at the moment.

c _____ He's waiting at the bus stop.

d _____ You aren't getting enough exercise.

e _____ We're spending too much money.

f _____ It isn't raining.

g _____ She's working very hard at college.

h _____ You aren't listening!

Link

Vietnam, Asia ⟳38

2 What are these people doing at the moment? Complete the sentences, using verbs from the box in the present continuous.

a She's a travel writer. At the moment, ___she's writing___ a book about Vietnam.

b I usually drive to work, but this week _____ the bus.

c I love Agatha Christie. _____ 'Murder on the Nile' at the moment.

d They go away a lot. At the moment _____ around Asia.

e He's an architect. At the moment, _____ a new airport.

f We're doing a lot of work in the house. At the moment, _____ the living room.

design
paint
read
take
travel
✓write

The future

We can also use the present continuous to talk about the future:

What's the programme for Wednesday?

Well, Professor Liu is arriving in the morning, and she's taking a taxi to her hotel. Then we're meeting her at the hotel at around 1.00 ...

These things are happening on Wednesday – not now, but in the future.

Visitor's programme: Prof. Liu	
11.00	Arrive. Taxi to Hotel Concorde.
13.00	Meet at hotel. Lunch.

To talk about the future we can also use going to and will (see Units 77–79)

3 Complete the text. Use the verbs in brackets, in the present continuous.

13.00	Meet at hotel. Lunch.
15.00	Lecture: World Economy
– 16.30	
18.30	Dinner: Old College
20.00	Concert: New Hall
Thursday	
09.00	City University
– 12.00	4th year students
13.00	Lunch
15.00	Taxi to airport

On Wednesday afternoon, Prof. Liu
(a) _is giving a lecture_ (give) on the World
Economy. Then they (b) _____
(have) at Old College, and in the evening, they
(c) _____ (go to) at New Hall. The
next morning, Prof Liu (d) _____
(visit) and (e) _____ (meet). At 3.00
in the afternoon she (f) _____ (get)
to the airport.

4 Read the examples. Write true sentences about you.

Now _____
_____

Around now _____
_____

The future _____
_____

Now
I'm wearing jeans and a jumper.

Around now
I'm doing exams at the moment.

The future
I'm not going to work tomorrow.

C Grammar Questions

Are you making a film here?

What are you doing in London?

Is your family travelling with you?

How long are you staying?

Yes/no questions	
Am I	
Are you/we/they	...-ing?
Is he/she/it	

Wh- questions		
How	am I	
When	are you/we/they	...-ing?
What	is he/she/it	

5 Write questions for the answers. Use the notes in the box.

a – _What are you doing this weekend?_ – Nothing.
b – _____ – Yes, thanks.
c – _____ – By taxi, I think.
d – _____ – Yes, she is.
e – _____ – Tomorrow night.
f – _____ – No – that's OK.

how / she / get here?
I / sit / your seat?
Anna / come / to the meeting?
when / he / leaving?
you / have / a good time?
✓ what / you / do / this weekend?

Write in your language

I'm working quite hard at the moment.

We're not going out this weekend.

What time are they arriving?

83 *was* and *were*

was, *were*

Link

the 1950s   ➲ 2

> Here's a photo of us in the 1950s. We were very young – I was about 21, and Mary was only 19. Of course, we weren't married then. Life wasn't easy in those days …

Present: positive and negative

I am		He/She	is	We	are
I'm not		It	isn't	You	aren't
				They	

Past: positive and negative

I	was	We	were
He/She	wasn't	You	weren't
It		They	

1 Here are some other things the man says about the 1950s. Add **was** or **were** to the sentences where necessary.

         was   *was*

  a I ⋏ a student, and Mary ⋏ a nurse in London.

  b Mary's parents shop assistants. They quite poor.

  c I in a flat with six other people. They all students too.

  d All the rooms very small, and the flat always cold.

Links

Mexican, Greek ➲ 38

artist, actor, band
            ➲ 54A

2 Correct these mistakes. Use **wasn't** or **weren't**.

  a | **Tolstoy, the Russian artist**   *He wasn't an artist. He was a writer.*

  b | the Mexican band, *The Beatles*   *They*

  c | the famous writer, Pablo Picasso

  d | Marlon Brando, the Greek actor

  e | the Chinese leaders, Lenin and Stalin

  f | the Brazilian tennis-player, Pelé

yes/no questions

Last week, this person was on holiday.

> Was the water warm?

> Yes, it was.

> Were the beaches crowded?

> No, they weren't.

Link

short answer   ➲ 97A

Question			
Was	I he/she it	…?	

Short answer			
Yes,	I he/she it	was.	
No,		wasn't.	

Question			
Were	we you they	…?	

Short answer			
Yes,	we you they	were.	
No,		weren't.	

3 Write more questions with **Was …?** or **Were …?**, and give short answers.

a <u>Was the weather good</u> ?
(weather).

Yes, it was.   Yes. It was really sunny.

d _____ ?
(the rooms?)

_____   Yes. Very clean.

b _____ ?
(the people?)

_____   No, not very friendly.

e _____ ?
(the restaurants?)

_____   No. They were quite expensive.

c _____ ?
(the hotel?)

_____   Yes. It was a very comfortable hotel.

f _____ ?
(the food?)

_____   Yes. It was very good.

C Grammar   *Wh–* questions

50,000 AT 'PEOPLE'S CONCERT'

When was the concert?   On Saturday.

Where was **it**?   In London.

How much were the tickets?   They were £1 each.

Links

When …?
Where …?   ➲95
visited   ➲43C
parents, grandfather   ➲44

4 Write questions with **was** and **were**. Use question words from the box.

How …?   How much …?   How old …?   ✓ What … like?   What time …?   Where …?

a – I was at Nick's party last night.
– <u>What was it like</u> ?
– It was very good.

b – Her grandfather died last year.
– Really? _____ ?
– He was about 75, I think.

c – I visited my parents last weekend.
– _____ ?
– They were fine.

d – I called last night, but you weren't at home. _____ ?
– I was at the cinema.

e – Do you like my new shoes?
– Yes. _____ ?
– They weren't very expensive. About £40.

f – The meeting wasn't at 10.30.
– Oh? _____ ?
– It was at 9.30.

Write in your language

The water was clean, but it wasn't very warm.	
Were the restaurants good?	
What was the weather like?	

There was, there were

Link

➲83 **was and were**

Link

different ➲31

A Grammar

There was, there were

Dubai is a large, modern city. But in 1900, it was very different. There was a harbour, and there were a lot of fishing boats. But there wasn't an airport, and there weren't even any schools.

The harbour at Dubai, 1900

Dubai, 2000

There was There wasn't	+ singular

There were There weren't	+ plural

1 Fill the gaps with **there was**, **there wasn't**, **there were** or **there weren't**.

The photo shows Dodgetown, Wyoming, in 1865. In Dodgetown, (a) _there was_ a railway station, (b) _____ four shops and (c) _____ a bank. (d) _____ lots of horses, of course, but (e) _____ any cars. It was quite hot in summer: (f) _____ any swimming pools, but (g) _____ a large lake near the town. And of course (h) _____ any electricity.

2 Add the missing verbs. Write the correct forms of **was/were** or **There was/were**.

a When we ʌ young our house ʌ always cold. ʌ any central heating.
   were   *was*   *There wasn't*

b In 1985, one computer in our office. By 2005, twenty-five.

c only three people at the meeting. All the others busy.

d In the 1990s, lots of good bands, but Nirvana and REM the best.

e I remember my grandmother's house. It quite big: five bedrooms, but a bathroom – and the toilet outside in the garden.

B Grammar — *Was there ...?, Were there ...?*

–Were there any cars when you were young?
–Yes, there were.

–Were there any mobile phones?
– No, there weren't.

–Was there a shower in the house?
– No, there wasn't.

–Was there a toilet?
–Yes, there was.

Link

short answers ➲97A

Questions		Short answers			
Was Were	there ...?	Yes, there	was. were.	No, there	wasn't. weren't.

Link

dishwasher, lights, washing machine ➲34

3 Complete these other questions. Guess the woman's answers!

a – _Were there_ any dishwashers?
– _No, there weren't._

b – .... any electricity?
– ....

c – .... any computer games?
– ....

d – .... a radio in the house?
– ....

e – .... a washing machine?
– ....

f – .... any lights?
– ....

C Grammar — *How much...? How many ...?*

Links

How many ...? ➲15C
How much ...? ➲14C
uncountable nouns ➲13C

How many people were there on the Titanic?

2,227.

How much coal was there?

About 6,000 tonnes.

How much … was there?
How many …s were there?

WHAT WAS THERE ON THE TITANIC?

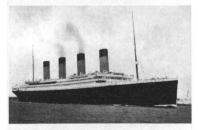

- 2,227 people
- 6,000 tonnes of coal
- .... car (a Renault 35)
- .... grand pianos
- _15,000_ sheets
- .... eggs
- .... of milk
- .... of meat

4 Write more questions. Can you match them with the answers?

a – _How many sheets were there?_ – 15,000.
b – .... – 40 tonnes.
c – .... – Five.
d – .... – 40,000.
e – .... – 70,000 litres.
f – .... – One.

Write in your language

There were 40 children in my class at school.

There wasn't a television in the hotel room.

Was there a shower in the room?

A Grammar · Regular verbs

Read this newspaper article.

Link
⟳86 **Past simple (2)**

Link
last (weekend) ⟳5A

1200 km BY FREIGHT TRAIN

Last weekend a 14-year-old boy travelled over 1000 kilometres to see his uncle – by freight train. The boy, Miles Jackson, lives in the small town of Westville, near Chicago, and he often watches the freight trains go by on their way to the east coast. Last Saturday, he decided to take a train to visit his uncle in Boston – 1,200 kilometres away. 'It was easy. I just waited for a train, and when it stopped, I jumped on in the middle. The next morning, we arrived in Boston.'

The verbs in blue are all in the past simple tense.

To form the past simple, add *-ed*:

Verb	Past simple	
wait jump	I He/She They	waited jumped

If the verb ends in *-e*, just add *-d*:

Verb	Past simple	
decide arrive	I He/She They	decided arrived

With some verbs, we double the last letter:

Verb	Past simple	
travel stop	I He/She They	travelled stopped

Links
chat, talk ⟳55A
goal ⟳41
wash, clean, brush ⟳43B

1 Write the past simple form of these verbs. (* = double the letter!)

a We (stay) _stayed_ at home last night and (play) _____ cards until 11.00.

b She (live) _____ all her life in London, and (die) _____ there in 1910.

c At 6.00, we (turn) _____ the radio on and (listen) _____ to the news.

d I (wash) _____ my face, (clean) _____ my teeth and (brush) _____ my hair.

e She (slip*) _____ on the steps and (drop*) _____ her shopping bag.

f I (phone) _____ this morning, but nobody (answer) _____ .

g The club (open) _____ last April, but it (close) _____ again a few months later.

h Bradley (push) _____ Makkinen, Makkinen (drop*) _____ the ball, and Barossa (kick) _____ it into the goal.

i We (chat*) _____ for more than an hour. Most of the time, he (talk) _____ and I (listen) _____ .

j He (type) _____ 'Dear Sir', then he (stop*) _____ 'What shall I write next?', he (ask) _____ .

Irregular verbs

Here is more of the newspaper article.

Before he left, Miles Jackson bought two bars of chocolate for the journey, and he also took a bottle of water.

'I had a warm coat,' he told reporters, 'so I was quite warm. I slept most of the time.'
In Boston, he got off the train and went straight to his uncle's house. 'He was really surprised to see me,' said Miles.

The verbs in blue are in the past simple tense. They are irregular verbs: they don't add -ed, but change in other ways.

Verb	Past simple	
leave		left
buy		bought
take		took
have	I	had
tell	He/She	told
sleep	They	slept
get	We	got
go		went
say		said

2 Many common verbs in English have irregular past forms. Do you know the past forms of these verbs? Check your answers in the list of irregular verbs on page 224.

come _came_ drive _ _ _ _ _ make _ _ _ _ hear _ _ _ _ _
drink _ _ _ _ _ give _ _ _ _ read _ _ _ _ see _ _ _
eat _ _ _ ring _ _ _ _ do _ _ _ put _ _ _
write _ _ _ _ _ find _ _ _ _ _ sit _ _ _

3 Here are parts of **four** stories. Write past forms in the gaps. Use the verbs in the box each time.

a

I _went_ into the café, _____ a table in the corner, and _____ down. After a few minutes, the waitress _____ over to my table. 'Sorry,' she _____, 'but you can't sit here.'

sit come say
✓go find

b

It was Boris's big day. He _____ up at 6.00, _____ a shower and _____ on his best suit and a white shirt. He _____ into the kitchen, quickly _____ a piece of bread and butter, _____ some coffee, and _____ the flat.

go put get
leave drink
eat have

c

At about 2.30, a man and a woman _____ out of the house. The man _____ something on a piece of paper and _____ it to the woman. The woman _____ it quickly, then _____ it in her pocket. Then she _____ into a black car and _____ away.

read put get
come write
drive give

d

'After dinner, I _____ the washing up and _____ some coffee, and then I _____ a noise in the living room. I _____ in and _____ a body on the floor – and then I _____ the police.'

ring do see
hear make go

Link

get up, put on ➲RU1

Write in your language

We left London at 6.00 and arrived home at 7.30.

They went out and saw a film ...

... and I stayed at home and watched TV.

A Grammar — We didn't go to ...

Link

⇨ 85 Past simple (1)

We visited Buckingham Palace, but we didn't go to Trafalgar Square. And we didn't visit the British Museum – the children didn't want to go there. They wanted to go to the Zoo, but we didn't have time for that. We went on the London Eye instead, and had a fantastic view of the whole city – and then it was time to leave. So we didn't do very much, but we had a good time.

London Zoo

The London Eye

Trafalgar Square

British Museum

Buckingham Palace

Links

infinitive   ⇨ RU2

The family went to two of the places in the pictures. Which were they? ....

To form the past simple negative, use *didn't* + infinitive:

Verb	Past simple		Past simple negative		
visit	I	visited	I		visit
want	We	wanted	We		want
go	He/She	went	He/She	didn't	go
do	They	did	They		do
have	You	had	You		have

NOT ~~didn't visited~~

didn't = did not

1 Complete the sentences with negative forms. Use verbs from the box.

a We _didn't visit_ St Paul's Cathedral. It was too far away.

b We went to the shops in Oxford Street, but we .... anything.

c We .... lunch, so the children got really hungry.

d We stood outside Buckingham Palace, but we .... the Queen.

e We had a camera with us, but we .... many photos.

f The weather was very good. It .... all day.

have
see
rain
buy
take
✓ visit

2 Think of a city you visited. Write about two things you did, and two things you didn't do.

....

....

....

....

PRAGUE
I saw Wenceslas Square.
I didn't go on a river boat.

B Grammar — *Did you go to …?*

Link

short answers ⮕97A

> Did **you** visit Buckingham Palace?

> Yes, we **did**.

> Did **you** go to Trafalgar Square?

> No, we **didn't**.

Questions	Did	you he/she they	visit …? go …?	Short answers	Yes,	I we he/she they	did.	No,	I we he/she they	didn't.

3 Look at A and Exercise 1. Complete the questions and write short answers.

a – *Did you see* Nelson's Column?   – *No, we didn't.*

b – .... to Oxford Street?   – ....

c – .... any clothes?   – ....

d – .... to the theatre?   – ....

e – .... the pandas in London Zoo?   – ....

f – .... a good time?   – ....

C Grammar — *Where did he grow up?*

Link

Where …?, When …?
⮕95

Links

grow up, study, become ⮕45

> Where did Alfred Hitchcock grow up?

> When did he make his first film?

> In London.

> In 1925.

Where When	did	you he/she they	+ verb

Alfred Hitchcock (1899–1980)

Alfred Hitchcock grew up in London, and studied engineering at university.

He made his first film in 1925.

He moved to the USA in 1939, and in 1955 he became a US citizen.

He made *Psycho* (his most famous film) in 1960.

He directed over 50 films, but he never won an Oscar.

He died in Los Angeles in 1980.

4 Write more questions about Alfred Hitchcock.

a *How many films did he direct* ?
Over 50.

b .... ?
In 1960.

c .... ?
Engineering.

d .... ?
In 1939.

e .... ?
In Los Angeles.

f .... ?
None!

Write in your language

He didn't win an Oscar.

Did you visit the British Museum?

When did they move to England?

87 Past continuous (1)

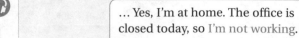

A Grammar   *was/were + -ing*

Links

⮑ 85 **Past simple (1)**

⮑ 82 **Present continuous (1)**

⮑ 83 **was and were**

> … Yes, I'm at home. The office is closed today, so I'm not working.
>
> … He's visiting his parents in London …
>
> No, the children aren't here. They're staying with friends …

The woman is talking about NOW. She uses the present continuous tense.

It was Friday afternoon, and Jane was at home. The office was closed, so she wasn't working. Her husband was visiting his parents in London, and the children were staying with friends. She was alone.

The story is about the PAST. It uses the past continuous tense.

Link

⮑ RU3   **-ing forms**

Past continuous

I He She	was wasn't	working visiting staying	We You They	were weren't	working visiting staying

1 Here are parts of four stories. Complete the sentences using the past continuous. Use verbs from the box.

a The lesson was nearly finished. The teacher _was talking_ about earthquakes. But James _____. He _____ about Maria's letter.

b The beach was almost empty. A few people _____ on the beach, and one woman _____ in the sea. But it was late, and most people _____ home.

c I was very cold. It _____, but I _____ a coat or a hat.

d It was 1968. My sister and I _____ in Paris. I _____ French, and she _____ as a waitress. And we _____ a very good time.

go
live
sit
snow
study
swim
✓ talk
think
work
have
not listen
not wear

Link

fire, was damaged
    ➜50

Art gallery fire

There was a fire at an art gallery at 2.00 p.m. yesterday, near a crowded café and a street market. Several paintings in the gallery were damaged in the fire, but no-one was injured. Police are looking for a woman who was wearing a blue dress and carrying a black sports bag. They are also looking for a man in a red T-shirt.

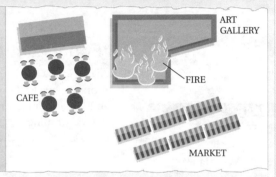

The police are asking questions …

– Where were you at 2.00 p.m.?
  – I was in the café.
– Were you sitting inside?
  – No, outside.
– Where were you sitting exactly?
  – Just by the door.

– I saw a woman come out of the café.
  – What was she wearing?
– Er, a blue dress.
  – Was she carrying anything?
– Yes – a black sports bag …

Questions

(Where) (What)	was	he she	…-ing?		(Where) (What)	were	we you they	…-ing?

2 The police talk to two other people. Write questions using the past continuous.

– (a) _What were you doing?_ (What / do)
– I was selling clothes at the market.
– Did you see a woman in a blue dress?
– Yes, I did.
– (b) _____ (buy / clothes?)
– No, she was talking to someone on a mobile.
– (c) _____ (Where / stand?)
– Just outside the art gallery.

– I saw a man and a woman.
– (d) _____ (Where / sit?)
– Next to my table. They were talking.
– (e) _____ (What / talk about?)
– I don't know. I couldn't hear.
– (f) _____ (wear / T-shirt?)
– Yes, he was – a red one.

Write in your language

They were sitting in the corner, by the window.

He was wearing jeans and a green shirt.

I wasn't working yesterday afternoon.

88 Past continuous (2)

A Grammar — Past continuous and past simple

Links

➲ 87 **Past continuous (1)**

➲ 85 **Past simple (1)**

➲ 83 **was and were**

> I got on the bus and sat down.
> Then I looked round and saw an old friend of mine.
> She was sitting near the back, and she was reading a newspaper.

> I first met my husband in 1998, at a party.
> I was living in London, and he was staying with friends there.

got, sat, looked, saw = past simple
was sitting, was reading = past continuous

met = past simple
was living, was staying = past continuous

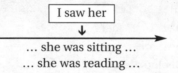

I saw her
↓

… she was sitting …
… she was reading …

I met him
↓

… I was living …
… he was staying …

1 Choose the correct form: past simple or past continuous.

a I *drove* / *was driving* along the road. Suddenly,   <u>was driving</u>
   a man *ran* / *was running* into the road and
   shouted / *was shouting* 'Stop the car!'

b I *found* / *was finding* this ring in the bedroom.
   I *cleaned* / *was cleaning* the room and I
   saw / *was seeing* it under the bed.

c I *saw* / *was seeing* Bob yesterday. He
   stood / *was standing* at the bus stop and he
   talked / *was talking* to a young woman.

B Grammar — *when* and *while*

I was living in London. I met my husband.

⇩

I was living in London when I met my husband.

or

I met my husband while I was living in London.

Links

cut, slipped, broke
⮑ 49A

lost, found ⮑ 58A

2 Find pairs of sentences.

a She was writing an email.   **1** She lost her passport.

b He was shaving.   **2** She slipped and broke her leg.

c He was cleaning the kitchen.   **3** The police stopped him.

d She was running down some steps.   **4** He cut his face.

e She was staying in Tokyo.   **5** He found £50 behind the fridge.

f He was driving home from a party.   **6** The computer crashed.

3 Join the sentences using **when** or **while**.

a _She was writing an email when the computer crashed._

_or_ _The computer crashed while she was writing an email._

b ....

c ....

d ....

e ....

f ....

C Grammar   *What were you doing? What did you do?*

– What were you doing **when**   (= at that time)
   the plane crashed?
– I was walking by the river.
– And what did you do?   (= next, after that)
– I rang the police on my
   mobile.

the plane crashed		I rang the police
↓		↓

… I was walking by the river …

Links

after that ⮑ 100
accident ⮑ 49A
crash, police ⮑ 50

4 Write questions in the gaps.

a – _What were you doing_ ...... when you heard the news? – We were having dinner.

b – .... when she found the money? – She put it in the bank.

c – .... when the police arrived? – They were watching TV.

d – .... when she found the money? – She was cleaning the car.

e – .... when you saw the accident? – I was walking home.

f – .... when you saw the accident? – I phoned an ambulance.

Write in your language

We were having lunch when they arrived.

I met them while I was working in London.

What were you doing when you heard the news?

89 *used to*

A Grammar | *used to*

Join a sports club - and change your life!

Links

table tennis, basketball,
snooker   ➲ 41

'I used to stay at home in the evening and watch TV. I also used to eat too much.

Then last year I joined a sports club. Now I play table tennis and basketball in the evenings, and I go swimming twice a week. I feel much better, and I meet people.'

A year ago

Now

Link

infinitive   ➲ RU2

used to + infinitive

I used to	stay at home. eat too much.

(= I did this before, but not now.)

We only use *used to* in the past. We can't say 'I use to …'.

Link

start/stop + verb
+ -ing   ➲ 65C

1 Write sentences with **used to**.

a They don't have a car. They sold their car last week. _They used to have a car._

b We don't live in Cairo any more. We moved last year. _____

c She doesn't teach English now. She's got a new job. _____

d I broke my arm, so I can't play snooker now. _____

e He stopped smoking about a year ago. _____

f I've started driving to work, so I don't go by bus any more. _____

B Grammar | *didn't use to*

Look at the man in Section A again.

Now he plays table tennis in the evenings.   →   He didn't use to play table tennis.

Positive

I He	used to + infinitive

Negative

I He	didn't use to	+ infinitive

2 **used to** or **didn't use to**? Write more sentences about the man in Section A.

a _He didn't use to go out in the evenings._ (go out in the evenings)

b _____ (be overweight)

c _____ (play basketball)

d _____ (eat a lot)

e _____ (meet many people)

f _____ (feel good)

There used to be

Link
➲ 84   **There was, there were**

Link
ago   ➲ 5C

NOW

In our street, there's a big supermarket.

20 YEARS AGO

There didn't use to be a supermarket.
There used to be a park and trees.

There	used to be / didn't use to be	a park. / trees. / a supermarket.

3 Look at the pictures. Say what there used to be and what there didn't use to be.

trams   factory   buses   office block

50 YEARS AGO

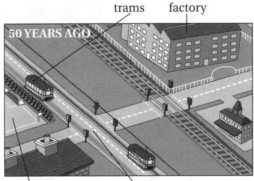

football ground   crossroads

NOW

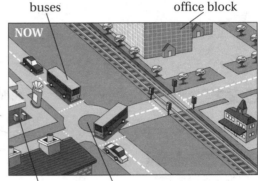

petrol station   roundabout

a *There used to be trams.* (trams)
b *There didn't use to be a petrol station.* (a petrol station)
c (a football ground)
d (a crossroads)
e (a roundabout)
f (a factory)
g (an office block)

4 Think about your town fifty years ago. Look at the examples, and write two sentences.

> There used to be a theatre.
>
> There didn't use to be an airport.

Write in your language

She used to be a school teacher.

I didn't use to like coffee, but now I love it.

There used to be a cinema here.

Present perfect (1)

A Grammar — *have/has* + past participle

Look at these situations.

To talk about them, we can use:

1 the present tense: The taxi is here. | They're at the theatre. | The window is open.

2 the present perfect tense: The taxi has arrived. | They've gone to the theatre. | Someone has opened the window.

Present perfect

I We You They	have	arrived gone opened

He She	has	arrived gone opened

Short forms
have → *'ve* *has* → *'s*
They have gone → They've gone
She has gone → She's gone

Link
➜RU4 **Past participles**

Link
someone, anyone
➜16

1 Match the sentences.

Now

a They're awake.
b The house is dark.
c There isn't anyone in the room.
d My hands are clean.
e The police are at the front door.
f The plates are all clean.

What has happened

1 I've done all the washing up
2 The police have arrived.
3 Someone has turned all the lights off.
4 They've woken up.
5 I've washed my hands.
6 Everyone has left.

2 Write sentences in the present perfect tense. Use verbs from the box.

Now

a They're in bed.
b The postman is at the door.
c She has a computer now.
d He's wearing a tie.
e They aren't at home.
f All the windows are closed.

What has happened

a *They've gone* _____ to bed.
b The postman _____ .
c _____ a computer.
d _____ a tie on.
e _____ out.
f We _____ .

| come |
| gone |
| closed |
| put |
| bought |

B Phrases — *The film has just started*

Link
just ➜6B

just = a short time ago

The film has just started.   She's just had a baby.

3 Complete the sentences with **just** and the present perfect.

a    b    c

d    e    f

a They _have just bought_ some food.
b The train _____ the station.
c He _____ his hair.
d She _____ a text.
e They _____ married.
f They _____ lunch.

Verb	Past participle
buy	✓ bought
finish	finished
get	got
leave	left
receive	received
wash	washed

C Grammar   Present perfect or past simple?

Link
⮕ 85 **Past simple (1)**

Link
past time expressions
⮕ 5

Compare these sentences:

Present perfect tense

> The President's plane has landed.
>
> – Is he still in the office?
> – No, he's just left.
>
> – Let's go and see *Love Story* tonight.
> – No. I've already seen it.

We use the present perfect tense with:
– no time expression
– just
– already

Past simple tense

> The President's plane landed at 5.45.
>
> – Is he still in the office?
> – No, he left a few minutes ago.
>
> – Let's go and see *Love Story* tonight.
> – No. I saw it last Saturday.

We use the past simple tense with past time expressions:
– at 5.45, on Monday, in 1960
– a few minutes ago, 5 years ago
– last Saturday, yesterday, last year

4 Choose the best verb form.

a ~~We missed~~ / (We've missed) the train. It *just left* / *has just left*.

b *I went* / *I've been* to the theatre last weekend.

c I know that book. *I already read* / *I've already read* it.

d My hair's wet. *I just had* / *I've just had* a shower.

e Mr Jones is in his office. *He came in* / *He's come in* ten minutes ago.

Write in your language

He's parked the car and he's getting out.

They've just got married.

I've already seen that film.

A Grammar — *haven't/hasn't* + past participle

Links

⮕90 **Present perfect (1)**

yet ⮕6A

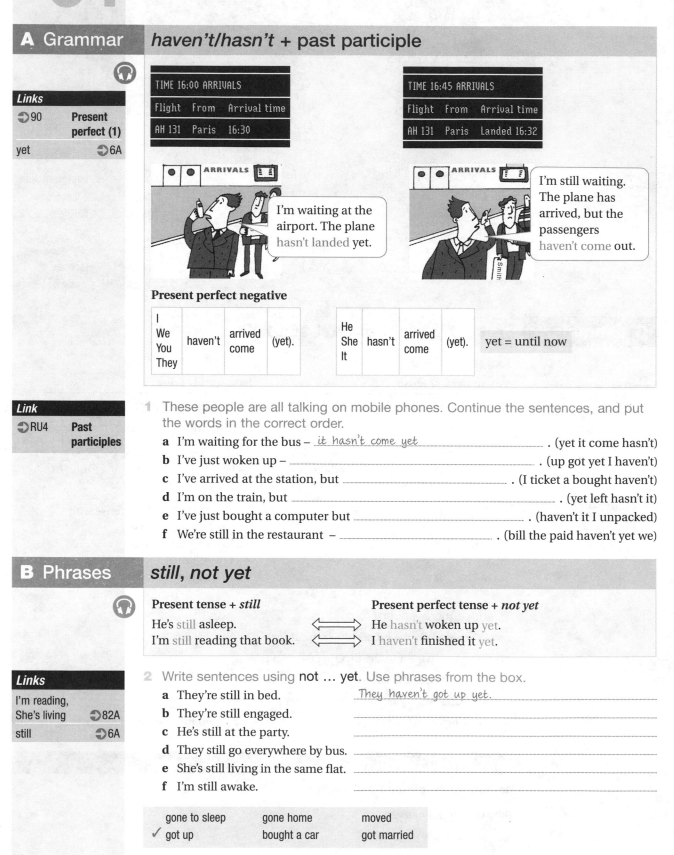

```
TIME 16:00 ARRIVALS

Flight  From   Arrival time

AH 131  Paris  16:30
```

I'm waiting at the airport. The plane hasn't landed yet.

```
TIME 16:45 ARRIVALS

Flight  From   Arrival time

AH 131  Paris  Landed 16:32
```

I'm still waiting. The plane has arrived, but the passengers haven't come out.

Present perfect negative

I We You They	haven't	arrived come	(yet).

He She It	hasn't	arrived come	(yet).

yet = until now

Link

⮕RU4 **Past participles**

1 These people are all talking on mobile phones. Continue the sentences, and put the words in the correct order.

a I'm waiting for the bus – *it hasn't come yet* . (yet it come hasn't)

b I've just woken up – _____ . (up got yet I haven't)

c I've arrived at the station, but _____ . (I ticket a bought haven't)

d I'm on the train, but _____ . (yet left hasn't it)

e I've just bought a computer but _____ . (haven't it I unpacked)

f We're still in the restaurant – _____ . (bill the paid haven't yet we)

B Phrases — *still, not yet*

Present tense + *still*		**Present perfect tense + *not yet***
He's still asleep.	⟺	He hasn't woken up yet.
I'm still reading that book.	⟺	I haven't finished it yet.

Links

I'm reading, She's living ⮕82A

still ⮕6A

2 Write sentences using **not … yet**. Use phrases from the box.

a They're still in bed.   *They haven't got up yet.*

b They're still engaged. _____

c He's still at the party. _____

d They still go everywhere by bus. _____

e She's still living in the same flat. _____

f I'm still awake. _____

gone to sleep	gone home	moved
✓ got up	bought a car	got married

C Grammar   Questions

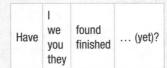 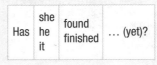

What are you doing these days? Have you found a flat yet? Or are you still living at home? And how's Robert? Has he finished university? Is he working now? Write and tell me your news.

Have	I we you they	found finished	… (yet)?

Has	she he it	found finished	… (yet)?

Link

retire, look for a job ➲42C

move to, live in ➲45A

3 Complete the questions in these letters, emails and texts. Use verbs from the table.

a
How's Gerald? _Has he got_ married yet, or is he still single?

b
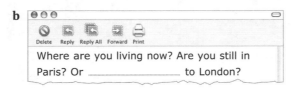
Where are you living now? Are you still in Paris? Or .... to London?

Verb	Past participle
come	come
find	found
✓get	got
move	moved
retire	retired
visit	visited

c
Do you like Athens?
.... the Acropolis yet?

e
I hope Anna is better now. .... out of hospital yet?

d
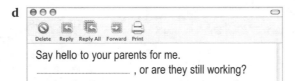
Say hello to your parents for me. .... , or are they still working?

f
Are you still looking for a job? Or .... one?

4 What is the woman asking? Ask questions, using verbs from the table.

Link

iron, wash, make ➲35

I've done everything now.

Are you sure …?

a _Have you made_ .... the beds?
b .... the sheets?
c .... the kitchen?
d .... the dishes?
e .... the car?
f .... lunch?

Verb	Past participle
iron	ironed
wash	washed
make	made
clean	cleaned

Write in your language

The plane hasn't arrived yet.

They haven't gone yet – they're still here.

Have you washed the dishes?

A Grammar

He has lived ...

Carlos Ramirez has lived in Mexico, France and the USA.

He has written two plays, and he has made three films. He has also written a book about his life.

Present perfect

He has	lived ...
	made ...
	written ...

(= at some time in his life)

Links

➲90   **Present perfect (1)**

➲RU4   **Past participles**

Link

➲85   **Past simple (1)**

Carlos Ramirez: Writer and film director	
1975–96	Guadalajara, Mexico Play: *The Shop Assistant*
1996–1998	Paris, France Film: *Summer Nights* Film: *Under the Bridges*
1998–2001	Los Angeles, USA Film: *On the Edge*
2001– now	Mexico City, Mexico Play: *South of the Border* Book: A *Mexican Life*

We are not saying *when* he did these things. Compare:

Present perfect	**Past**
Carlos Ramirez has lived in Mexico.	Carlos Ramirez lived in Mexico until 1996.
He has written two plays.	He wrote his first play while he was in Mexico.

1   What has Flora Miles done in her life? Complete the sentences.

She has worked	She has written
She has lived	✓ She has done
She has studied	She has taught

Flora Miles: Writer	
1976–1998	London, England Student, London University
1998–1999	Montreal, Canada Student, Concordia University Waitress, Le Canard Restaurant
1999–2003	Bern, Switzerland Receptionist, Hotel Commodore Novel: *White River*
2003–now	Ankara, Turkey Teacher, ABC English School Novel: *Sun in the Afternoon.*

a   _She has done_   several different jobs.

b   _____ two novels.

c   _____ as a hotel receptionist.

d   _____ in England and Canada.

e   _____ English.

f   _____ in several countries.

B Phrases

I've never been to ...

Links

I haven't (been) ➲91A

(five) times   ➲10A

I've never been to Ibiza.

I've been there five or six times. It's lovely.

I've been to Spain several times, but I haven't been to Ibiza.

| I've been to | Ibiza | twice.
five times. | I haven't been to
I've never been to | Ibiza. |

I've *been to* = I've visited

2 Read the examples and write true sentences about yourself and your family. If you like, write about some of the places in the box.

....

....

....

....

....

> I've been to England twice.
> My brother has never been to England.
> My parents have been to Australia several times.

| London | China | the USA | Moscow | Australia | Italy |
| Egypt | Greece | Thailand | India | Paris | Brazil |

C Grammar

Have you ever ...?

Have you ever done a bungee jump?

No, I haven't.

Have you ever been to a rock festival?

Yes, I have.

| Have you ever | done
been | ...? | Yes, I have.
No, I haven't. |

ever = at any time in your life

3 What are the questions? Use participles from the box.

| been | climbed | done |
| eaten | ✓slept | driven |

a _Have you ever slept_ .... in a tent?

b .... rabbit meat?

c .... a mountain?

d .... a parachute jump?

e .... a racing car?

f .... to an opera?

4 What are your answers to questions a–f? Write **Yes, I have.** or **No, I haven't.**

a ....   b ....   c ....

d ....   e ....   f ....

Write in your language

I've lived in three different countries.	
I've never been to India.	
Have you ever worked in a restaurant?	

93 Present passive

A Grammar — Active and passive

Links

➲81 **Present simple (1)**

➲94 **Past passive**

The supermarket closes every day at 7.00 pm.

They lock the doors ...
or
The doors are locked ...

... and they switch on the alarm.
or
... and the alarm is switched on.

ACTIVE:	They lock the doors.	They switch on the alarm.
PASSIVE:	The doors are locked.	The alarm is switched on.

Present passive | is / are | + past participle

Links

turn on/off, switch on/off ➲34B

past participles ➲RU4

1 Here are some other things that happen. Write passive sentences.

a They turn off the heating. _The heating is turned off._
b They lock the windows. ....
c They switch off the lights. ....
d They turn off the music. ....
e They clean the floor. ....
f They take the money to the bank. ....

Verb	Past participle
lock	locked
switch	switched
turn	turned
clean	cleaned
take	taken

B Phrases — Common verbs: *is made, is grown, is produced*

Links

Finland ➲38

20%, 35% ➲1B

Link

make ➲63A

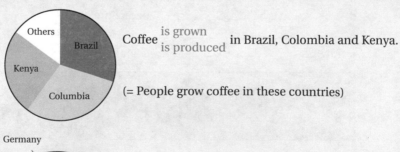

Coffee is grown / is produced in Brazil, Colombia and Kenya.

(= People grow coffee in these countries)

20% of all cars are made / are produced in Japan.

Verb		Passive form
grow	→	is/are grown
make	→	is/are made
produce	→	is/are produced

2 Here are some more facts. Correct the mistakes.

a Cotton grown in India and Egypt. _is grown_

b 35% of all mobile phones is make by Nokia. ....

c Rolex watches are grown in Switzerland. ....

d Sugar produced in the USA and the Caribbean. ....

e Toyotas are in Japan produce. ....

f 30% of all tea are grow in China. ....

C Phrases	**Common verbs: *is spoken*, *is written***

Links

Arabic	➲ 38D
Middle East, North Africa	➲ 37A
by	➲ 24A

FACT FILE: Arabic

→ Arabic is spoken by about 206 million people, mainly in the Middle East and North Africa.

→ Books and newspapers are written in Modern Standard Arabic. This is different from the spoken language.

→ Arabic is written from right to left, but numbers are written from left to right.

Verb		Passive form
speak	→	is/are spoken
write	→	is/are written

3 Complete the sentences.

a English _is written_ from left to right ...

b ... and English numbers .... from left to right.

c About 500 languages .... in Nigeria.

d Chinese .... by more than a billion people.

e Two languages .... in Belgium: French and Flemish.
Most signs .... in both languages.

f In Greece, most menus .... in English as well as Greek.

Write in your language

The heating is turned off every evening.	
20% of cotton is grown in India.	
Portuguese is spoken in Brazil.	

94

Past passive

A Grammar | Past passive

Links
⮕85 **Past simple (1)**
⮕93 **Present passive**

A painting by M. J. Heade, 1880

This painting was found in a house near Boston.
It was sold for $1 million.

Two paintings by Canaletto, 18th century

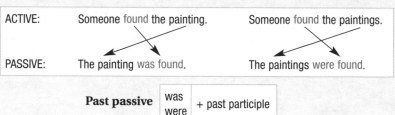

These two paintings were found in a farmhouse in England.
They were sold for £6 million.

Links
was and were ⮕83
past participles ⮕RU4

| ACTIVE: | Someone found the painting. | Someone found the paintings. |
| PASSIVE: | The painting was found. | The paintings were found. |

| Past passive | was were | + past participle |

Links
find, keep ⮕58
painting, art gallery ⮕54A
someone ⮕16

1 Read about the paintings, and write passive sentences.

The M. J. Heade painting:

a He painted it in 1880.

   It was painted in 1880.

b Someone kept it an attic.

   ....

c Someone found it in 2003.

   ....

d They sold it to a New York art gallery.

   ....

The Canaletto paintings:

e He painted them in the 18th century.

f Someone gave them to a family in England.

g Someone put them in a cellar.

h Someone found them in 2002.

Verb	Past tense	Past participle
find	found	found
sell	sold	sold
paint	painted	painted
give	gave	given
keep	kept	kept
put	put	put

Common verbs: *was built, was written ...*

The Taj Mahal was built in the 17th century.

Macbeth was written by William Shakespeare in 1606.

The Mona Lisa was painted by Leonardo da Vinci.

Fireworks were invented by the Chinese about 1000 years ago.

rings

The rings of Saturn were discovered in 1610.

Verb		Past passive
paint		painted
invent	was	invented
discover	were	discovered
write		written
build		built

Macbeth was written	by Shakespeare.	(= who)
	in 1606.	(= when)

2 Write sentences using the past passive.

   a 'Sunflowers' <u>was painted by</u> Van Gogh.

   b The telephone _____ Alexander Bell.

   c The Great Pyramid _____ 2560 BC.

   d *War and Peace* _____ Leo Tolstoy.

   e The Eiffel Tower _____ 1889.

   f Radium _____ Marie Curie.

   g The parking meter _____ 1932.

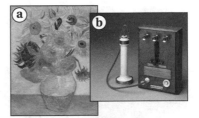

3 Think of a **building**, a **book** and a **painting** you know. Write sentences about them.

   a _____

   b _____

   c _____

Write in your language

The painting was found in an attic.	
This book was written by my father.	
Their house was built in 1800.	

95 Question words

A Phrases — Question words

> When **does** the plane leave?
> Whose **bag** is this?
> Where **do** we check in?
> Who **are** you travelling with?
> How **can** I get to the town centre?
> What's **our** flight number?
> Why **is** the plane late?

1 Match the questions with the answers. Add question words.

1 – Excuse me. _Where_ are the toilets?	**a** – A bit nervous. I've never flown before!
2 – .... is the next bus to the centre?	**b** – We got here too late.
3 – .... jacket is this?	**c** – Go down those steps, and you'll see them.
4 – .... didn't we get a window seat?	**d** – No-one. I'm taking a taxi.
5 – .... are you feeling?	**e** – It's 16F.
6 – .... 's meeting you at the airport?	**f** – In about 15 minutes.
7 – .... 's your seat number?	**g** – Oh, it's my husband's. Thanks.

B Phrases — Questions with *What ...?*

Link
What size ...? ➔ 51D

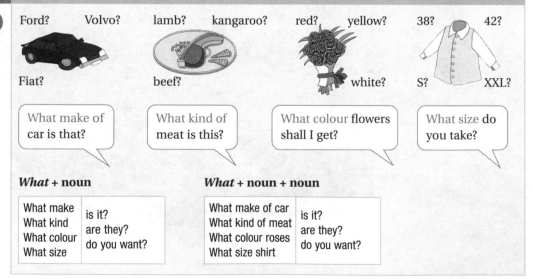

Ford?   Volvo?   lamb?   kangaroo?   red?   yellow?   38?   42?
Fiat?   beef?   white?   S?   XXL?

> What make of car is that?
> What kind of meat is this?
> What colour flowers shall I get?
> What size do you take?

What + noun

What make What kind What colour What size	is it? are they? do you want?

What + noun + noun

What make of car What kind of meat What colour roses What size shirt	is it? are they? do you want?

2 Complete the questions.

a – _What kind of_ meat is this?
– It's beef, I think.

b – .... mobile phone do you have?
– Nokia.

c – .... curtains shall we buy?
– Let's get white ones, to go with the carpet.

d – .... music does she like?
– Mainly classical: Bach, Mozart, Beethoven ...

e – .... is your CD player?
– I think it's a Sony.

f – .... shoes do you wear?
– 42.

C Phrases

Questions with *How ...?*

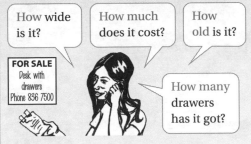

How wide is it?

How much does it cost?

How old is it?

FOR SALE
Desk with drawers
Phone 836 7500

How many drawers has it got?

How well do you know them?

How often do you see them?

How + adjective

How	wide ...?
	old ...?

How + adverb

How	well ...?
	often ...?

How + much/many

How	much ...?
	many ...?

3 Write questions with **How ...?**

a Do the trains go every hour? Every two hours?   *How often do the trains go?*

b Are these trainers £30? £40? Or more?

c Do you like your coffee strong? Very strong? Weak?

d Are you 1.60m tall? 1.65? 1.70 ...?

e Is the water deep? Or is it shallow?

f Does he speak English well? Very well?

D Phrases

Questions with *Which ...?*

Or do we go right?

Which way do we go?

Do we go left?

Which floor do you want?

2nd?

3rd?

4th? 5th?

Which way ...? = one of two ways

Which floor ...? = one of five floors

4 Complete the questions. Use **Which ...?** and a noun from the box.

house	train	leg	cinema	part	magazine

He broke his left leg and had to go to hospital.

a   *Which cinema*   is showing White River?

b   _____ is Sue arriving on?

c   _____ is for sale in John Street?

d   _____ of Australia is Perth in?

e   _____ did Paul break?

f   _____ is giving away a free CD?

FOR SALE
House with garage, 36 John Street

FREE CD!!
with this week's Music Maker

See you at the station at 4.30! Sue

ABC CINEMA
| White River | 18.00 |

PERTH Town in Western Australia.

Write in your language

Which way do we go now?

What kind of shoes do you want to buy?

How well do you know her?

96 Questions (1)

A Grammar — Object and subject questions

Links

object, subject ➡ RU6

Who …? What …?
➡ 95A

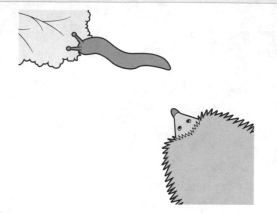

In many countries, slugs are a problem in gardens because they eat flowers and vegetables. Unfortunately, very few animals eat slugs because they taste terrible.

But one animal loves eating slugs – the hedgehog. An adult hedgehog can eat over 200 slugs in one night.

The story of the film *Who Loves You?* is very simple. Alex loves Sheila, a colleague at work. But Sheila loves Alex's brother Richard …

Q: What do slugs eat?
A: Flowers and vegetables.

Q: What eats slugs?
A: Hedgehogs.

Q: Who does Sheila love?
A: Richard.

Q: Who loves Sheila?
A: Alex.

Object questions
These questions are about the object of the sentence:

Slugs eat **flowers and vegetables**.	→	**What** do slugs eat?
Sheila loves **Richard**.	→	**Who** does Sheila love?

Subject questions
These questions are about the subject of the sentence:

Hedgehogs eat slugs.	→	**What** eats slugs?	NOT ~~What does eat slugs?~~
Alex loves Sheila.	→	**Who** loves Sheila?	

Links

How many …? ➡ 15

How much …? ➡ 14

Which …? ➡ 95

1 Are these subject questions or object questions? Write S or O.

a Who came to the party? _____S_____

b What did you wear? _____O_____

c What books does she read? _____

d What did he say to you? _____

e What happened last night? _____

f Who are you taking to the party? _____

g How many people work for you? _____

h Who phoned just now? _____

i Which train do we want? _____

j How much money do you have? _____

2 Read this newspaper report, and write the questions in the correct order. (The answers are in brackets.)

a to the match came people how many?

How many people came to the match?

(32,000)

b goal the who first scored?

....

(Loroso)

c City did score many more how goals?

....

(Two)

d happened half time after what?

....

(Things started going badly)

e Kopf kicked who?

....

(Borossa)

f did the do what referee?

....

(He gave him a yellow card)

32,000 people came to the match between City and United. It was an exciting match from the beginning. After only 10 minutes, Loroso scored the first goal for City. City scored two more goals in the first half, making the score 3–0.

But after half time, things started going badly. Borossa kicked Kopf, and the referee gave him a yellow card.

B Grammar   Questions with prepositions

What are you looking at?

Who is she talking to?

You're looking at something. → What are you looking at?   NOT At what are you looking?
She's talking to someone. → Who is she talking to?

Links

something, someone ➲16

last week/night ➲5A

3 Reply to these remarks with a question.

a – They're waiting in the next room. (*for someone*) – *Who are they waiting for?*

b – I'm just writing an email. (*to someone*) – *Who are you writing to?*

c – Ssh! I'm thinking. (*about something*) – ....

d – My brother got married last week. (*to someone*) – ....

e – I'm going out tonight. (*with someone*) – ....

f – I need to talk to you. (*about something*) – ....

g – I played cards last night. (*with someone*) – ....

Write in your language

How many people came to the party?	
Who scored the first goal?	
What are you looking at?	

A Grammar — Short answers

Links

Have you (been)?
➔ 91C

Did you (arrive)? ➔ 86B

Are you + verb
+ -ing …? ➔ 82B

– Excuse me. Are you travelling to London?
– Yes, I am. Why?

– Can I ask you a few questions?
– Yes, you can.

– OK. Have you been to this airport before?
– Yes, I have. Several times.

– Did you arrive here by car?
– No, I didn't. I came by train.

– Are you travelling on business?
– No, I'm not.

Question	Answer	
Are you …?	Yes, I am.	No, I'm not.
Can I …?	Yes, you can.	No, you can't.
Have you …?	Yes, I have.	No, I haven't.
Did you …?	Yes, I did.	No, I didn't.

1 Here are some more short answers. Complete the table.

a Yes, we are.	No, _we aren't_ .	**f** Yes, _____ .	No, she wasn't.
b Yes, _he is_ .	No, he isn't.	**g** Yes, I can.	No, _____ .
c Yes, they do.	No, _____ .	**h** Yes, _____ .	No, it won't.
d Yes, I did.	No, _____ .	**i** Yes, I would.	No, _____ .
e Yes, _____ .	No, we haven't.	**j** Yes, _____ .	No, they weren't.

2 Complete the replies. Choose sentences from the table.

a – Have you got children? – _No, we haven't_ .

b – Do they like fish? – No, _____ .

c – Was she at home when you called? – No, _____ .

d – Would you like a biscuit? – Yes, _____ .

e – Can you swim? – No, _____ .

f – Did you know her well? – No, _____ .

g – Will you be at work tomorrow? – Yes, _____ .

3 Answer these questions about yourself. Write short answers.

a Do you live in a big city? _____

b Did you go out last night? _____

c Do people eat much rice in your
   country? _____

d Can you ski? _____

e Did it rain yesterday? _____

f Have you got a car? _____

g Are you married? _____

h Have you ever been to the USA?
   _____

Tag questions

Links

I've/I haven't +
past participle ➲ 90

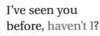 I've seen you before, haven't I?

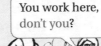 You work here, don't you?

 You don't work here, do you?

You aren't married, are you?

You work here, don't you? =
I think you work here (but I'm not sure).

You don't work here, do you? =
I think you *don't* work here (but I'm not sure).

To make tag questions, we add a question 'tag' to a sentence:

Positive

You're married, aren't you?
You work here, don't you?
I've seen you before, haven't I?

Negative

You aren't married, are you?
You don't work here, do you?
I haven't seen you before, have I?

After a positive sentence, add a negative tab.

After a negative sentence, add a positive tab.

4 Complete these tag questions.

a You're Eva, *aren't you* ?

b You don't work here, _____?

c I know your husband, _____?

d He works in the London office,
_____?

e You've got two children, _____?

f I've met one of them, _____?

g They're both at university, _____?

h Your daughter is studying Chinese,
_____?

i It's a difficult language, _____?

j You haven't got a drink, _____?

Tag questions: making conversation

Link

conversation ➲ 55

We often use tag questions to 'make conversation':

It's a lovely day, isn't it?

= I think it's a lovely day.

The food isn't very good, is it?

= I don't think the food is good.

5 Find **two** sentences to go with each picture. Add question tags at the end of each sentence.

a The music isn't very good, *is it* ? _3_

b It was a good film, _____? _____

c It's crowded in here, _____? _____

d The water isn't very warm, _____? _____

e The actors were good, _____? _____

f It's a lovely day, _____? _____

Write in your language

– Did you come by car? – Yes, I did.	
I don't know you, do I?	
It's a lovely day, isn't it?	

98 and, but, so …

A Grammar — and, but, or

Link

near, a long way
from   ➲12A

There are two good hotels in Starigrad: you can stay at the Carlton or you could try the Windsor.
The Windsor is just by the river and it's near the Old Town. The Carlton is quite near the railway station but it's a long way from the Old Town.

Links

several, lots of   ➲15A
millions of   ➲1C
for (a week)   ➲7

1 Here are some more sentences about Starigrad. Write **and**, **but** or **or** in the gaps.

a Only 250,000 people live in Starigrad, <u>but</u> millions of tourists go there every summer.

b You can get to the Old Town by bus _____ you can take a taxi.

c In the Old Town there's a 15th century castle _____ several beautiful churches.

d You can walk through the Old Town _____ you can't drive your car there.

e The town centre has some very nice shops _____ there are lots of restaurants and cafés.

f Most tourists only stay for one _____ two nights, _____ some people stay for more than a week.

B Grammar — also, too, as well

 THE NEW EXTET   ✳ printer   ✳ photocopier   ✳ scanner

The Extet is a printer and it's *also* a photocopier.
The Extet is a printer and photocopier, and it *also* scans pictures.
The Extet is a printer and photocopier, and it scans pictures *too*.
The Extet is a printer and photocopier, and it's a scanner *as well*.

also comes

| – after the verb *be*: | … it's also a photocopier |
| – before a main verb: | … it also scans pictures |

too and *as well* come at the end:

| … it scans pictures too. |
| … it's a scanner as well. |

2 Correct these sentences. Write **also**, **too** or **as well** in the correct places.

a I'm a student, but I work <del>as well</del> in a café _∧.   *as well*

b They live in London and they have also a house in the country .

c I watch TV a lot , but I as well enjoy reading .

d It rains a lot in the winter , and it also is windy .

e She works all day and she sometimes works too in the evenings .

C Grammar — *so, because, as*

Compare these sentences:

	A	B
	Our room was at the front of the hotel,	so it was very noisy.

`A,` `so` `B`

	A	B
As	our room was at the front of the hotel,	it was very noisy.
Because		

`As` `A,` `B`
`Because`

	B	A
	Our room was very noisy	because it was at the front of the hotel.

`B` `because` `A`

3 Write these sentences in a different way, using the word in brackets.

a They've got a large garden, so they can grow vegetables. (as)

As they've got a large garden, they can grow vegetables.

b As my new printer didn't work, I took it back to the shop. (because)

....

c I speak Spanish fluently because I studied it at university. (so)

....

d They didn't see the traffic lights because they were talking. (so)

....

e The room's nice and cool because it faces north. (as)

....

f I was in the garden, so I didn't hear the phone. (because)

....

D Grammar — *so that*

Why are you leaving your job?

I want to spend more time with my family.

MINISTER LEAVES

Government minister Robin Smith is leaving his job so that he can spend more time with his family, he told reporters yesterday.

Link

should, ought to ➲ 75C

4 Complete these sentences with **so that** and phrases from the box.

a Let's get to the cinema by 7.00 *so that we can get tickets* .

b They're buying a flat in town ....

c He's joining a sports club ....

d You should lock your bike ....

e You ought to take an umbrella ....

f I'll take my mobile ....

you can text me
he can meet new people
you don't get wet
✓ we can get tickets
they'll be nearer the shops
no-one steals it

Write in your language

The room faces north, so it's quite cold.	
As it was late, we decided to go home.	
Give me a cloth so that I can clean the table.	

205

A Grammar — *who, which, where*

Link

architect, pilot ⟳42

> **architect** (n.) a person who designs buildings.

> **newsagent's** (n.) a shop which sells newspapers.

> **wardrobe** (n.) a large cupboard where you keep clothes.

(= An architect is a person. He/She designs buildings.)

(= A newsagent's is a shop. It sells newspapers.)

(= A wardrobe is a large cupboard. You keep clothes there.)

The parts in blue are relative clauses. They begin with:

who (for people)

which (for things)

where (for places)

> We can also use that for people and things:
> a person that designs buildings.
> a shop that sells newspapers.

1 What are these people, things and places? Complete the sentences with phrases from the box. Add **who**, **which**, **that** or **where**.

  a A microwave is an oven _which cooks food quickly_ .

  b A pilot is a man or woman _____ .

  c Neighbours are people _____ .

  d A hurricane is a strong wind _____ .

  e An art gallery is a building _____ .

  f Nokia is a company _____ .

  g A library is a place _____ .

> can destroy buildings
> live next door to you
> makes mobile phones
> ✓cooks food quickly
> you can look at paintings
> flies planes
> you can borrow books

B Grammar — Subject and object relative clauses

Link

subject, object ⟳RU6

> These are some friends who came with us ...

(= they came with us)

> ... and this is a dog that followed us.

(= it followed us)

> These are some people (who) we met ...

(= we met them)

> ... and this is an old castle (which) we visited.

(= we visited it)

These are subject relative clauses.

We can say:

some friends	who / that	came with us

a dog	which / that	followed us

These are object relative clauses.

We can say:

some people	who we met / that we met / we met	NOT ~~who we met them~~

an old castle	which we visited / that we visited / we visited	NOT ~~that we visited it~~

2 These sentences all have mistakes. Write them correctly, using relative clauses.

a You can see the house we stayed there. _You can see the house where we stayed._

b This is a photo of a man I met him at a party. _____

c This is the car which I used to drive it. _____

d We found a beach who had a lovely little café. _____

e Is that the woman lives next door? _____

f There's a boat which it leaves every morning. _____

C Grammar — Giving more information

Notice how we can join these sentences:

Links

go to see, visit ➲43C

was/were (built) ➲94

THINGS TO DO IN EGYPT

Go to Luxor and visit the tomb of Tutankhamun. He died in 3500 BC.

➡ **1** Go to Luxor, and visit the tomb of Tutankhamun, who died in 3500 BC.

See the Pyramids at Giza, near Cairo. They were built in 4000 BC.

➡ **2** See the Pyramids at Giza, near Cairo, which were built in 4000 BC.

Visit Ismailiya. You can sit there and watch the ships on the Suez Canal.

➡ **3** Visit Ismailiya, where you can sit and watch the ships on the Suez Canal.

These relative clauses just give more information. We write a comma (,) before *who*, *which* or *where*.

Link

century ➲2C

3 Here are some more sentences about Egypt. Complete them with relative clauses.

a In Cairo you can visit the tomb of President Nasser, _who died in 1972._
He died in 1972.

b In Cairo there are large street markets, _____ .
You can buy carpets and jewellery there.

c The Suez Canal, _____ , is used by 50 ships every day.
It was built in the 19th century.

d The Sakkara Pyramid, _____ _____ , is about 30 km south of Cairo.
It is one of the oldest pyramids.

e In the summer, many people go to Alexandria, _____ .
It is cooler there.

f In Memphis, there is a statue of Rameses II, _____ .
He lived in the 13th century BC.

Write in your language

This is a family we met on holiday.	
Are those the people who live next door?	
Cairo, which is the capital, is on the Nile.	

100 *before, after …*

A Grammar — *and, then, after that*

Link
went, bought, had
➲ 85B

I went into town.
I bought some shoes.

I went to a café.
I had some lunch.

We can join these ideas in two sentences:

I went into town and bought some shoes.
Then
After that, I went to a café and had some lunch.

or in one sentence:

I went into town and bought some shoes, and then I went to a café and had some lunch.

Link
turned on, online ➲ 53

1 Put these ideas in the best order. Join them using **and**, **then**, and **after that**.

a I started reading the paper. I bought a ticket. I got to the station. I went onto the platform.

I got to the station and

b Put it in the oven. Wait until it's hot. Take the pizza out of the box. Turn the oven on.

c He read his emails. He turned the computer on. He went online. He replied to one of them.

d She printed it out. She saved it. She took it to the meeting. She finished her report.

B Phrases — *… later*

Tutankhamun died in about 1,300 BC. His tomb was discovered by Howard Carter in 1922. ⇨ Tutankhamun died in about 1,300 BC. His tomb was discovered by Howard Carter over 3,000 years later.

Tutankhamun

Apollo 11

Neil Armstrong and Edwin Aldrin took off in Apollo 11 on 16th July, 1969. On July 20th, they landed on the Moon. ⇨ Neil Armstrong and Edwin Aldrin took off in Apollo 11 on 16th July, 1969. Four days later, they landed on the Moon.

…	minutes hours days	later		…	weeks months years	later

2 Complete the sentences. Use phrases from the table.

a The plane left Istanbul at 2.00, and arrived in Cairo _3 hours later_ . (at 5.00)

b They got married in 1990, and _____ they had their first child. (in 1994)

c She phoned me at 4.00, and she phoned again _____ . (at 4.20)

d She left university in July. _____, she got a job with IBM. (in October)

e They met on February 14th, and got engaged _____ . (on February 28th)

f The picture was painted in 1886. _____, it was sold for £2 million. (In 1986)

C Grammar · *before, after*

Neil Armstrong and Edwin Aldrin landed on the Moon on July 20th, 1969. After putting on spacesuits, they opened the door and climbed down the steps onto the Moon.

They put on spacesuits. Then they opened the door.

⟹ After putting on / After they put on spacesuits, they opened the door.

⟹ Before opening / Before they opened the door, they put on spacesuits.

before/after + -*ing*

before after	putting … opening … going …

before/after + past simple tense

before after	they	put … opened … went …

3 Before or after? Write sentences with **before/after** + **-ing** or **before/after** + past simple tense.

a we paid the bill – we left the restaurant
   After paying the bill, we left the restaurant.

b she went out – she turned off all the lights
   Before

c he got dressed – he had a shower

d I saw a documentary about chicken farms – I decided to stop eating meat

e he took his driving test five times – he passed it

Write in your language

I read my emails, and then I wrote a letter.	
I met them again five years later.	
After turning the lights off, she went out.	

Reference units

Phrasal verbs

What is a phrasal verb?

A phrasal verb (or two-word verb) has two parts: 1 a verb (get, go, sit ...)
                                                  2 a small word (up, on, off ...)

```
 1    2
wake up:   I always wake up at 7.30.
 1    2
sit down:   We all sat down and started eating.
```

Common phrasal verbs:

get on/off	stand up	wake up	go away
get in/out	sit down	get up	drive away/off
go in/out	lie down	(➲43)	take off
come in/out	(➲59)		(➲59)
(➲57, 59)			
grow up	start up		
(➲45)	shut down		
	print out		
	(➲53A)		

1 Complete the sentences.

  a 'Come _in_ and sit _____,' he said.
  b I grew _____ in the country, but then we moved to a large city.
  c I woke _____ at 6.00, got _____ quickly, had breakfast, and went _____ .
  d Hurry _____! We'll be late.
  e The front door opened. Two people came _____, got _____ a car, and drove _____ .

Phrasal verbs with an object

Look at the sentences. These phrasal verbs have a *noun* after them (an object).

switch on: He switched on *the light*.
take off: Take off *your coat*.
throw away: I think I'll throw away *these old shoes*.

We can also say:

              He switched *the light* on.
              Take *your coat* off.
              I think I'll throw *these old shoes* away.

Common verbs:

turn ... up/down	try ... on	throw .... away	pick ... up
turn ... on/off	put ... on	give ... away	put ... down
switch ... on/off	(➲ 51)	(➲ 58)	(➲ 60)
(➲ 34)			

2 You can write these sentences in two ways. Add the missing sentences.

	A	B
a	Take off your shoes.	_Take your shoes off._
b	_She tried on the dress._	She tried the dress on.
c	Why don't you turn on the TV?	
d		Let's throw these magazines away.
e		She gave all her money away.
f	Put on a coat – it's cold.	
g	Could you turn down the music?	

C Phrasal verbs with pronouns

Phrasal verb + noun
Take off your coat.
or   →
Take your coat off.

Phrasal verb + pronoun
Take it off.

(NOT ~~Take off it.~~)

I'll throw away these old shoes.
or   →
I'll throw these old shoes away.

I'll throw them away.

(NOT ~~I'll throw away them.~~)

Object pronouns
me
you
him
her
it
us
them

3 Write the words in brackets in the correct order.

a Your jacket is on the floor. (up/it/could/pick/you) _Could you pick it up?_

b Those jeans look nice. (try/going/them/I'm/on/to) ....

c I need those bags. (away/don't/throw/them) ....

d There's no hot water. (I/to/switch/forgot/on/it) ....

e Your shoes are dirty. (off/them/take/you/can?) ....

f I can't hear the music. (turn/it/you/a bit/can/up?) ....

Write in your language

He took off his coat and sat down.

Hurry up! We'll be late.

Could you switch the light on?

2 Infinitives

A What is an infinitive?

Look at the dialogues. The verbs in blue are all **infinitive** forms.

The infinitive looks like the present simple, but it doesn't change its form:

Infinitive	Present simple
have	I have, he has
come	I come, she comes

With the verb *be*, the infinitive and present simple are different:

Infinitive	Present simple
be	I am, he is

– I didn't see you at the party last night.
– No, I couldn't come. I had to finish some work. Was it good?
– It was all right, but I didn't know many people there.

– We're going to play basketball this afternoon. Do you want to come?
– I'd like to play, but I'm not sure if I'm free. Can I phone you later?

1 What is the infinitive form of the verbs in *italics*?

a She *gets* up at 7.00 and *makes* coffee, and then she *has* breakfast. _get up_ , _____ , _____

b Last year I *went* to Malaysia. We *enjoyed* it, but it *was* very hot. _____ , _____ , _____

c They *live* in the country, but their son *studies* in London, so he *comes* home at weekends. _____ , _____ , _____

d He *ate* three burgers, *drank* two cans of lemonade, and then *had* an ice-cream. _____ , _____ , _____

B Using infinitives

Links

Do you …?	⮕81B
She doesn't	⮕81A
We didn't	⮕86A

Links

going to	⮕79A
I'd like to	⮕67C
have to	⮕72C

Link

⮕RU5 **Modal verbs**

We use infinitives:

1 After *do*, *does*, and *did*, in negatives and questions:

Do you play chess?

She doesn't live here any more.

We didn't go swimming – the water was too cold.

2 After *to*:

We're going to play basketball this afternoon.

I'd like to be a lorry driver when I grow up.

College starts at 8.00, so I have to get up at 6.30.

Spanish is quite easy to learn.

Is there anything to eat?

3 After these verbs:

can	will	shall	may	must
could	would	should	might	

These are called **modal verbs**. After them, we use an infinitive without *to*.

I can swim.   (NOT I can to swim)

I couldn't come to the party.

You must be hungry.

Would you open the door, please?

2 Circle the infinitive forms.

a We must (be) at the station at 7.00.

b I'll phone you if I can't be there.

c Why didn't you tell me that they're going to get married?

d I want to learn Spanish, so I'm going to live in Barcelona for a month.

e If you've got a temperature, you should drink plenty of water.

f I saw him at the meeting, but I didn't speak to him.

C Verb + *to* + infinitive

Some common verbs with *to* + infinitive:

want to	Wait a minute. I just want to have a quick shower.
would like to	We'd like to pay the bill, please.
have to	She has to work in the evenings to earn enough money.
(I'm) going to	We're going to play badminton this afternoon.
try to	I tried to learn Russian, but it was very difficult.
decide to	We've decided to get married.
tell (someone) to	I told you to wake me in the morning.
ask (someone) to	The neighbours asked us to look after their plants.
offer to	He offered to do the washing up.

Links

would like to	➜67C
have to	➜72C
going to	➜79
decide to	➜77B
offer to	➜74B

3 Choose the correct form in each sentence.

a Do you want *see* / *to see* my holiday photos?

b Sorry. I can't *give* / *to give* you any more money.

c We were at school together, but I didn't *know* / *knew* him well.

d Did you *went* / *go* anywhere interesting last night?

e Would you like *to see* / *seeing* the menu?

f You must *thank* / *to thank* them for the present.

Write in your language

They asked me to buy some bread.	
I tried to phone you, but you weren't at home.	
I'd like to get up early tomorrow.	

-ing forms

What are *-ing* forms?

In English we often add *-ing* to the verb. Look at these examples:

We're staying with friends at the weekend.

An old man was sitting in the corner, reading a newspaper.

Do you like living in Egypt?

Stop talking and listen to me!

We make *-ing* forms like this:

Verb	*-ing* form
stay	staying
talk	talking
wait	waiting
write	writing
live	living
sit	sitting
swim	swimming
lie	lying
die	dying

1 Most verbs: add *-ing*

2 Verbs that end in consonant + *-e*
(*-te, -se, -ne, -me* ...): ~~e~~ + -ing   NOT ~~writeing~~

3 Verbs with a short vowel:
t → tt, m → mm, b → bb ...   NOT ~~siting~~

4 Verbs that end in *-ie*: *-ie → -y* + *-ing*   NOT ~~lieing~~

---

1 Add **-ing** to these verbs:

try   *trying*   smile   ....   give   ....

take   ....   do   ....   get   ....

buy   ....   hit   ....   speak   ....

Using *-ing* forms

Links

present continuous
⮕82

past continuous
⮕87, 88

We use *-ing* forms in two main ways:

1 In **continuous tenses**:

Present continuous: *am/is/are* + verb + *-ing*

She's staying with friends in Italy.

Are you going to the match on Saturday?

Past continuous: *was/were* + verb + *-ing*

People were singing in the street.

I was driving to work when I heard the news.

Links

after + verb + -ing
⮕100

good at + verb + -ing
⮕73C

2 When we use the verb **like a noun**. Compare these sentences:

Noun	**Verb + *-ing***
I like the rain.	I like walking in the rain.
Golf is an expensive sport.	Sailing is an expensive sport.
After breakfast, we went out.	After having breakfast, we went out.
She's good at English.	She's good at learning languages.

2 Are these -ing forms (1) part of a tense or (2) used like a noun? Write **1** or **2**.

a _2_ speaking   *Speaking* is easy, but I'm not very good at *listening*.
b .... listening
c .... climbing   He loves *climbing*. He climbed Mont Blanc while he
d .... staying   was *staying* in France last year.
e .... feeling   She's not *feeling* very well, so she's *lying* down in
f .... lying   her room.
g .... studying   He's *studying* maths and computer *programming* at
h .... programming   the university.

C   Verbs + *-ing* form

Links

like, love, hate, enjoy
➲67A

finish, stop, start, begin
➲65

remember, forget ➲69

Link

infinitives ➲RU2

We use *-ing* forms after these verbs:

like	I don't really like getting up early.
love	She loves watching old films on TV.
hate	I hate waiting at airports – it's so boring.
enjoy	Does he enjoy living alone?
finish	Here are your shirts. I've finished ironing them.
stop	Let's stop working now and have a rest.
give up	I really must give up smoking.

After these verbs, we can use an *-ing* form or *to* + infinitive:

start	*or*	It started raining. It started to rain.
begin	*or*	She took a pen and began writing. She took a pen and began to write.
remember		I remember living in Singapore as a child. (= in the past) I must remember to post this letter (= now; I mustn't forget)

3 Each sentence has one mistake. Correct it by adding **-ing** to a verb.

a You really should stop ~~eat~~ so much.   *eating*
b Ski is fun, but I can't do it very well.   ....
c The baby was cry all night, so I didn't sleep much.   ....
d I'll just finish eat, then I'll wash the dishes.   ....
e Sorry – this is a no smoke restaurant.   ....
f I don't remember see her here before.   ....

Write in your language

I love cooking, but I hate ironing.	
She gave up smoking last year.	
I hope it stops raining soon.	

Past participles

What is a past participle?

A **past participle** is a form of the verb:

He has gone to London.

They've finished the stadium.

These computers are made in Korea.

Verb		Past participle
go	→	gone
finish	→	finished
make	→	made

Forming past participles

Link

same, different 31

Regular verbs
The past participle is the same
as the past simple tense (verb + -*ed*):

Verb	Past simple	Past participle
finish	finished	finished
play	played	played
wait	waited	waited

Irregular verbs
Sometimes the past participle
is the same as the past simple tense:

Verb	Past simple	Past participle
make	made	made
put	put	put
say	said	said
lose	lost	lost

Sometimes it is different:

Verb	Past simple	Past participle
see	saw	seen
swim	swam	swum
come	came	come
go	went	gone
take	took	taken

1 Find the past participles and add them to the lists.

Verb	Past simple	Past participle
a speak	spoke	_spoken_
b give	gave	
c begin	began	
d get	got	
e wear	wore	
f have	had	
g buy	bought	
h write	wrote	
i be	was/were	

given	been
begun	worn
had	✓spoken
written	bought
got	

C   Using past participles

We use past participles in:

1 Present perfect tense: *have* + past participle
   They **have gone** to London.
   Have you **seen** the new film at the Film House?
   I **haven't finished** eating yet.

2 Passive sentences: *be* + past participle
   Coffee **is grown** in Colombia.
   These shoes **were made** in Poland.
   English **is spoken** all over the world.

2 Circle the past participles.

   a The rooms are (cleaned) and the clothes are (washed) every morning.

   b These hard disks are made in China, and they are sold all over the world.

   c I haven't been to Africa, but I've travelled a lot in Asia.

   d I haven't seen him. I think he's gone swimming.

   e They've arrived in London and they've just left the station.

   f I've lost my mobile. I think someone has taken it.

3 Add past participles. Use verbs from the box.

wear	go
make	see
lose	✓take
write	

   a You've _taken_ my dictionary – give it back!

   b This is a new coat. I haven't _____ it yet.

   c He's _____ his gloves. Have you _____ them?

   d *Hamlet* was _____ by Shakespeare.

   e That's a beautiful table. When was it _____?

   f Sorry, she isn't here. She's _____ out.

Write in your language

Have you finished yet?

They aren't here. They've gone to the cinema.

When was this book written?

Modal verbs

What is a modal verb?

The verbs in the box are called **modal verbs**. They usually come before another verb:

> I can swim.
> It might rain tomorrow.

After modal verbs, we use the infinitive without *to*:

> I can speak English.   NOT ~~I can to speak~~ …

> We must go home now.   NOT ~~We must to go~~ …

can	could
will	would
shall	should
may	might
must	

Forming modal verbs

Positive sentences

All the forms are the same.

I You He/She We They	must can should	go home now.

NOT ~~He musts, She cans~~

Negative sentences

Add not (or n't) after the modal verb.

Positive	**Negative**
You should tell her.	You shouldn't tell her.
It might rain tomorrow.	It might not rain tomorrow.

Questions

Change the word order.

Sentence	**Question**
He can swim.	Can he swim?
It will rain tomorrow.	Will it rain tomorrow?

Negative forms	
Long	**Short**
cannot	can't
could not	couldn't
will not	won't
would not	wouldn't
should not	shouldn't
must not	mustn't
may not	–
might not	–

1 Write the words in the correct order.

  a Japanese I speak can't .   <u>I can't speak Japanese.</u>

  b me will tomorrow phone you ?   ....

  c up get tomorrow early must I .   ...

  d water have I some can ?   ....

  e home they might at be not .   ...

2 Correct these sentences.

a The train will arriving soon.   _The train will arrive soon._

b Would you to like a drink?

c You don't should work so hard.

d Can I to help you?

e Did you can swim when you were a child?

C

Using modal verbs

Examples of modal verbs in this book:

can	She can play the piano, but she can't sing very well.	(➡73)
	Can I carry your suitcase?	(➡74)
could	I could read when I was four.	(➡73)
	Could you open the window, please?	(➡74)
will	Will the shops be open tomorrow?	(➡78)
	I think I'll have a cup of tea.	(➡77)
would	Would you stop talking, please?	(➡74)
	Would you like something to eat?	(➡74)
	He would see you if he wasn't so busy.	(➡80)
shall	Where shall we go this evening?	(➡75)
should	You look tired. You should go to bed.	(➡75)
may	I may be a bit late for the meeting.	(➡71)
might	I don't know where he is. He might be at home.	(➡71)
must	I really must go now. It's late.	(➡72)

3 Test yourself. Cover the sentences. What verbs go in the gaps?

a I don't know where he is. He _might_ be at home.

b _____ you like something to eat?

c I really _____ go now. It's late.

d She _____ play the piano, but she _____ sing very well.

e _____ the shops be open tomorrow?

f You look tired. You _____ go to bed.

g I _____ read when I was four.

h _____ you open the window, please?

Write in your language

I must talk to you. Can I phone you tonight?

It was dark, so I couldn't see very well.

The train might be a bit late.

Subject, verb, object

What is a subject?

English sentences always have a subject and a verb:

SUBJECT   VERB
| Kangaroos | live in Australia.

    SUBJECT   VERB
| The train from London | is late.

   SUBJECT   VERB
| His brother | is studying medicine at London University.

SUBJECT   VERB
| They | arrived last night.

The subject can be

– a noun (kangaroos)
– a noun phrase (the train from London, his brother)
– a pronoun (they)

> The subject tells us who or what:
> – What is late?
> (The train from London.)
> – Who is studying
> medicine?
> (His brother.)

1 Find the **subject** and **verb** in these sentences. Circle the subject, and underline the verb.

a (Shakespeare) died in 1616.

b I start work at 7.00 in the morning.

c The people in the next flat are having a party.

d The President of the USA is flying to Moscow tomorrow.

e His sister lives in Canada.

f Too much coffee is very bad for you.

What is an object?

Sometimes (but not always) there is also an object after the verb.

SUBJECT   VERB   OBJECT
| The flat | has | three rooms and a balcony |.

   SUBJECT   VERB   OBJECT
| His brother | is studying | medicine | at London University.

SUBJECT   VERB   OBJECT
| We | will see | you | tomorrow.

SUBJECT   VERB
| They | arrived last night. *(no object)*

The object can be
– a noun (medicine)
– a noun phrase (three rooms and a balcony)
– a pronoun (you)

> The object also tells us who or what:
> – What does the flat have?
> (Three rooms and a
> balcony.)
> – What is he studying?
> (Medicine.)

2 Which sentences have an object? Write **No**, or circle the object.

a I love (chocolate ice-cream.)

b The bus is leaving at 6.00. No.

c They've got six children.

d I usually get up late at the weekend.

e Do you smoke?

f The children are watching TV.

g Have you seen John?

C Verbs with two objects

Some verbs have two objects: a person and a thing. Look at these examples:

Verb + thing + *to* + person
I gave this CD to my brother.
I gave it to my brother.
I gave it to him.

Verb + person + thing
I gave my brother a CD.
I gave him a CD.

NOT ~~I gave to my brother a CD.~~

NOT ~~I gave to him a CD.~~

We can use these verbs in the same way:

Present	Past		Present	Past		Present	Past
send	sent (➜53)		pay	paid (➜47)		show	showed
sell	sold (➜47)		take	took (➜56A)		tell	told (➜55)
lend	lent (➜47)		offer	offered (➜74)		read	read

After *get*, *buy* and *make*, we use *for* (not *to*):

Verb + thing + for + person
I'll buy a present for John.
I've made a cake for my mother.

Verb + person + thing
I'll buy John a present.
I've made my mother a cake.

3 Are these sentences correct? Write **Ok** or add **to** or **for** if necessary.

a I've lent my car to a friend.

b I must show you my holiday photos. Ok

c I think I'll send a postcard my sister.

d Shall I buy some food you?

e He pays his secretary $1000 a week.

f I usually read a story the children before they go to bed.

g Excuse me – can you tell me the time?

Write in your language

Shall we buy her a present?	
I'll show you where they live.	
I'm giving this book to my father.	

7 Phrases with prepositions

A   What is a preposition?

Look at the examples. The words in blue are all prepositions. Prepositions come before nouns, pronouns or noun phrases.

We often use prepositions:

– to say when or how long:
  in the summer, on Tuesday, for 5 days, since September
  (➜2, 4, 5, 7, 8)

– to say where or where to:
  in London, to the station, under the tree, behind you,
  past our house (➜22, 23)

– to say how:
  with a sharp knife, by bus, without a coat (➜24, 40)

> I'm going to London in September.
>
> Your bag is under the table by the front door.
>
> We stayed with friends in France for a few days.
>
> I bought a packet of biscuits for the children.
>
> I'm reading an interesting book about Egypt.

1   Circle the prepositions. (There are **three** in each sentence).

   a   Are you coming (with) us to the theatre on Tuesday?

   b   The post office is quite near my office – it's in the next street, opposite the cinema.

   c   We're staying at the Hilltop Hotel in Tokyo for a week.

   d   Go across the river and up the hill, and you'll see it on the left.

B   Verb + preposition

Some verbs are followed by a preposition. Look at these examples:

They arrived.	They arrived at the station.	NOT ~~They arrived the station~~
Listen!	Listen to me!	
I'm waiting.	I'm waiting for the bus.	

Common verbs with prepositions:

look at	arrive at	get in(to) (a car)	talk
listen to	get to	get out of (a car)	chat to (someone)
look for	get on (a bus)	move to	argue about (something)
search for	get off (a bus)	(➜45, 57)	write
(➜42, 61)			(➜55)

spend … on	belong to	(➜20)	taste of (➜62)
pay for	worry about	(➜29)	smell of (➜62)
apply for	know about	(➜68)	
look after	break into	(➜50)	live in/at (a place)
work in/for	help … with	(➜74)	stay with (someone)
(➜39, 42, 47)			(➜43, 45)

2 Match the phrases on the left with those on the right, and add a preposition.

a	My neighbour and I were chatting	....	the 6 o'clock news.
b	I'm going to apply	....	a new flat.
c	Before going out, I listened	....	my grandmother.
d	We've decided to move	_about_	the weather.
e	The train is arriving	....	a job in a bank.
f	This coat used to belong	....	Platform 16.

3 Add prepositions to these sentences.

a How much did you pay _for_ those shoes?

b I don't know much .... art.

c She comes to their flat every morning to look .... the children.

d Can I help you .... anything?

e My cousin is staying .... us at the moment.

f Don't worry .... the children – I'm sure they'll be OK.

g Look .... this table. It's really beautiful.

C   Adjective + preposition

Some adjectives in English are followed by a preposition. Look at these examples:

He's interested in old films.

I'm quite good at English.

I'm very sorry about last night.

Common adjectives with prepositions:

Feelings:	**Others:**	
worried about	late for	(➔4)
keen on	(not) far from	(➔12)
interested in	good at	(➔73)
frightened of	similar to	(➔31)
afraid of	different from	(➔31)
sorry about	full of	(➔25)
(➔46, 76)		

4 Complete the sentences with an adjective + preposition from the box.

a Let's go, or we'll be _late for_ the meeting.

b He's very .... jazz. He's got about 50 jazz CDs at home.

c I'm really .... your mother. I hear she's in hospital.

d The dog won't hurt you. You don't need to be .... it.

e My sister is quite .... me. We both enjoy the same things.

f He's very .... chess. He always beats me.

Write in your language

He's very keen on football, but he isn't very good at it.	
I'm quite worried about her. Will you talk to her?	
I'll stay in the car and wait for you.	

Irregular verb list

Infinitive	Simple past	Past participle	Infinitive	Simple past	Past participle
be	was/were	been	lie	lay	lain
beat	beat	beat	lose	lost	lost
become	became	become	make	made	made
begin	began	begun	meet	met	met
break	broke	broken	pay	paid	paid
bring	brought	brought	put	put	put
build	built	built	read	read	read
burn	burnt	burnt	ride	rode	ridden
buy	bought	bought	ring	rang	rung
can	could	been able	run	run	run
catch	caught	caught	say	said	said
come	came	come	see	saw	seen
cost	cost	cost	sell	sold	sold
cut	cut	cut	send	sent	sent
do	did	done	shine	shone	shone
drink	drank	drunk	shoot	shot	shot
drive	drove	driven	show	showed	shown
eat	ate	eaten	shut	shut	shut
fall	fell	fallen	sit	sat	sat
feel	felt	felt	sleep	slept	slept
find	found	found	smell	smelt	smelt
get	got	got	speak	spoke	spoken
give	gave	given	spend	spent	spent
go	went	gone (been)	stand	stood	stood
grow	grew	grown	steal	stole	stolen
have	had	had	swim	swam	swum
hear	heard	heard	take	took	taken
hit	hit	hit	teach	taught	taught
hold	held	held	tell	told	told
hurt	hurt	hurt	think	thought	thought
keep	kept	kept	throw	threw	thrown
know	knew	known	understand	understood	understood
learn	learnt	learnt	wake	woke	woken
leave	left	left	wear	wore	worn
lend	lent	lent	win	won	won
let	let	let	write	wrote	written

Verb tables

Present

Positive

Full form
I am
You are
He/She is
It is
We are
They are

Short form
I'm
You're
He's/She's
It's
We're
They're

Negative

I'm not	–
You're not	You aren't
He's/She's not	He/She isn't
It's not or	It isn't
We're not	We aren't
They're not	They aren't

Questions and short answers

Am I	
Are you	
Is he/she/it	...?
Are we	
Are they	

	I am.
	you are.
Yes,	he/she/it is.
	we are.
	they are.

	I'm not.
	you aren't.
No,	he/she/it isn't.
	we aren't.
	they aren't.

Wh- questions

	am I?
	are you?
Where	is he/she/it?
	are we?
	are they?

Past

Positive

I was
You were
He/She/It was
We were
They were

Negative

I wasn't
You weren't
He/She/It wasn't
We weren't
They weren't

Questions and short answers

Was I	
Were you	
Was he/she/it	...?
Were we	
Were they	

	I was.
	You were.
Yes,	he/she/it was.
	we were.
	they were.

	I wasn't.
	you weren't.
No,	he/she/it wasn't.
	we weren't.
	they weren't.

Wh- questions

	was I?
	were you?
Where	was he/she/it?
	were we?
	were they?

Positive

Present	There is (There's)	a shop.
Past	There was	a man in the room.

Present	There are	lots of shops.
Past	There were	two men in the room.

Negative

There isn't	a shop.
There wasn't	a man in the room.

There aren't	any shops.
There weren't	any people in the room.

Questions and short answers

Is Was	there a shop near here?

Yes, there	is. was.
No, there	isn't. wasn't.

Wh- questions

How much money	is was	there?

Are Were	there any men in the room?

Yes, there	are. were.
No, there	aren't. weren't.

How many people	are were	there?

Present simple   Unit 81

Positive

I You We They	live go have

He She It	lives goes has

Negative

I You We They	don't	live go have

He She It	doesn't	live go have

Questions and short answers

Do	I you we they	live …? go …? have …?

Yes,	I you we they	do.

No,	I you we they	don't.

Does	he she it	live …? go …? have …?

Yes,	he she it	does.

No,	he she it	doesn't.

Wh- questions

Where do	I you we they	live?

Where does	he she it	live?

-s endings

Verb + -s		Verb + -es			-y → -ies			Irregular		
work	→ works	go	→	goes	study	→	studies	have	→	has
live	→ lives	watch	→	watches						

Present continuous & going to   Units 77, 78, 79, 82

Positive

I'm You're He's/She's/It's We're They're	eating

Negative

I'm not You aren't He/She isn't It isn't We aren't They aren't	eating

226

Questions and short answers

Am I		eating?
Are you		
Is he/she/it	eating?	
Are we		
Are they		

Yes,	I am.
	you are.
	he/she/it is.
	we are.
	they are.

No,	I'm not.
	you aren't.
	he/she/it isn't.
	we aren't.
	they aren't.

Wh- questions

What	am I	eating?
When	are you	
	is he/she/it	
	are we	
	are they	

-ing forms

+ *-ing*			e + *-ing*			+ consonant + *-ing*		
listen	→	listening	write	→	writing	sit	→	sitting
go	→	going	come	→	coming	swim	→	swimming
do	→	doing	have	→	having	run	→	running

NOTE: *going to* is a form of the present continuous, e.g. *I'm going to see him. They aren't going to come. Are you going to stay for dinner? What are we going to do?*

Past simple Units 85, 86

Positive

I	
You	watched
He/She/It	saw
We	went
They	

Negative

I		watch
You		
He/She/It	didn't	see
We		go
They		

Questions and short answers

	I	
	you	watch ?
Did	he/she/it	see ?
	we	go ?
	they	

Yes,	I	did.
	you	
	he/she/it	
No,	we	didn't.
	they	

Wh- questions

What	did I	watch?
	did you	
	did he/she/it	
Where	did we	go?
	did they	

Past forms: Regular verbs

Verb + *-ed*	Verb + *-d*	-y → *-ied*	+ consonant + *-ed*
watch → watched	live → lived	carry → carried	stop → stopped
play → played	close → closed	try → tried	chat → chatted

For irregular verbs, see page 224.

Past continuous Units 87, 88

Positive

I was	
You were	
He/She/It was	going
We were	
They were	

Negative

I wasn't	
You weren't	
He/She/It wasn't	going
We weren't	
They weren't	

Questions and short answers

Was I						
Were you						
Was he/she/it	going?	Yes,	I was. you were. he/she/it was. we were. they were.	No,	I wasn't. you weren't. he/she/it wasn't. we weren't. they weren't.	
Were we						
Were they						

Wh- questions

Where	was I were you was he/she/it were we were they	going?

Passive forms   Units 93, 94

Present passive: *is* or *are* + past participle (See RU4)
Past passive: *was* or *were* + past participle (See RU4)

	Positive			Negative		
Present Past	The floor	is was	cleaned.	The floor	isn't wasn't	cleaned.
Present Past	The doors	are were	locked.	The doors	aren't weren't	locked.

QUESTION FORMS: See the verb *be* (page 225).

Present perfect tense   Units 90, 91, 92

Present perfect: *have* or *has* + past participle (See RU4)

Positive

Full form			Short form	
I have You have He/She/It has We have They have	watched gone got		I've You've He's/She's/It's We've They've	watched gone got

Negative

I haven't You haven't He/She/It hasn't We haven't They haven't	watched gone got

Questions and short answers

Have I Have you Has he/she/it Have we Have they	watched ...? gone ...? got ...?	Yes,	I have. he/she/it has. we have. they have.
		No,	I haven't. he/she/it hasn't. we haven't. they haven't.

Wh- questions

Where	have I have you	gone?
What	has he/she/it have we have they	got?

Past participle forms: Regular verbs

Verb + *-ed*	Verb + *-d*	-y → -ied	+ consonant + *-ed*
watch → watched	live → lived	carry → carried	stop → stopped
play → played	close → closed	try → tried	chat → chatted

For irregular verbs, see page 224.

will, *would* and other modal verbs — Units 72, 73, 77, 78, 80, RU5

Positive

Full form		
I		
You		
He/she/it	will	go.
We	would	
They		

Short form: will	
I'll	
You'll	
He'll/She'll/It'll	go.
We'll	
They'll	

Short form: would	
I'd	
You'd	
He'd/She'd/It'd	go
We'd	
They'd	

Negative

I	will not	
You	won't	
He/She/It		go.
We	would not	
They	wouldn't	

Questions and short answers

	I	
	you	
Will	he/she/it	go?
Would	we	
	they	

Yes,	I	will.
	you	would.
	he/she/it	
No,	we	won't.
	they	wouldn't.

Wh- questions

		I	
		you	
Where	will	he/she/it	go?
	would	we	
		they	

NOTE: Other modal verbs (can, could, may, might, must, should ...) have similar forms: e.g. *It might rain*; *You mustn't tell them*; *Can I go? What should we do?* (See RU5)

Answer key

1 Numbers

1
b What's the temperature;
   5 degrees
c How big / What size;
   30 metres by 20 metres.
d How big / What size;
   90 square metres
e do … weigh?
   82 kilos / kilograms

2
b twenty-three per cent
c nought point seven per
   cent / zero point seven
   per cent
d half a kilo; a quarter of a
   glass
e two and a half kilos

3
Possible answers:
b exactly 62 kilometres per
   hour
   just over 60 kilometres per
   hour
c almost one metre
   a bit less than one metre
d exactly 8,850 metres
   nearly 9,000 metres

4
b Hundreds of planes
c Millions of / Billions of
   bacteria
d thousands of pounds
e Millions of people
f hundreds of emails

2 Years and centuries

1
b two thousand and four
c nineteen hundred and one
   / nineteen oh one
d sixteen hundred
e nineteen ninety-nine
f nineteen fourteen

2
b the seventeen twenties
c the eighteen seventies
d the nineteen thirties
e the nineteen sixties *or* the
   sixties
f the nineteen nineties *or* the
   nineties

3
b in the (nineteen) nineties
c in the (nineteen) twenties
d in the (nineteen) sixties
e in the eighteen thirties

4
b was invented in the (early)
   19th century
c were invented in the (late)
   18th century
d was invented in the (early)
   17th century
e was invented in the (early)
   20th century
f was invented in the (early)
   14th century

3 Age

1
b in his seventies
c in his forties
d in her thirties
e in her sixties
f in his eighties

2
Marco: 20
Riccardo: 13
Paula: 13
Roberto: 16

3
b older brothers; older sister
c years younger than
d younger than; older than
e older brother

5
b children; teenagers; adults
c A middle-aged woman
d teenagers
e children; babies

4 Time phrases (1)

1
b early   e on time
c early   f late
d in time

2
a on Monday; in the morning;
   at 9.00
b in April; by the end; on
   Friday
c at 6.30; in the afternoon; on
   Tuesday morning; by
   lunchtime

3
b … we won't get there
   till/until the evening
c … the meeting didn't start
   until/till 12.00
d … they didn't finish it
   till/until 2006
e … we won't see you until/till
   Monday
f … it won't open till/until
   next week

5 Time phrases (2)

1
b last   f next
c last   g this
d next   h next
e this

2
b tomorrow; in three days'
   time
c the day before yesterday;
   today
d yesterday
e four days ago; the day after
   tomorrow

3
Answers depend on current date.

6 already, just, only …

1
b already
c still
d yet
e already
f still
g yet

2
b I'm just about to get on the
   bus.
c I'm just having a (cup of)
   coffee.
d I've just bought some
   flowers.
e I've just had an accident.
f I'm just watching the news.

3
b She's only 30 …
c … it's only 9 o'clock.
d … she only works …
e Only 50 people …
f He only lives …

7 *How long?* (1): past and future

1
- b for 2 years
- c for 3 years
- d from 1998 to 2003
- e for 4 years

2
- b for
- c from
- d to/until
- e until
- f for
- g until
- h for
- i for
- j from
- k to / until

They can all meet on 26th April.

3
- b How long did you stay (there) (for)?
- c How long did you live there (for)?
- d How long is she staying (for)?
- e How long did you play (for)?
- f How long will you be there (for)?

8 *How long?* (2): up to now

1
- b I've known
- c I've had
- d she's been
- e We've had
- f He's lived (He's been)
- g he's worked (he's been)

2
b for	f since
c since	g since
d since	h for
e for	

4
- b How long has she been …
- c How long has she lived / been …
- d How long have they been …
- e How long have they worked …
- f How long have they been …

9 *always, usually …*

1
Possible answers:
- a I usually get up early.
- b I'm hardly ever tired in the morning.
- c I always leave the house by 7.30.
- d I'm never late for work.
- e I don't usually have a big lunch.
- f I sometimes go to bed early.
- g I'm not usually asleep by 10.30.

2
- b The curtains aren't often open.
- c They don't get letters very often.
- d I often see a green taxi outside the house.
- e The house is often empty in the winter. *or*
  In the winter, the house is often empty.
- f They don't often go into the garden.

3
Possible answers:
- b … I watch DVDs from time to time
- c … we meet for coffee occasionally
- d … I go swimming every now and then
- e … stir it with a spoon occasionally
- f … I go by car from time to time

10 *How often …?*

1
- b twice a day
- c four times a day
- d three times a year
- e once a week
- f twice a day

2
- b every two hours
- c every 76 years
- d every month
- e every morning
- f every 4 years

3
- b every three days
- c every two years
- d every Sunday / every week / every 7 days
- e every four hours
- f every 50 years

4
- b How often are there concerts?
- c How often do they clean the apartments?
- d How often is there a boat to the island?
- e How often do planes fly to Madrid?
- f How often does the postman come?

11 *How high …?*

1
- b narrow feet
- c thin glass
- d a wide river
- e a short piece of rope
- f a tall tree / a high tree
- g deep water
- h a high wall

2
- b short
- c narrow
- d low
- e thin
- f long

3
- a It's 1 metre high.
  It's 1.5 metres wide.
- b It's 2 metres long.
- c It's 100 metres long.
  It's 70 metres wide.
- d He's 1 metre tall.

4
- 2 How tall is
- 3 How high is
- 4 How long is
- 5 How tall is
- 6 How wide is

(Answers: 1c, 2b, 3c, 4a, 5a, 6b)

12 Distance
Possible answers:

1
- b a long way from
- c close to
- d a long way from
- e close to
- f close to
- g not far from

2
- b My house is 5 km from the town centre.
  It's about 20 minutes from the town centre by bus.
- c The station is 400 m from my office.
  It's about 10 minutes from my office on foot.
- d Moscow is 1000 km from Kiev.
  It's about 2 hours by aeroplane from Kiev.

3

Possible answers:

b How far is it to the car park?
c How far away is the station?
d How far away is the town centre?
e How far is it to the airport?

4

b Kalgoorlie
c Albany
d Mount Bruce
e Sydney
f Mount Bogong

13 Countable and uncountable nouns

1

b	U	f	U
c	C	g	U
d	U	h	C
e	U		

2

b a small coffee
c some paper
d glass
e hair
f wood

3

b slice, piece
c piece, bar
d litre, jug
e slice, loaf

4

b a piece of cheese
c loaves of bread
d pieces of wood
e a piece / kilo of meat
f slices of pineapple

14 How much …?

1

b A lot / Lots / Plenty
c A little / A bit
d A little / A bit
e A lot / Lots / Plenty
f A lot / Lots / Plenty

2

b We've got a lot of / lots of / plenty of rice.
c We've got a little / a bit of cheese.
d We've got a little / a bit of sugar.
e We've got a lot of / lots of / plenty of yoghurt.
f We've got a lot of / lots of / plenty of butter.

3

b people eat lots of sugar.
c people eat quite a lot of sugar.
d people don't eat much / a lot of rice.
e people eat very little sugar.
f people eat a lot of / lots of rice.
g people don't eat much / a lot of sugar.

4

b How much space
c How much water
d How much money
e How much petrol
f How much work

15 How many …?

1

b a few friends
c several different colours
d lots of people / a lot of people
e a lot of photos / lots of photos
f a few people

2

b Very few people live
c Quite a lot of people live
d A lot of / Lots of people live
e Very few people live
f Quite a lot of people live

3

b How many goals (2)
c How many languages (About 6,000)
d How many people (69,000)
e How many languages (500)
f How many bones (206)

16 someone, something …

1

b someone / somebody
c something
d somewhere.
e somewhere
f Someone / Somebody

2

b anywhere; 3
c anyone / anybody; 5
d anything; 1
e anyone / anybody; 6
f anyone / anybody; 2

3

b Nothing.
c None.
d Nowhere.
e No-one. / Nobody.
f Nothing.

4

b had no money
c didn't see anybody all day
d was nowhere to go
e had nobody to talk to
f weren't any videos to watch

17 every, all, the whole

1

b every country
c All the shops
d all the plates
e Every house
f all the newspapers
g all the books
h Every room

2

b We talked all night / the whole night.
c They stayed in London the whole week / all week.
d I'd love to stay in bed all morning / the whole morning.
e We spent the whole summer / all summer in Italy.
f He watched TV all afternoon / the whole afternoon.

3

b Everyone / Everybody
c everything
d Everything
e everywhere
f everybody / everyone
g everything

18 all, both, most, some …

1

b most
c Some of
d None of
e all
f most

2

b None of them are sitting.
c Some of them have glasses.
d Most of them have short hair.
e All of them are over 40.
f Some of them are smiling.

3

Mike's luggage: 1, 4
Irina's luggage: 3, 8

4

b All of us
c None of them
d Both of us
e Neither of them
f Neither of them

19 *other, another …*

1

c … any other books …
d … some other friends.
e … here's another picture …
f … he's got another brother …
g … my other friends …

2

b some more
c another
d another
e some more
f another
g some more

3

b someone else / somebody else
c somewhere else
d something else
e someone else / somebody else
f somewhere else

20 *mine, yours …*

1

a the coffee is mine.
the tea is Maria's.
b The Honda is his.
the VW is hers.
c better than ours.
Ours is bigger.
theirs is nearer the centre.

2

b They belonged to Princess Diana.
c It belongs to Bill Gates.
d They belong to Prince Charles.
e It belonged to Elvis Presley.
f They belonged to William Shakespeare.

3

b Whose cigars are these? *or*
Who do these cigars belong to?
c Whose earrings are these? *or*
Who do these earrings belong to?

d Whose book is this? *or*
Who does this book belong to?
e Whose key is this? *or*
Who does this key belong to?
f Whose ring is this? *or*
Who does this ring belong to?

21 *myself, my own …*

1

b introduce myself
c enjoyed ourselves
d looked at himself
e help yourself / help yourselves
f hurt herself

2

b ourselves
c yourself
d myself
e himself
f themselves

3

b their own car
c our own vegetables
d its own shower
e my own flat
f your own language

4

c without help
d alone
e alone
f without help

22 *at the front, in the middle*

1

b Florian
c Julia
d Jana
e Philip
f Friederike

2

Possible answers:

b on the left, and she's next to me.
c She's in the middle row, and she's behind Jana.
d He's on the right of the photo, and he's behind Philip.
e She's in front of Claudia, and she's beside Max.

3

b at the top of a building
c at the bottom of a page
d in the middle of a road
e at the side of a road
f in the middle of a field
g at the end of a corridor

4

b outside
c out of doors
d downstairs
e upstairs
f outside

23 Direction

1

b under
c round
d through
e into
f under
g out of
h towards
i past

2

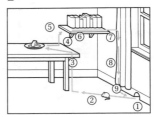

3

b across, under
c a river, a railway
d a hotel, a church
e up, down
f past, towards

4

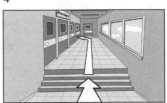

5

Possible answer:

… down the stairs. Then go along the corridor, past two doors, and you'll see a door in front of you. Go through the door, into a courtyard, and you'll come to a pond. Go round the pond and through a gate. Then go along a path, past some trees on your left, and you'll see a statue straight ahead. …

24 by, with, without

1
b It's a painting by / It was painted by Picasso.
c It's a book by / It was written by Lao Tse.
d It's a play by / It was written by Shakespeare.
e It's a book by / It was written by Tolstoy.
f It's a film by / It was made/directed by Kirosawa.

2
We went: by bus, by plane, by taxi;
Send it: by email, by post;
You can pay: by credit card

4
b with a sharp knife
c with a large spoon
d with soap and water
e with an old toothbrush
f with glue or sellotape

5
b without
c with
d without
e with; with
f without

25 Adjectives

1
b noisy, dangerous
c full, heavy
d light, dark
e difficult, slow
f dark, wet

2
b quite a big balcony
c a very small bathroom
d a really nice beach near the hotel
e a very interesting town
f quite a relaxing holiday

3
b such e so
c so   f so
d such

4
Possible answers:
b I thought it was difficult.
c I think it's very useful.
d I found it boring / difficult.
e I think it's really funny.
f I found it quite easy.

26 Adverbs

1
adj.: e, g, j
adv.: b, c, d, f, h, i

2
b fast, quietly
c clearly, beautifully
d safely, easily
e late, hard

3
b 3 Fortunately
c 5 Unfortunately
d 4 Eventually
e 1 Suddenly
f 6 Apparently

4
b … Fortunately, I had plenty of money …
c … suddenly a car came …
d … Naturally, it's very difficult …
e … unfortunately I didn't get it.
f … eventually, I started to enjoy

27 Comparatives

1
warm – warmer
short – shorter
easy – easier
difficult – more difficult
comfortable – more comfortable

2
Possible answers:
b … is cheaper, and it's easier
c … more expensive, but it's more comfortable
d … is more powerful, and it's faster

3
Possible answers:
b Have you got anything thinner?
c I need something smaller.
d Have you got anything lighter?
e I need something cheaper.
f Have you got anything bigger?

4
b Fewer
c fewer
d less
e fewer
f more

28 Superlatives

1
the youngest
the tallest
the shortest
the thinnest
the laziest
the fittest
the most intelligent
the most hard-working

3
b the longest river
c the hottest place
d the largest country
e the richest woman
f the largest / heaviest animal

5
a the most
b the least
c the fewest
d the most
e the most
f the most
g the fewest
h the least

29 too

1
a are too short
b is too big
 is too small
c is too high
 is too short / is too small
d is too low / is too small
 are too long

2
b He sleeps too much.
c She works too much.
d He eats too much.
e She spends too much.
f They cost too much.

3
a too much
b too much, too many, too much
c too many
d too many, too much

4
b … he talks too much.
c … there are always too many people there.
d … I've got too much work.
e They spend too much money …
f … it's too strong.
g … they paid too much …

30 enough

1
b He's hasn't got enough
c He's hasn't got enough
d He's got enough
e He's got enough
f He hasn't got enough

2
b enough food
c enough time
d enough chairs
e enough money
f enough films

3
b aren't old enough
c 'm not tall enough
d aren't strong enough
e isn't big enough
f isn't wide enough

4
a Nina
b Anna
c Rose
e Nina is old enough to leave school.
f Anna isn't old enough to buy fireworks.
g Rose is old enough to vote.

31 the same, different …

1
b They're (completely) different.
c They're the same.
d They're similar.
e They're (completely) different.

2
b the same town
c different streets
d the same age
e different jobs
f the same school

3
b at a different time from me
c the same age as ours
d different programmes from me
e the same price as mine

4
b 6
c 2
d 1
e 5 It's similar to / like a cup …
f 4 It's similar to / like a bicycle …

32 Food and cooking

1
Meat: chicken, beef, pork
Vegetables: tomatoes, beans, cabbage, lettuce, onions, carrots, aubergines, peas, mushrooms
Others: pasta, eggs, rice

4
b pour
c add
d Boil / Cook
e stir
f put
g cook / boil

5
Possible answer:
Cut the onions and potatoes into slices. Pour some oil into a pan, and fry the chicken, potatoes and onions for 10 minutes. Then add water and some salt and pepper. Put a lid on the pan, and cook it slowly for one hour. Stir it occasionally with a spoon.

33 Rooms, flats and houses

1
Floor: rug, mat
Window: blind
Washing: bath, sink, washbasin
Electricity: cooker, stereo
Keep things: wardrobe, drawer, bookshelves

2
The bedroom
Part 2 possible answers:
Living room: It's got a comfortable sofa and an armchair. There's a stereo in the corner, and a large carpet on the floor. There are pictures on the wall, and some bookshelves.
Kitchen: There's a sink, a small fridge and a nice cooker. There are drawers, and there are cupboards on the wall. There's a blind in the window.
Bathroom: It's got a washbasin and a bath, and there's a big shower in the corner. There's a small mat on the floor by the shower.

3
b on the top floor
c a view of
d four large rooms
e on a main road
f near a station

34 Electricity

1
b 10 washing machine
c 5 radiator
d 1 air conditioning unit
e 7 computer
f 12 microwave
g 13 cooker
h 9 iron
i 4 television (or TV)
j 6 radio
k 11 vacuum cleaner
l 15 refrigerator (or fridge)
m 3 stereo (or hi-fi)
n 8 telephone (or phone)
o 2 light

3
b turn the radiator up
c turn the radio down
d switch / turn the light on
e switch / turn the radio on
f turn / switch the TV off *or* turn the TV down

4

torch	✓	✓	–
hairdrier	–	–	✓
lamp	✓	–	✓
MP3 player	–	✓	–

5
b torch
c camera
d MP3 player
e hairdrier

35 Housework

1
b she made the beds.
c she cooked / made lunch.
d she washed the dishes.
e she ironed / washed the shirts.
f she cleaned the kitchen windows.

2
Ed didn't do any housework today.
b Bill did the washing up.
c Chris did the cleaning.
d Bill did the ironing.
e David did the shopping.
f Alex did the cooking.

4

b B; put/clear
c A; tidied
d B; untidy; put/clear
e A; tidy; puts

36 In the street

1

b 5   e 4
c 1   f 3
d 2

2

a cash
b post; letterbox/postbox; bus
c cross; crossing
d make; box/booth

4

Possible answers:

b Where can I get a cup of coffee?
c Where's the nearest phone box?
d Is there anywhere I can buy stamps near here?
e Is there a toilet near here?

6

a 1
b 3
c 4

Possible answers:

d Go along this road until you come to the main road. Cross the main road and then take the first turning on your left. Go along that road, and you'll see it on the right.
e Go down this road and take the first turning on the right. Then carry on until you come to a crossroads. Turn right at the crossroads, and you'll see it on your left.

37 The world

1

Continents: Europe, Africa, North America, South America, Australia
Regions: Southeast Asia, Central America
Oceans and seas: the Atlantic Ocean, the Pacific Ocean, the Indian Ocean, the Mediterranean, the South China Sea

2

b Spain
c Panama
d Vietnam
e Chile
f Mongolia
g Nigeria

4

Possible answers:

b Herat is in the northwest of Afghanistan, not far from the border with Iran.
c Kandahar is about 500 kilometres southwest of Kabul.
d Lagos is in the southwest of Nigeria, on the south coast.
e Ibadan is about 100 kilometres northeast of Lagos.
f Kano is in the north of Nigeria, not far from the border with Niger.

38 Countries and languages

1

We're Egyptian.
They're South African. He's Korean.
I'm Japanese. She's Vietnamese.
They're Israeli. She's Pakistani.

2

	Finnish	Belgian
Scottish	Polish	Portuguese
Irish	Spanish	Greek
Danish	Turkish	Swiss
Swedish	French	Dutch
Norwegian	German	

3

a Scottish; Irish
b Chinese, Vietnamese and Korean
c Italian, Greek and Turkish
d French, Dutch and Swiss
e Norwegian or Swedish; Danish
f Mexican, Colombian and Venezuelan

4

c No. She speaks a few words of Japanese.
d No. She speaks a bit of English.
e No. She speaks French quite well.
f No. She doesn't speak Chinese at all.

39 Places to stay

1

A3, B1, C2, D4

2

holiday: go on holiday, take a holiday, I've got a holiday
stay: stay with friends, stay in a cottage, stay in an apartment, stay at home
travel: travel round (Mexico)

3

b He's staying with his uncle in Berlin for two weeks.
c They're staying in a friend's house in Hawaii.
d I'm travelling round China for three weeks.
e I'm going on holiday to Egypt for a week.

4

2 R, 3 T, 4 R, 5 T, 6 T, 7 T, 8 T

5

b Is the room at the back?
c Can I see the room?
d How many nights / How long are you staying?
e Has the room got a TV?
f How much is the room?

6

b let
c own; rent
d pay; rent
e own; let (out)

40 Transport

1

a go by boat.
b You can go by / take a train
or
You can go by / take a bus.
c You can go by / take the underground *or*
You can go by / take a tram.
d You can go by / take a bus
or
You can go by / take the underground.

2

b flew
c cycled
d fly, drive
e drove

3

b takes
c single, costs
d change
e leaves (Poznań) from
f direct

4

b Do I have to change?
c How long does it take?
d What time does the train leave?
e Where does it leave from?
f How much does it cost?

41 Sport

1

a He often watches 6, 4, 3
b He sometimes watches 8, 1
c He doesn't watch 9, 12
d He's never watched 7
f 5
g 10
h 2

3

1 RACE
2 POINTS
3 MATCH
4 LOST
5 BEAT
6 TEAM
7 WIN
8 SCORE
9 LOSE
10 ATHLETICS

4

+ -er: swimmer, boxer, racing driver
+ -player: basketball player, tennis player
others: cyclist

42 Work

1

b	6	g	5
c	9	h	7
d	12	i	3
e	2	j	4
f	10	k	8

2

b writes
c works in / runs
d make / design; do a lot of work for
e works for
f writes / designs

3

a 4; b 3; c 2; d 1

5

b got/found
c left
d got/found
e lost
f find
g applied for
h interviews

i unemployed
j found/got
k retired

43 Everyday activities

1

b asleep
c woke
d go to sleep / fall asleep
e went to sleep / fell asleep
f woke up
g awake

3

b puts on her
c wash your
d brush my
e wash my
f clean / brush their

5

a going to see
b She's visiting
c she's going out for
d she's staying at home
e she's staying with / visiting

44 Family and friends

1

b my grandmother
c my aunt
d my uncle
e my cousin
f my grandson
g my granddaughter
h my nephew
i my niece
j my grandchildren

3

a ... got engaged a year later, but they only got married in 2001.
b We met at a party. We fell in love immediately, and got married a year later.
c They first met at university. They got married, but 5 years later they got divorced.

4

b colleague / friend
c friend
d fiancé
e girlfriend

45 Life events

1

b started writing
c moved
d went to live
e was born

f grew up
g started singing
h went to live

2

School, college, university: went to (Bristol) university; studied (Russian); left (university); did a course in (Business Studies)
Work: worked as (a secretary); got a job as (a teacher); started working for (IBM); became (a sales manager)

4

b failed
c took
d passed
e passed
f took; failed

5

b Elvis Presley died in Memphis, Tennessee at the age of 42.
c John Kennedy was shot in Dallas in 1963.
d Princess Diana died / was killed in a car crash at the age of 36.
e Che Guevara was killed in Bolivia in 1967.

46 *happy, angry, friendly …*

1

b I'm really disappointed.
c He feels very excited about it.
d I'm really worried about them.
e I was really angry about it.
f Everyone was really frightened.

2

b interested in; worried about
c afraid / frightened of; worried about
d interested in; keen on
e afraid / frightened of; worried about

3

b She's unfriendly.
c He's lazy.
d He's shy.
e She's clever / intelligent.
f He's hard-working.
g He's quiet.

47 Money

1
b ... pay for those shoes?
c ... all his money on CDs.
d ... €50 for the hotel room;
  €140 for the evening meal.
e ... on food; on clothes
f ... $50 for it.

2
b cost
c paid
d bought
e paid
f cost

3
a paid/gave
b lend
c borrowed
d lend; Give / Pay
e borrow
f borrow

4
a Can I pay by credit card?
b Can we have the bill, please?
c Can I have a receipt, please?
d Do you have any change?

48 Health and illness

1
1 BETTER
2 COLD
3 FEEL
4 TEMPERATURE
5 TOOK
6 VITAMIN
7 MEDICINE
8 SEE
9 STAY
10 FLU
11 FELT
12 ILL
13 TAKE
14 WELL

2
a 4; b 1; c 2; d 3

3
b neck
c shoulder
d chest
e back
f arm
g stomach
h leg
i foot

4
b feet hurt
c pain; leg
d stomach ache
e arm hurts/aches

49 Accidents and problems

1
b He burned his hand.
c She broke her leg.
d He cut his face.
e He cut his foot.
f She broke her arm.

2
b doesn't work
c doesn't work
d (leg) is broken
e won't / doesn't open
f is dirty

3
Possible answers:
b need to clean them
c needs repairing
d need washing
e should paint them
f needs cutting

50 Disasters and emergencies

1
b a flood / floods
c an earthquake
d a fire
e a plane crash

2
b killed
c injured
d damaged
e fires
f destroyed
g killed
h floods
i rescued

3
b fire engine
c ambulance
d thief
e police(men)
f police cars

4
1 POLICE
2 PUT
3 INTO
4 THIEF
5 CAUGHT
7 STARTED
8 HOSPITAL
9 ENGINE
10 FIRE
11 WAS
12 STOLE
13 CALLED

51 Clothes

1
b 8
c 4
d 2
e 5
f 9

2
Possible answer:
Formal: tie, jacket, suit, dress
Formal or casual: trousers, shirt, skirt, top
Casual: (old) jumper, jeans, T-shirt

3
Possible answers:
c ✓ d ✓ e ?! f ✓ g ✓
h ? i ✓

5
c two pairs of shorts
d three shirts
e two jumpers
f seven pairs of socks
g two pairs of shoes
h a pair of sandals
i a jacket

6
b 2 c 5 d 1 e 3

7
a try it on
b try it on; suits
c fit me; What size

52 Containers and materials

1
b a bottle of water
c a bag of apples
d a carton of milk
e a box of matches
f a can of tomatoes
g a packet of biscuits
h a jar of honey

3
b 3 They're made of plastic.
c 1 It's made of glass.
d 4 They're made of paper.
e 2 It's made of metal.
f 5 It's made of wood.

53 Communicating

1
b open
c save
d shut down
e print / print out
f start / start up

2

a type in the message; type in the address; click 'Send'
b pick up the phone; dial the number; talk to the person; put the phone down
c write the letter; put it in an envelope; write the address; put a stamp on it; post it

4

a send; receive
b download
c use
d connect to
e search for; visit
f type in

5

2 CONNECT
3 TYPE
4 USE
5 HARD
6 DOWNLOAD
7 REPLY
8 WEBSITES
9 INTERNET

54 Arts and entertainment

1

Where? cinema
What? play; exhibition; concert, music
Who? actors; actors, director; artists; band, singer

2

b concert hall
c film
d actors
e exhibition (of paintings)
f artist
g play

3

Possible answers:

b What's on at the cinema
c What's on at the theatre
d What plays are on
e What's on at the Bond Gallery

55 Talking

1

b had a terrible argument with her father
c talk to you about the office party
d had an interesting conversation about China

e had a long discussion about the new sports centre
f discuss money with my parents

2

Possible answers:

b He said he was having a good time.
c He told me he had a lot of friends in London.
d He said he was going back to Canada in June.
e He told me he needed to earn some money.
f He said he was starting university in September.

3

b ... you didn't like football.
c ... he was studying Arabic.
d ... she wasn't married.
e ... they were leaving on Sunday.
f ... they lived in a flat.

56 bring, take, give ...

1

b took; give/bring
c gave
d took; put; brought/got
e taken; fetch/get

3

c –
d to
e to
f –
g for

57 get

1

b get = bring
c get = receive
d get = receive
e get = buy
f get = arrive

3

3 b, 2 c, 5 d, 1 e, 4 f

4

b get dressed
c got engaged; get married
d got undressed
e get changed
f get lost

5

get on/off: a train, a horse, a plane
get into/out of: a taxi; bed

58 find, lose, keep ...

1

a found
b lost
c find; lost
d lose

2

b forgotten
c left
d forgotten
e left
f forget

59 stand, sit, walk ...

1

b 11 walking
c 8 lying
d 6 sitting
e 10 standing
f 9 running

2

b lay down
c stood up / got up
d lie down
e stood up / got up
f sat down

3

a got; rode; chased
b came; walked; followed; got; drove
c followed; stopped; waited
d took; landed; got; went; waited

60 Moving things

1

b a car, their bikes
c your car, these books
d clothes, magazines
e suitcases, bags

2

b carried
c picked; up
d pushed
e put; down
f moved

3

b won't open
c can't open / can't close; locked
d won't move
e won't turn; stuck

4

b He's going to hit
c She's going to catch
d He's going to kick
e He's going to drop
f She's going to miss

61 see, hear …

1
b saw
c looking
d see
e looked
f saw
g looking at
h see
i watched

2
a the news
b someone in the street; the wind
c to me; carefully

3
c I heard them ring the bell.
d I heard one of them say 'I know she's there.'
e I saw Marlene put the photos in a drawer.
f I saw her get up.
g I saw her run out of the room.

62 look, sound …

1
b smells awful.
c sounds interesting.
d looks tired.
e tastes delicious.
f feels damp.

2
b sounds like
c tastes like / looks like
d smells like / looks like
e looks like
f feels like

3
b What does she sound like? (4)
c What does it taste like? (1)
d What does it smell like? (3)
e What do they feel like? (2)

4
Some possible answers:
I love the smell of fried onions.
I like the sound of the sea.
I don't like the taste of raw fish.
I don't like the sound of motorbikes.
I like the taste of garlic.

63 make and do

1
b make a phone call
c made a note
d make a salad
e made a mistake
f Make a list
g made a cake

2
b It's made of plastic.
c It's made in Japan.
d It's made by Mercedes.
e It's made in Switzerland.
f They're made by Esprit.
g They're made of gold.
h They're made by Gucci.
i It's made of paper.
j They're made in Turkey.

3
c ~~made~~ done your homework
d ✓
e ~~make~~ do much sport
f ✓
g ~~do~~ make a list
h ✓
i ~~does~~ makes lots of mistakes
j ~~done~~ made an appointment

4
b What are you doing?
c What are you doing this evening?
d What did you do at the weekend?
e What shall we do?
f What do you do?

64 use

1
c 3 You use it to / It is used to
d 1 You use it to / It is used to
e 2 You use it for / It is used for
f 6 You use it for / It is used for
g 7 You use it to / It is used to

2
b a knife
c scissors
d string
e a brush
f a cloth
g glue

3
b for cutting
c for sticking
d for tying
e for cleaning
f for cutting

4
Possible answers:
b very useful (you could light a fire)
c very useful (you could catch fish)
d quite useful (you could use it for lots of things)
e quite useful (you could use the bottle)
f quite useful (you could sleep in it)
g not very useful
h completely useless
The most useful: b or c
The least useful: a or h

65 start and finish

1
b begins at / starts at
c finishes at / ends at
d begin on / start on
e ends at / finishes at
f finishes on / ends on

2
b at the end of
c in the middle of
d at the end of
e in the middle of
f At the beginning of

3
b arriving / to arrive
c to write / writing
d raining
e thinking
f reading / to read; to ring / ringing; reading

66 have got

1
b Ten million people in Britain have got a car.
c I've got two tickets for the film.
d All the rooms have got satellite TV.
e I hope you've got enough money with you.
f My computer has got a 250GB hard disk.

2
b hasn't got a lift.
c hasn't got an email address.
d haven't got passports.
e haven't got any milk.
f hasn't got a ticket.
g haven't got much hot water.

3

b Have you got
c Has she got
d Have you got
e Has he got
f Has it got

4

b Yes, I have. *or* No, I haven't.
c Yes, they have. *or* No, they haven't.
d Yes, it has. *or* No, it hasn't.
e Yes, it has. *or* No, it hasn't.
f Yes, I have. *or* No, I haven't.

67 *I like ...*

1

b I love sitting in cafés.
c I love chocolate.
d I hate doing the ironing.
e I like getting up late on Saturdays.
f I don't like milk.
g I really enjoy cooking.

3

b your favourite city
c our favourite room
d her favourite sport
e my favourite drinks
f their favourite writers

5

b He likes
c Would you like
d like walking
e I'd like
f Do you like
g to pay

68 *know*

3

Possible answers:

a I don't know anything about sport.
b I know a lot about music.
c I don't know much about films.

4

Possible answers:

b They're not sure what his job is.
c They have no idea where he comes from.
d They know what languages he speaks.
e They don't know who his friends are.
f They're not sure how tall he is.

5

b I know them very well.
c I know them by sight
d I don't know them very well.
e I know them quite well.

69 *remember* and *forget*

1

b memory; remembers
c forgotten
d forgot; remember
e remember; remember; forget
f memory; remember

2

b I remember the other children looking at me.
c I remember arriving at school late one day.
d I remember playing football at lunchtime.
e I remember my grandmother meeting me after school.
f I remember my teacher falling off her desk.

4

Possible answers:

b Don't forget to take your passport.
c Remember to take a key.
d Remember to buy some bread.
e Don't forget to ask for a receipt.
f Don't forget to write the date.

70 *think, expect, hope ...*

1

b I'm sure they'll be all right.
c I think I've got flu.
d I don't think she likes them.
e I'm sure I left it on this chair.
f I don't think they'll win the match.

2

The real answers are:
a No (It's in Mali.)
b No (He was a writer.)
c Yes
d No (It's 'knives'.)
e No (They were in Sydney, Australia.)
f Yes
g No

3

b I hope we don't get wet.
c I don't expect she'll remember me.
d I expect they will get lost.
e I hope he finds it.
f I expect they will be late.

71 *probably, perhaps ...*

1

Possible answers:

b There is probably life on other planets.
c We will definitely travel to other planets.
d We are certainly the most intelligent animals on Earth.
e The world will definitely get warmer over the next century.
f There probably isn't a monster in Loch Ness.

2

a ... maybe / perhaps he's just had a shower.
b Maybe / Perhaps he didn't switch it on or maybe / perhaps he left it at home.
c Perhaps / Maybe he didn't see you, or maybe / perhaps he doesn't like you.

3

Possible answers:

c We may go out tomorrow.
d John might phone this evening.
e I may not stay very late.
f Take a coat – you might be cold.
g You may need some money.

72 *must* and *have to*

1

b I must buy him a present.
c I must go to bed.
d We must buy the tickets.
e I must have a shower.
f We must go shopping.

2

2 f, 3 d, 4 c, 5 b, 6 a
b You mustn't
c You must
d You mustn't
e You mustn't
f You mustn't

3

b don't have to
c don't have to
d have to
e have to
f don't have to

4

b have to
c mustn't
d don't have to
e must
f mustn't

73 can, could, know how to …

1

Expected answers:

b couldn't
c could
d could
e couldn't
f could

2

Expected answers:

b don't know how to
c know how to
d know how to
e don't know how to
f know how to

3

Possible answers:

b She's very good at cooking.
c He's quite good at (playing) basketball.
d He's not very good at driving.
e I'm not very good at (playing) the guitar.
f She's very good at listening.
g She's very good at (speaking) French.

74 Requests and offers

1

Possible answers:

b Could you lend me 50 euros?
   Would you mind lending me 50 euros?
c Can you drive me to the station?
   Would you mind driving me to the station?
d Could you move your car?
   Would you mind moving your car?

2

Possible answers:

b Would you like a cold drink?
c Can I carry your suitcase?
d Would you like me to get you a taxi?
e Do you want a room with a balcony?
f Shall I show you the room?

3

b Do you need any help?
c Shall I clean the flat for you?
d Can you help me with my homework?
e Would you help me with these suitcases?
f Would you like me to help you?

75 Suggestions

1

a a good idea; shall we
b How about; Let's
c Why don't we; That's; Let's
d shall we do; could

2

b about buying me dinner?
c don't you try it on?
d could sleep on the sofa.
e about turning the lights on?
f don't you throw them away?

3

b shouldn't / ought not to   2
c shouldn't / ought not to   1
d should / ought to   2
e shouldn't / ought not to   1
f shouldn't / ought not to   4
g should / ought to   4
h shouldn't / ought not to   3

4

b you could call
c You ought not to
d why don't you
e he should get
f Let's play

76 Everyday expressions

1

a about; mind
b sorry; That's; matter
c I'm; about; worry

2

Possible answers:

a Many thanks for a lovely evening.
b Thank you very much for your help.
   Thanks for helping me.
c Many thanks for the flowers.
   Thank you so much for the present.
d Thanks for calling.
   Thank you for talking to me.

3

b Be careful! Good luck! Have a good trip! Have a safe journey!
c Well done! Congratulations!
d Good luck!
e Look out! Be careful!

4

Good: That's great. I'm glad to hear that.
Bad: That's terrible. That's a pity. I'm sorry to hear that.
Interesting: Oh, really? That's interesting.

5

Possible answers:

b That's great. I'm glad to hear that.
c Oh, really? That's interesting.
d Oh, dear. That's terrible.

77 will and going to (1): decisions

1

Possible answers:

b I think I'll have a sandwich.
c I won't go for a swim.
d I'll get a taxi home.
e I think I'll print it out.
f I don't think I'll eat there again.

2

b I decided to have a sandwich.
c I decided not to go for a swim.
d I decided to get a taxi home.
e I decided to print it out.
f I decided not to eat there again.

3

b He's going to make some shelves.
c They're going to paint the kitchen.
d She's going to learn English.
e He's going to write some letters.
f She's going to clean the car.

4

b I'll
c I won't
d I'll
e We're going to
f I'm going to

78 will and going to (2): the future

Presentation questions:
Gassi; Stankova

1

b will probably
c probably won't
d probably won't
e will probably
f probably won't

3

b If   e If
c When   f If
d when

4

b you leave the motorway
c when you arrive
d If we're out
e when we see you
f If the weather is nice

5

b are going to crash.
c are going to get wet.
d is going to break.
e is going to have
f is going to fall asleep.

79 going to

1

b is going to
c isn't going to
d isn't going to
e aren't going to
f are going to

2

b are going to get married
c I'm not going to spend; I'm going to save
d are going to build
e is going to leave; I'm going to stay
f he's not going to retire

3

b Are you going to hire a car?
c How are you going to get to Naxos?
d Are you going to go by boat?
e Are you going to visit Mykonos?
f When are you going to come back?

4

b are they going to see?
c are you going to cook it?
d are you going to wear?
e is he going to do?
f is she going to live?

80 would

1

Question 1:
a would *or* 'd
b would *or* 'd; would *or* 'd
c wouldn't
Question 2: Would
a would *or* 'd; would *or* 'd
b would *or* 'd; wouldn't
c would *or* 'd

2

b knew   e had
c weren't   f wasn't
d didn't live

3

a … I'd go home by taxi.
  … I'd buy a new mobile.
b … I'd get some exercise.
  … I'd clean my flat.

5

c … if they were more interesting.
d … if it wasn't so long.
e … if the water was warmer.
f … if it wasn't so far.

81 Present simple

1

b fly; costs
c don't have
d sell; buy
e don't earn
f works; sends

2

b Do you like
c does he take
d Do you play
e Does she work
f do they sell

3

b Where do they spend the summer?
c How many languages does she speak?
d What does she do in the evenings?
e How many houses does she own?
f What kind of car does she drive?

82 Present continuous

1

b N   f N
c N   g AN
d AN   h N
e AN

2

b I'm taking
c I'm reading
d they're travelling
e he's designing
f we're painting

3

b are having dinner
c are going to a concert
d is visiting City University
e is meeting 4th year students
f is getting a taxi

5

b Are you having a good time?
c How is she getting here?
d Is Anna coming to the meeting?
e When is he leaving?
f Am I sitting in your seat?

83 was and were

1

b were shop assistants; were quite poor
c was in a flat; were all students
d were very small; was always cold

2

b They weren't Mexican. They were English / British.
c He wasn't a writer. He was a painter / an artist.
d He wasn't Greek. He was American.
e They weren't Chinese. They were Russian.
f He wasn't Portuguese. He was Brazilian.

3

b Were the people friendly? No, they weren't.
c Was the hotel comfortable? Yes, it was.
d Were the rooms clean? Yes, they were.
e Were the restaurants cheap? No, they weren't.
f Was the food good? Yes, it was.

4

b How old was he?
c How were they?
d Where were you?
e How much were they?
f What time was it?

84 *There was, there were …*

1

b there were
c there was
d There were
e there weren't
f there weren't
g there was
h there wasn't

2

b … there was one computer … there were twenty-five.
c There were only three … were busy.
d … there were lots …. were the best.
e It was quite big. There were five bedrooms … there wasn't a bathroom … the toilet was outside.

3

b Was there; Yes, there was.
c Were there; No, there weren't.
d Was there; Yes, there was.
e Was there; No, there wasn't.
f Were there; Yes, there were.

4

b How much meat was there?
c How many grand pianos were there?
d How many eggs were there?
e How much milk was there?
f How many cars were there?

85 Past simple (1)

1

a played
b lived; died
c turned; listened
d washed; cleaned; brushed
e slipped; dropped
f phoned; answered
g opened; closed
h pushed; dropped; kicked
i chatted; talked; listened
j typed; stopped; asked

2

drove; made; heard
drank; gave; read; saw
ate; rang; did; put
wrote; found; sat

3

a found; sat; came; said
b got; had; put; went; ate; drank; left
c came; wrote; gave; read; put; got; drove
d did; made; heard; went; saw; rang

86 Past simple (2)

Presentation questions:
Buckingham Palace; The London Eye

1

b didn't buy
c didn't have
d didn't see
e didn't take
f didn't rain

3

b Did you go; Yes, we did.
c Did you buy; No, we didn't.
d Did you go; No, we didn't.
e Did you see; No, we didn't.
f Did you have; Yes, we did.

4

b When did he make Psycho?
c What did he study at university?
d When did he move to the USA?
e Where did he die?
f How many Oscars did he win?

87 Past continuous (1)

1

a wasn't listening; was thinking
b were sitting; was swimming; were going
c was snowing; wasn't wearing
d were living; was studying; was working; were having

2

b Was she buying clothes?
c Where was she standing?
d Where were they sitting?
e What were they talking about?
f Was he wearing a T-shirt?

88 Past continuous (2)

1

a ran; shouted
b found; was cleaning; saw
c saw; was standing; was talking

2

b 4; c 5; d 2; e 1; f 3

3

b He was shaving when he cut his face. / He cut his face while he was shaving.
c He was cleaning the kitchen when he found £50 behind the fridge. / He found £50 behind the fridge while he was cleaning the kitchen.
d She was running down some steps when she slipped and broke her leg. / She slipped and broke her leg while she was running down some steps.
e She was staying in Tokyo when she lost her passport. / She lost her passport while she was staying in Tokyo.
f He was driving home from a party when the police stopped him. / The police stopped him while he was driving home from a party.

4

b What did she do
c What were they doing
d What was she doing
e What were you doing
f What did you do

89 *used to*

1

b We used to live in Cairo.
c She used to teach English.
d I used to play snooker.
e He used to smoke.
f I used to go (to work) by bus.

2

b He used to be overweight.
c He didn't use to play basketball.
d He used to eat a lot.
e He didn't use to meet many people.
f He didn't use to feel good.

3

c There used to be a football ground.
d There used to be a crossroads.
e There didn't use to be a roundabout.
f There used to be a factory.
g There didn't use to be an office block.

90 Present perfect (1)

1

b 3; c 6; d 5; e 2; f 1

2

b has come.
c She has bought / She's bought
d He has put / He's put
e They have gone / They've gone
f have closed all the windows.

3

b has just left
c has just washed
d has just received
e have just got
f have just finished

4

a has just left
b I went
c I've already read
d I've just had
e He came in

91 Present perfect (2)

1

b I haven't got up yet
c I haven't bought a ticket
d it hasn't left yet
e I haven't unpacked it
f we haven't paid the bill yet

2

b They haven't got married yet.
c He hasn't gone home yet.
d They haven't bought a car yet.
e She hasn't moved yet.
f I haven't gone to sleep yet.

3

b have you moved
c Have you visited
d Have they retired
e Has she come
f have you found

4

b Have you washed / ironed the sheets?
c Have you cleaned the kitchen?
d Have you washed the dishes?
e Have you cleaned / washed the car?
f Have you made lunch?

92 Present perfect (3)

1

b She has written
c She has worked
d She has studied (lived)
e She has taught
f She has worked (lived)

3

b Have you ever eaten
c Have you ever climbed
d Have you ever done
e Have you ever driven
f Have you ever been

93 Present passive

1

b The windows are locked.
c The lights are switched off.
d The music is turned off.
e The floor is cleaned.
f The money is taken to the bank.

2

b are made
c are made in Switzerland
d Sugar is produced
e are produced in Japan
f of all tea is grown

3

b are written
c are spoken
d is spoken
e are spoken; are written
f are written

94 Past passive

1

b It was kept in an attic.
c It was found in 2003.
d It was sold to a New York art gallery.
e They were painted in the 18th century.
f They were given to a family in England.
g They were put in a cellar.
h They were found in 2002.

2

b was invented by Alexander Bell
c was built in 2560 BC
d was written by Leo Tolstoy.
e was built in 1889
f was discovered by Marie Curie
g was invented in 1932

95 Question words

1

2 When   f
3 Whose   g
4 Why   b
5 How   a
6 Who   d
7 What   e

2

b What make of / What kind of
c What colour
d What kind of
e What make
f What size

3

b How much are these trainers?
c How strong do you like your coffee?
d How tall are you?
e How deep is the water?
f How well does he speak English?

4

b Which train
c Which house
d Which part
e Which leg
f Which magazine

96 Questions (1)

1

c O; d O; e S; f O; g S; h S; i O; j O

2

b Who scored the first goal?
c How many more goals did City score?
d What happened after half time?
e Who kicked Kopf?
f What did the referee do?

3

c What are you thinking about?
d Who did he get married to?
e Who are you going with?
f What do you need to talk about?
g Who did you play with?

97 Questions (2)

1
c they don't
d I didn't
e we have
f she was
g I can't
h it will
i I wouldn't
j they were

2
b they don't
c she wasn't
d I would
e I can't
f I didn't
g I will

3
a Yes, I do. *or* No, I don't.
b Yes, I did. *or* No, I didn't.
c Yes, they do. *or* No, they don't.
d Yes, I can. *or* No, I can't.
e Yes, it did. *or* No, it didn't.
f Yes, I have. *or* No, I haven't.
g Yes, I am. *or* No, I'm not.
h Yes, I have. *or* No, I haven't.

4
b do you
c don't I
d doesn't he
e haven't you
f haven't I
g aren't they
h isn't she
i isn't it
j have you

5
b wasn't it   1
c isn't it   3
d is it   2
e weren't they   1
f isn't it   2

98 *and, but, so …*

1
b or
c and
d but
e and
f or; but

2
b … and they also have …
c … but I enjoy reading as well.
d … and it is also windy.
e … works in the evenings too.

3
b Because my new printer didn't work, I took it back to the shop. *or* I took my new printer back to the shop because it didn't work.
c I studied Spanish at university, so I speak it fluently.
d They were talking, so they didn't see the traffic lights.
e As the room faces north, it's nice and cool. *or* As it faces north, the room is nice and cool.
f I didn't hear the phone because I was in the garden. *or* Because I was in the garden, I didn't hear the phone.

4
b so that they'll be nearer the shops
c so that he can meet new people
d so that no-one steals it
e so that you don't get wet
f so that you can text me

99 *who, which …*

1
a *or* that cooks food quickly
b who / that flies planes
c who / that live next door to you
d which / that can destroy trees and buildings
e where you can look at paintings
f which / that makes mobile phones
g where you can borrow books

2
b … a man I met ~~him~~ at a party.
c … which I used to drive ~~it~~.
d … a beach which had … *or* … a beach that had …
e … the woman who lives … *or* … the woman that lives …
f … which ~~it~~ leaves …

3
b where you can buy carpets and jewellery
c which was built in the 19th century
d which is one of the oldest pyramids
e where it is cooler
f who lived in the 13th century BC

100 *before, after*

1
Possible answers:
a … bought a ticket. Then I went onto the platform and started reading the paper.
b Turn the oven on and wait until it's hot. Then take the pizza out of the box and put it in the oven.
c He turned his computer on and went online, and then he read his emails and replied to one of them.
d She finished her report and saved it. After that, she printed it out and took it to the meeting.

2
b four years later
c twenty minutes later
d Three months later
e two weeks later
f A hundred years later / A century later

3
b Before going out / Before she went out, she turned off all the lights.
c Before he got dressed / Before getting dressed, he had a shower.
d After seeing / After I saw a documentary about chicken farms, I decided to stop eating meat.
e After he took / After taking his driving test five times, he passed it.

RU1 Phrasal verbs

1
a down
b up
c up; up; out
d up
e out; in/into; away/off

2
c Why don't you turn the TV on?
d Let's throw away these magazines.
e She gave away all her money.
f Put a coat on – it's cold.
g Could you turn the music down?

3

b I'm going to try them on.
c Don't throw them away.
d I forgot to switch it on.
e Can you take them off?
f Can you turn it up a bit?

RU2 Infinitives

1

a make, have
b go, enjoy, be
c live, study, come
d eat, drink, have

2

b phone, be   e drink
c tell, get   f speak
d learn, live

3

b give   e to see
c know   f thank
d go

RU3 *-ing* forms

1

–   smiling   giving
taking   doing   getting
buying   hitting   speaking

2

b 2, c 2, d 1, e 1, f 1, g 1, h 2

3

b skiing
c crying
d eating
e smoking
f seeing

RU4 Past participles

1

b given
c begun
d got
e worn
f had
g bought
h written
i been

2

b made, sold
c been, travelled
d seen, gone
e arrived, left
f lost, taken

3

b worn
c lost; seen
d written
e made
f gone

RU5 Modal verbs

1

b Will you phone me tomorrow?
c I must get up early tomorrow.
d Can I have some water?
e They might not be at home.

2

b Would you like a drink?
c You shouldn't work so hard.
d Can I help you?
e Could you swim when you were a child?

3

The answers are on page 219, section C.

RU6 Subject, verb, object

1

b *Subject:* I
   Verb: start
c *Subject:* The people in the next flat
   Verb: are having
d *Subject:* The President of the USA
   Verb: is flying
e *Subject:* His sister
   Verb: lives
f *Subject:* Too much coffee
   Verb: is

2

c six children
d No
e No
f TV
g John

3

c … a postcard to my sister.
d … some food for you?
e OK
f … a story to the children …
g OK

RU7 Phrases with prepositions

1

a to; on
b near; in; opposite
c at; in; for
d across; up; on

2

b … for a job in a bank.
c … to the 6 o'clock news.
d … to a new flat / into a new flat
e … at Platform 16.
f … to my grandmother.

3

b about
c after
d with
e with
f about
g at

4

b keen on / interested in
c sorry about
d frightened of / afraid of
e similar to
f good at

Phonemic symbols

Vowel sounds

Symbol	Example
/iː/	sleep
/i/	happy
/ɪ/	dinner
/ʊ/	foot
/uː/	shoe
/e/	red
/ə/	arrive father
/ɜː/	work
/ɔː/	walk
/æ/	cat
/ʌ/	sun
/ɒ/	clock
/ɑː/	car
/eɪ/	name
/aɪ/	my
/ɔɪ/	boy
/eə/	where
/ɪə/	hear
/əʊ/	home
/aʊ/	cow
/ʊə/	euro

Consonant sounds

Symbol	Example
/p/	put
/b/	book
/t/	take
/d/	dog
/k/	car
/g/	go
/tʃ/	church
/dʒ/	age
/f/	for
/v/	video
/θ/	three
/ð/	this
/s/	sport
/z/	zoo
/ʃ/	shop
/ʒ/	usually
/h/	hear
/m/	make
/n/	name
/ŋ/	bring
/l/	look
/r/	road
/j/	young
/w/	wear

Index

The numbers in the Index are unit numbers, not page numbers.

all /ɔːl/
    all (day) **17B**
    all (of) 17A, **18**
    not … at all **38C**
all, both, most, some … 18
almost /ˈɔːlməʊst/ **1C**
alone /əˈləʊn/ **21D**
along /əˈlɒŋ/ **23B**
already /ɔːlˈredi/ **6A**, **90C**
already, just, only 6
also /ˈɔːlsəʊ/ **98B**
always /ˈɔːlweɪz/ **9A**
always, usually … 9
am /æm/ **83A**
ambulance /ˈæmbjələnts/ **50C**
America /əˈmerɪkə/ **37A**
American /əˈmerɪkən/ **37A**
ancient /ˈeɪntʃənt/ **81A**
and /ænd/ **98A**, **100A**
    and then … **100A**
and, but, so … 98
angry /ˈæŋgri/ **46A**
another /əˈnʌðə/ **19A**, **19B**
any /ˈeni/ **14A**
    not … any **16D**
anybody /ˈeniˌbɒdi/ **16B**
    not … anybody **16D**
anyone /ˈeniwʌn/ **16B**
    not … anyone **16D**
anything /ˈeniθɪŋ/ **16B**
    anything + adj. + -er **27B**
    don't know anything **68B**
    not … anything **16D**
anywhere /ˈenihweə/ **16B**
    Is there anywhere …? **36B**
    not … anywhere **16D**
apparently /əˈpærəntli/ **26B**
apply for /əˈplaɪ fɔː/ **42C**, **RU7B**
appointment /əˈpɔɪntmənt/ **63A**
Arabic /ˈærəbɪk/ **38C**
architect /ˈɑːkɪtekt/ **42A**
are /ɑː/ **83A**
    are + past participle **93A**
    …, are you? **97B**
    …, aren't you? **97B**
argue /ˈɑːgjuː/ **55A**, **RU7B**
argument /ˈɑːgjəmənt/ **55A**
arm /ɑːm/ **48B**
armchair /ˈɑːmtʃeə/ **33A**
around (time) /əˈraʊnd/ **2B**
around now /əˈraʊnd naʊ/ **82A**
art college /ɑːt ˈkɒlɪdʒ/ **6A**
art gallery /ɑːt ˈgæləri/ **54A**
article /ˈɑːtɪkl/ **79A**, **85A**
artist /ˈɑːtɪst/ **54A**
Arts and entertainment 54
as (= because) /æz/ **98C**
    the same as **31C**
as well /æz wel/ **98B**
Asia /ˈeɪʒə/ **37A**
Asian /ˈeɪʒən/ **37A**
ask (someone to) /ɑːsk/ **RU2C**

asleep /əˈsliːp/ **43A**
at /æt/
    at (8.00) **4B**
    at the (front) **22A**, 39B
    at the age of **45D**
    at the beginning of … **65B**
    at the bottom of **22C**
    at the end of **22C**, **65B**
    at the moment **82A**
    at the top of **22C**
    look at **61A**
    turn (right) at **36C**
    What's on at …? **54B**
at the front, in the middle … 22
at all /æt ɔːl/ **38C**, **68D**
athlete /ˈæθliːt/ **41C**
athletics /æθˈletɪks/ **41A**
Atlantic Ocean /ətˈlæntɪk ˈəʊʃən/ **37A**
attic /ˈætɪk/ **58C**
aubergine /ˈəʊbəʒiːn/ **32A**
aunt /ɑːnt/ **44A**
Australia /ɒsˈtreɪliə/ **37A**
Australian /ɒsˈtreɪliən/ **37A**
awake /əˈweɪk/ **43A**
away /əˈweɪ/
    How far away … ? **12C**
baby /ˈbeɪbi/ **3C**
back (part of body) /bæk/ **48B**
back /bæk/
    at the back (of) **22A**, **22B**, 39B
backache /ˈbækeɪk/ **48B**
backpack /ˈbækpæk/ **13A**
bad /bæd/ 27A
    a bad memory **69A**
badly /ˈbædli/ **26A**
bag /bæg/ **18C**, **52A**
bake (v) /beɪk/ **32B**
baked (potatoes) /beɪkt/ **32B**
balcony /ˈbælkəni/ **33B**
band /bænd/ **54A**
bank card /bæŋk kɑːd/ **47C**
bank manager /bæŋk ˈmænɪdʒə/ **42A**
bar of (chocolate) /bɑː ɒv/ **13C**
bark (v) /bɑːk/ **65B**
basketball /ˈbɑːskɪtbɔːl/ **41A**
basketball player /ˈbɑːskɪtbɔːl ˈpleɪə/ **41C**
bath /bɑːθ/ **33A**
battery /ˈbætəri/ **2C**, **34C**
Be careful! /bi ˈkeəfəl/ **76C**
beans /biːnz/ **32A**
beat (v) /biːt/ 41B
beautifully /ˈbjuːtɪfəli/ **26A**
became (past simple) /bɪˈkeɪm/ 45B
because /bɪˈkɒz/ **98C**
bed /bed/ **35A**
bee /biː/ **23A**
beef /biːf/ **32A**
been (past participle) /biːn/ **8A**, **8B**, **92B**
before /bɪˈfɔː/
    before + -ing **100C**
    before + verb **100C**
    the day before yesterday **5B**
before, after … 100

got /gɒt/ **57A, 85B**
    Have/Has … got …? **66C**
    have/has got **66A**, 33B
    haven't/hasn't got **66B**
government minister /ˈgʌvənmənt ˈmɪnɪstə/ **98D**
grand piano /grænd piˈænəʊ/ **84C**
granddaughter /ˈgrænd,dɔːtə/ **44A**
grandfather /ˈgrænd,fɑːðə/ **44A**
grandmother /ˈgrænd,mʌðə/ **44A**
grandparent /ˈgrænd,peərənt/ **44A**
grandson /ˈgrændsʌn/ **44A**
great /greɪt/ **76D**
Greece /griːs/ **38B**
Greek /griːk/ **38B**
grill (v) /grɪl/ **32B**
grilled (meat) /grɪld/ **32B**
ground /graʊnd/
    ground floor **33B**
grow /grəʊ/ **42A**
    grow up **45A**, RU1A
grown (past participle) /grəʊn/ **93B**
hair /heə/ 13B, 43B
hairdrier /ˈheədraɪə/ **34C**
hairstyle /ˈheəstaɪl/ **31B**
half /hɑːf/ **1B**
handle /ˈhændl/ **60B**
hands /hændz/ **43B**
happy /ˈhæpi/ **46A**
    Happy birthday! **76C**
happy, angry, friendly … 46
hard (adv) /hɑːd/ **26A**
hard disk /hɑːd dɪsk/ **53C**
hard work /hɑːd wɜːk/ **42B**
hardly (ever) /ˈhɑːdli/ **9A**
hard-working /ˈhɑːdˈwɜːkɪŋ/ **46C**
has /hæz/
    has got **66A**
    Has he (+ past participle) …? **91C**
    Has it got …? **66C**
    has + past participle **90A**
    Yes, it has. **66C**
hasn't /ˈhæzənt/
    hasn't + past participle **91A**
    hasn't got **66B**
    No, it hasn't. **66C**
hat /hæt/ **13A, 51B**
hate (v) /heɪt/ **67A**
    hate …-ing **67A**, RU3C
have /hæv/
    have (a job) **42C**
    have a (shower) **43B**
    have a chat **55A**
    have a conversation **55A**
    have a discussion **55A**
    Have a good trip **76C**
    have an argument **55A**
    have been to … **92B**
    have got **33B, 66A**
    …, have I? **97B**
    have just + past participle **90B**
    have no idea **68C**
    have + past participle **90A**

have to + infinitive **72C, 72D**, RU2C
    Have you ever …? **92C**
    Have you got …? **66C**
    Have you + past participle **91C**
    Yes, I have. **66C, 92C**
had (past simple) /hæd/ **85B**
have got 66
haven't /ˈhævənt/
    haven't got **66B**
    …, haven't I? **97B**
    haven't + past participle **91A**
    No, I haven't. **66C, 92C**
head /hed/ **48B**
headache /ˈhedeɪk/ **48B**
Health and illness 48
hear /hɪə/ **61B, 62A**
    hear (the door) (open) **61C**
heard /hɜːd/ **61C, 85B**
heavy /ˈhevi/ **25A**
hedgehog /ˈhedʒhɒg/ **96A**
helicopter /ˈhelɪkɒptə/ **40B**
help (n) /help/ **21D, 74C**
help (v) /help/ **74C**
    help (me) + verb **74C**
    help (me) with **74C**, RU7B
    help yourself **21A**
her (pronoun) /hɜː/ **RU1C**
her (possessive) /hɜː/ **20A**
    her own /hɜː əʊn/ **21C**
hers /hɜːz/ **20A**
herself /hɜːˈself/ **21A**
hi-fi /ˈhaɪfaɪ/ **34A**
high /haɪ/ **11A**, 29A
    (30 metres) high **11B**
    How high? **11C**
him /hɪm/ **RU1C**
himself /hɪmˈself/ **21A**
his /hɪz/ **20A**
    his own **21C**
hit /hɪt/ **60C**
hole /həʊl/ **23B**
holiday /ˈhɒlədeɪ/
    be/go on holiday **39A**
    take a holiday **39A**
homework /ˈhəʊmwɜːk/ **63C**
honey /ˈhʌni/ **52A**
hook /hʊk/ **64A**
hope /həʊp/
    I hope not. **70D**
    I hope + present **70C**
    I hope so. **70D**
horse-racing /hɔːs ˈreɪsɪŋ/ **41A**
hotel /həʊˈtel/ **39A**
hotel manager /həʊˈtel ˈmænɪdʒə/ **42A**
hour /aʊə/
    2 hours from … **12B**
    long hours **42B**
Housework 35
housework /ˈhaʊswɜːk/ **35**

Acknowledgements

We would like to thank Alison Sharpe for overseeing the development of Language Links Pre-intermediate, and our editors, Jamie Smith, Lynn Dunlop, Fiona Davis and David Baker, for all their hard work and support. We are also grateful to Studio AVP and Kamae Design, and to Cambridge University Press for making available the Cambridge International Corpus.

We would like to thank Gabriella Zaharias for her help with photos for the book.

Photographic Acknowledgements
The authors and publishers are grateful to the following photographic sources and illustrators:

(Key: t = top, b = bottom, l = left, r = right, c = centre)

Alamy pp 11l (Ulrike Preuss/Photofusion Picture Library), 16 (David Wall), 31tr (blickwinkel), 31cl (Rich Iwasaki/Stock Connection), 67 (Chad Ehlers), 86tl (David Robertson), 86bl (FAN travelstock), 89 (Ingemar Edfalk/pixonnet.com), 99tl (John Walmsley/Education Photos), 114b (Peter Griffin), 140 (Robert Francis/Robert Harding Picture Library Ltd), 150r (Popperfoto), 154 (Pat Behnke), 163 (e/PNRF), 168t (Liquid-Light Photography), 168cl (Nick Chaldakov), 168bl (Rod Edwards), 170b (David South), 176tl (Mary Evans Picture Library), 177t (imagebroker), 177b (Popperfoto), 180l (Paul Springett), 180r (Chris Andrews/Oxford Picture Library), 193tr (Hayley Madden/S.I.N), 193 (d/Profimedia International S.R.O.), 193 (e/Mark Scheuern), 197tr (Dennis Hallinan), 197 (c/AAD Worldwide Travel Images), 207c (Mark Crame/Christine Osborne Pictures), 208br (BL Images Ltd); Corbis pp 14r (Tim McGuire), 39r (Alberto Estevez/epa), 43b (Frithjof Hirdes/zefa), 48r (Ted Spiegel), 56tr (Edimédia), 78 (JLP/Sylvia Torres), 91l (Christian Liewig/Liewig Media Sports), 96bl (Bob Thomas), 96br (Tim Graham), 98tl (Alfredo Dagli Orti/The Art Archive), 98tr & 98cl (Bettmann), 99bl (Bettmann), 107l (PBNJ Productions), 108l (Frans Lanting), 142 (Chris Carroll), 159 (Rick Gayle Studio), 171 (Jim Craigmyle), 176tr (Jon Hicks), 180tr (Sandro Vannini), 181t (Bettmann), 181b (CinemaPhoto), 193 (a/Mark Bolton), 193 (f/Robbie Jack), 197 (a/Vincent van Gogh/Philadelphia Museum of Art), 207b (Dean Conger); Empics pp 43c (AP), 108r (Matt Rourke/AP); Getty Images pp 14cl (Gregory E Betz/Taxi), 31tl (Travel Pix/Taxi), 34tr (Alan Powdrill/Photonica), 39l (RNHRD NHS Trust), 42 (Manfred Mehlig), 51 (Chabruken/Taxi), 63t (Keystone/Hulton Archive), 85 (Pankaj & Insy Shah/Gulfimages), 86br (Gregory Kramer/The Image Bank), 91c (Christof Koepsel/Bongarts), 91r (Jeff Haynes/AFP), 97l (Mark Scott/Photographer's Choice), 97cr (David Lees), 99bc (Hulton Archive), 99br (STF/AFP), 138 (Kelley & Meyers/The Image Bank), 151 (Silvia Otte/Photonica), 166Julia (Gen Nishino/Taxi), 166Juan (Kaz Chiba/Photographer's Choice), 174 (Hulton Archive), 180cl (Hulton Archive), 180cr (Roy Rainford/Robert Harding World Imagery), 184l (Kim Steele/Photonica), 193tl (Andrew Shennan/Taxi), 193 (c/Philip & Karen Smith/The Image Bank), 197 (e/Todd Gipstein/National Geographic), 197 (g/Time Life Pictures), 201 (Martin Bureau/AFP), 204 (Occidor Ltd/Robert Harding World Imagery); iStockphoto.com pp 71 (texasmary), 86tr (Spanishalex), 197tl (dalan), 197cl (Bas Rabeling); Leonardo Hotels p 58; NASA pp 208bl, 209; Photolibrary.com pp 163 (a), 170t (Bill Bachmann Photography), 193 (b/Soleil Noir/Photononstop); Punchstock pp 14l (Purestock), 14cr (MedioImages), 20 (Photodisc), 31br (Blend Images), 70 (Digital Vision), 97cl (Digital Archive Japan), 97r (BananaStock), 107r (Brand X Pictures), 108cr (Photodisc), 114l (Glowimages), 114c (PhotoAlto), 133 (Digital Vision), 163 (b/Corbis Royalty-free), 163 (c/Photodisc), 164 (BananaStock), 166Paula (Image Source), 173 (UpperCut Images), 184r (Corbis Royalty-free), 207t (Corbis Royalty-free); Rex Features pp 31cr (Erik C Pendzich), 31bl (Albert Ferreira), 63b (Jonathan Hordle), 98bl (Sipa Press), 176b (Patrick Frilet), 178 (Jon Blumb); Science Photo Library pp 11r (Jerry Lodriguss), 29 (Richard J. Wainscoat/Peter Arnold Inc.), 61 (Stephen J. Krasemann), 108c (Sam Pierson Jr), 197cr (Detlev van Ravenswaay), 197 (f); Science & Society Picture Library pp 48l (Science Museum), 197 (b/Science Museum); Still Pictures pp 43t (Paul Glendell), 108cl (John Cancalosi); Topfoto p 150l (Charles Walker)

Photos sourced by Suzanne Williams/Pictureresearch.co.uk

Illustrated by Ferenc Bálint, Humberto Blanco, Julian Mosedale, Mark Duffin, Mark Watkinson, Matthew Robson and Nick Schon.

The authors and publishers are grateful to the following for permission to reproduce copyright material. While every effort has been made, it has not always been possible to identify the sources of all the material used, or to contact the copyright holders. If any omissions are brought to our notice, we will be happy to include the appropriate acknowledgements on reprinting.

p.56: Image from cover of *The House of the Spirits* by Isabel Allende, published by Black Swan, by permission of The Random House Group; p59: Image from cover of *The Swimmer* by Zsuzsa Bánk, translated from the German by Margot Bettauer Dembo, courtesy of Harcourt; p.163 Image from cover of *Language Links Beginner > Elementary* by Adrian Doff and Christopher Jones, published by Cambridge University Press, by permission of Cambridge University Press; p.195: Text from Arabic translation of *The Cambridge History of Literary Criticism*, Volume 9, edited by Christa Knellwolf and Christopher Norris, by permission of The Supreme Council of Culture, El Gezira, Cairo, Egypt; p.197: Image from cover of *Macbeth*, published by Cambridge University Press, by permission of Donald Cooper; p.197: Image from cover of *War and Peace* by Leo Tolstoy, by permission of Penguin Group UK.